Dementia in close-up

Dementia is an illness which causes the person with dementia to experience gradual powerlessness and estrangement from their surroundings, and is a confusing and frightening experience for the sufferers themselves and for their family and friends.

Drawing on Bère Miesen's extensive practical experience and research findings, this book uses first-hand accounts and real-life examples to examine common patterns of behaviour and responses of persons with dementia and their carers. Essential topics such as aggression, power, sexuality and attachment, the importance of acceptance of the condition, and effects of denial are explored, and a framework for understanding and working with those with gradual memory failure proposed.

Going beyond purely medical descriptions of dementia, *Dementia in close-up* combines compassionate insight into a difficult and isolating condition with practical advice for all those caring for or planning services for people with dementia, whether professional health care workers, home carers or family members.

Bère M. L. Miesen is a clinical old-age psychologist and an NIP registered clinical psychologist. In 1995 he was awarded the Old Age Psychology Award in the Netherlands.

Dementia in close-up

Understanding and caring for people with dementia

Bère M. L. Miesen

Translated by Gemma M. M. Jones

London and New York

First published 1999
by Routledge
11 New Fetter Lane, London EC4P 4EE

Simultaneously published in the USA and Canada
by Routledge
29 West 35th Street, New York, NY 10001

Typeset in Palatino by Routledge
Printed and bound in Great Britain by Creative Print and
Design (Wales), Ebbw Vale

British Library Cataloguing in Publication Data
A catalogue record for this book is available from the British
Library

Library of Congress Cataloguing in Publication Data
Miesen, Bère M. L.
[Dement. English]
Dementia in close-up / Bère M. L. Miesen.
Includes bibliographical references and index
1. Dementia. 2. Senile dementia. 3. Dementia – Patients – Care.
I. Title.
RC521 .M5413 1998   98-23238
616.8' 3–dc21   CIP

ISBN 0–415–12884–6 (hbk)
ISBN 0–415–12885–4 (pbk)

Contents

Contents

Translator's foreword

In this translation, two separate books, originally published in Dutch, have been brought together because, in combination, they offer a complete psycho-social description of dementia. This new book is not intended to be 'studied' so much as 'read'. It describes the perceptions of carers, persons with dementia and family members. The dependence that dementia causes leads to feelings of fear. Eventually, the 'closeness' of others is essential for the person with dementia . Sustained closeness in any human relationship can be difficult; in dementia even more so. This book is in many ways a detailed study of this closeness and the conflicts it causes.

Professional closeness is not the same thing as familial closeness, but where are the boundaries? This closeness is the dimension of care that the medical world has long avoided speaking about (except in unhelpful platitudes such as 'keep your work and your private life separate'). The reality is that having dementia, or caring for someone with dementia 'does' something to you, deep within you. This needs to be spoken about so that useful caring relationships and partnerships can be formed to help everyone involved. Sharing closeness in caring for a person with dementia goes far beyond doing one's 'work'. It is not obvious how to achieve it. It is never easy, but it can be done and has great rewards for everyone.

Part I, originally entitled 'Demented, but not that crazy', strives to give professional carers, family of persons with dementia, and 'fellow-residents of persons with dementia in care facilities' a clear understanding of dementia, and a much deeper understanding of the world of persons with dementia and their families. (See the Acknowledgements section for a description of the 'Substitution Project', which led to the development of the original version of this book.)

Part II , originally entitled 'Dementia at close up', was written to describe the complexity of caring. It is aimed at all carers (professional and family), but is especially relevant to 'home carers'. It deals with the varied types of relationships between the person with dementia, the family and carers, and with the most difficult issues of caring: power, adoption, sexuality, and aggression.

All names in the books are fictitious. Where the word 'he' appears, 'she' could be substituted. The word 'sufferer' has been used in places to replace the more wordy expression 'the person who has dementia'. We recognise that no suitable shorter term has yet been found.

This book uses most of the case material published in Miesen (1998a: 224), with different names and sometimes with different translations.

About Dr Bère Miesen

Bère Miesen, a clinical old-age psychologist, has long been known in the Netherlands and abroad for his pioneering work in helping society to understand the dementia process. He has been a ferocious proponent of the need to have 'life history information' available for all professional carers so that more humane, long-term care for dementia sufferers can be provided. Persons with dementia and family carers are largely invisible in our society. There has been a strong impetus in recent years by many, to inform society at large about the specific needs and difficulties that occur for all involved in the process of dementia. Bère Miesen has been educating the public and professional sectors of society about dementia since 1970. His 'consciousness-raising' efforts have not diminished with time.

Most recently, he has shaken up the 'status quo' by setting up an 'Alzheimer Café' on the university campus at Leiden. Persons with dementia, family members and friends are welcome here to start the evening with drinks and snacks, listen to some entertainment (sometimes a short talk about a dementia-related subject) and are then invited to end the evening with a communal toast. The Alzheimer Café is a great success; attendance and press-interest is soaring.

The message is:

> Come out of the woodwork, you are part of society and we want you to take your part in it. Dementia is a part of life for some, for which nothing yet can be done. You didn't ask to 'get' it; it could happen to anybody. Don't hide away.

The stigma around this illness is slowly being removed. Persons with dementia should not be seen as 'crazy'. They are human beings struggling with a chronic illness in the end phase of their life. There is no reason for them to be 'invisible' in a modern society; dementia is not contagious. More is needed than help in the form of 'custodial assistance'. If we do not take the global human needs seriously, simply because persons have a form of damage to their brain, we are guilty of 'metaphorical decapitation'. This is murderous and ethically unjust.

Translator's personal note

Bère Miesen has been a friend and a colleague for over twelve years. It has been a pleasure to translate these books, not only because of our long-standing efforts to gain recognition for the speciality of 'care-giving in dementia', but because of Bère's knack of explaining complex things vividly and simply.

This translation is a close rendering of Bère's original work. The idioms have been translated in the most accurate way possible. I confess that because of my Canadian roots, I have sometimes used idioms with which I was familiar when I was unsure of a more 'quintessentially' British version.

At a time when health authorities throughout the UK are struggling individually to generate training material for all types of carers, many professionals in the UK are concerned about the difficulties involved in providing 'nationally consistent' training. This book is a good starting point: it looks at dementia from the outside and the inside in a readily accessible way.

Gemma M. M. Jones, HBSc, BSN, CVT, PhD

Acknowledgements

Acknowledgements and thanks for Part I of this book

Brief history of Part I of this book

In 1989, in the provincial region of Zuid Holland Noord, the Netherlands, there were 240 persons with a diagnosis of dementia on a waiting list for placement into EMI nursing home settings. Some of them already lived in nursing homes, but needed additional, specialised EMI care. A 'substitution project' called 'Medio 1991', was set up aimed to meet their needs. Five nursing homes, thirty-six residential homes, family doctors, national assessors (RIAGG), and an 'intake/admissions committee' started working together under a contractual agreement.

The Medio 1991 Project had three aims: (1) to set up **care plans** for those in the substitution project, under the guidance of a family doctor and a psychologist; (2) to provide residential homes with **extra help** (hours, days per week), for example, activity therapists, care staff to help give extra care and guidance to persons with dementia; (3) to provide **mandatory education** and training for carers in residential homes, and **voluntary education** for residents (and their family) in residential homes.

Dr Bère Miesen, clinical old-age psychologist at the Old Age Research Centre and Nursing Home, Marienhaven, in Warmond, had been teaching a course, 'General Introduction to Dementia' since 1984, in a number of 'in-house' and 'open subscription' settings. Dr Miesen was given provincial funding to develop this book so that it could be used for the educational goals of the project, but also elsewhere in the country. The unique aspect of the educational aims of this project was that, for the first time ever, residents (and their families) were invited to take part in the educational settings. The existing residents, after all, were to be those who were 'most confronted' by suddenly having persons with dementia placed in their midst. The most important goal of the education programme was to increase the understanding of and tolerance to persons with dementia, by broadening the knowledge about dementia, particularly insight into the behaviours of persons with dementia.

The first part of this book (Chapters 1 to 7) were used as the workbook for the education programme. It was intended as an instrument to get staff and fellow residents prepared for and involved with the changes that were going to happen in their residential settings.

The author wishes to thank Lien Bulthuis, Tischa van der Cammen, Han Diesfeldt, Ries Kleijnen, Keetje Ruizeveld and Leintje Tanja for their critical comments on the first draft of the text. The editorial board of the 'Workbooks in Old Age and Life History' (Cahiers Ouderdom en Levensloop), especially Mia Duijnstee are thanked for their comments on the second draft.

Acknowledgements and thanks for Part II of this book

Part II of this book builds upon Part I, which was originally published as *Dement: zo gek nog niet*, Bohn Stafleu Van Loghum, 1992. Part II, originally published as: Dementie dichterbij, Bohn Stafleu Van Loghum, 1993, was not written without help and came about as a result of guidance from a reading group, whose members include: Diny Nooijen-van Asseldonk, Milly Scheepers-Zijlstra, Mia Duijnstee and Ilse Warners. I owe them many thanks. Without the firm editing hand of Mia Duijnstee, it would not have become what it is. Margaret Jansen's help in rounding off the manuscript was essential.

A separate word of recognition is required for my sources of information. The Attachment Theory of the family psychiatrist John Bowlby (1907–90) was an important source of inspiration. In writing Chapter 13, I made use of Chapter 8 in *Psychotherapy with Older Adults* (*Psychotherapie met Oudere Volwassenen*), Knight and Buijssen (eds) (Intro Publishers, 1989). Personal notes from Marika Engel and Paul Tjoa put me on the track for writing Chapters 14 and 15. Mia Duijnstee's published doctoral thesis, entitled *The Burden of Families of Dementia Sufferers* (*De belasting van familieleden van dementerenden*) (Intro Publishers, 1992), gave form to my thoughts in writing Chapter 16. Above all, I felt especially guided and supported by Ilse Warners. This book also breathes her spirit.

The contributions of the Psychogeriatric Research Centre, Marienhaven, Warmond, are herewith thankfully acknowledged – for both the development and translation of this text.

Part I

Dementia in close-up

The process

What is dementia? What is the truth? How do we get beyond the medical description of it? Is it possible to understand the behaviour of the person with dementia? Can we change our response to the person once we understand more? The behaviour of persons with dementia is not 'crazy', but it does require the will and time to try to understand it.

1 Introduction to Part I

Bound to each other

As a rule, belonging to a family brings with it a strong sense of bonding between members. This means that to a greater or lesser extent, some kind of close bond has gradually become securely anchored over time. When someone suffers from a dementing illness, the bond with his/her family is weakened. Unasked for and as a result of the illness, the person with dementia becomes separated from those who live with him/her. This separation occurs even when the person with dementia cannot express it directly. At the same time, family members are slowly forced to take their leave of someone who is still living. Sometimes the spouse of a person with dementia even lives in a care facility themselves.

For all involved – the person with dementia and the family – this means that the lifelong bond with one another gradually becomes diminished and is sometimes lost altogether.

A new bond

For professional care-givers, it can actually be an advantage not to have a historical bond anchored in the life history of a family. Care-givers can leave their work when it is finished for the day. Gathering knowledge about and experience with a person with dementia occurs spontaneously, without the simultaneous loss of someone to whom one is attached. Professional care-givers have little to lose, and much to profit. They can gain a new relationship. This new relationship can lead to feelings of loss eventually, for example, when a resident who was 'good' initially, becomes worse and needs to be transferred to another care setting. Usually, the age difference is quite large between carer and resident. At the beginning of a new relationship, carers do not usually become emotionally involved in thinking about dementia and what it must be like to suffer from this illness. Thoughts about the possibility that they themselves might one day suffer with dementia are far removed. Thoughts about the eventual death of their own (grand) parents strike closer to home.

Unasked for

Most residents in a residential care facility do not have a dementing illness. Likewise, residents are not linked to the families of their fellow residents, unless a spouse is involved. It was never intended that elderly persons should coexist in the last years of their life with a cohort of persons with dementia. And yet, the numbers of persons with dementia who live in residential care homes continues to increase.

Under one roof

For healthy persons, being in the immediate living environment of residents with dementia necessarily causes different types of conflict. The behaviour of persons with dementia can be an 'impediment' or sometimes 'jarring', particularly in company, or if one is trying to concentrate on something. Their behaviour is sometimes so strange and incomprehensible that it can evoke fear and anxiety in others. Even if you accept that death is an inescapable eventuality, you do not spend your time sitting around waiting for 'the end'.

Intolerant

It is clear that if you were a resident of a residential care home, you would not be too eager to meet, much less become well acquainted with persons with dementia. There are times when complaints about their disruptive behaviour come pouring into the director's office. Persons with dementia are often shunned, especially during group activities (usually unconsciously). It is understandable that, in an average residential care home, the tolerance for the behaviour of a fellow resident with dementia will be limited.

Why do things differently?

The range of options for caring long term for persons with dementia outside their family circle will be insufficient in the coming years. This has two consequences. If you should be living in a residential care home and eventually suffer from dementia, it will not necessarily be possible to move you elsewhere. If a fellow resident begins to suffer from dementia, it might not be easy to find other accommodation for him. The expectation is that increasing numbers of persons with dementia will need to remain in residential care homes – along with the inevitable consequences for others such as anxiety, fear, misunderstanding and intolerance. Residents who are cognitively healthy will continue to avoid persons with dementia. Later on in this book, we will discuss that precisely because of this situation, persons with dementia receive too little of the attention they so desperately need.

How?

If education about dementia is a way to impart knowledge, understanding and skills to professional care-givers, why not provide more information about dementia to the residents of residential care homes? Since persons with dementia remain 'fellow residents', even when professional care-givers are off duty, cognitively healthy residents might be especially well served by obtaining information about dementia.

Information

In my experience at any rate, in order to increase understanding about dementia in fellow residents, it is necessary to provide information about what it is like for the person with dementia to have this condition. This involves providing information that both enlightens and guides the fellow resident's experiences. It must be the kind of information that allows one to understand what is happening to the fellow resident with dementia, as well as their family. It must be information that provides personal answers to questions such as: 'How can I best act towards my fellow residents with dementia, not only for their sake, but also for my own wellbeing?'

Such information is best utilised if it is placed in a framework in which all aspects of the problems surrounding the dementia process are discussed together.

- How many elderly suffer from dementia; where do they live? (Chapter 2)
- What is dementia? How is it diagnosed? Can something be done about it? (Chapter 3)
- How does memory work in persons with dementia? What are the consequences of failing memory? How do you cope with this? (Chapter 4)
- How do persons with dementia respond to what is happening to them? (Chapter 5)
- What does it mean for families to experience this process? (Chapter 6).

2   If only I had known that

Concepts and contact

Before we immerse ourselves in studying the behaviours of persons with dementia, it is necessary to examine the notion or concept that we have already formed about dementia. Concepts are what we think about a certain person or group of persons. There are popular concepts (stereotypes), about political exiles, the police, film stars, pop musicians, immigrants, unmarried mothers and so on. Everyone knows people or groups of people about whom we have an opinion or judgement. In the same way, we have a concept about different generations and also about persons in residential care homes.

It is noteworthy that our concepts do not always match the truth. What we think about a group of persons does not always apply to individual members of that group. Generally speaking, the concept that we have is related to the contact that we have had with the person or persons about whom we have the concept. The less contact there has been, the more our imagination (or fantasy) embellishes our concept.

Notions about old age

Naturally, one has ideas about what old age might be like. There are several ways of demonstrating this. One well-known way is to ask school children to make drawings of old people. Considering the traits of old people described in fairy tales, some of these features can also be identified in children's drawings. Another way to get at perceptions of old age, is to ask persons to guess about percentages. For example:

How many persons in the UK are over the age of 65 now?
How many of them live in residential care homes?
How many of them live independently, so independently that they barely require any help?

Over 65?

How many persons are over the age of 65 now? Most people wouldn't know precisely. So if you don't know, guess. This is interesting with regard to your own ideas about old age. What would you guess right now?

In the UK at the present time, about 15 per cent of the population is over the age of 65.

In a residential care home?

What percentage of people over the age of 65 lives in a residential care home? This does not include: hospitals, nursing homes, sheltered accommodation or other care facilities. This really concerns past norms about care homes for elderly people. If you don't know for sure, guess again. What would you fill in next?

Of all of the UK population over 65 years of age, about 7 per cent are in residential or nursing homes.

As good as independent?

What percentage of all of those over the age of 65 presently live so independently that they barely require any assistance? What would you guess now?

Of all of those over the age of 65 in the UK right now, about 80 per cent are 'as good as' independent.

Undifferentiated

Specific questions and their answers only provide a very general insight into the ideas and perceptions about old age. They provide an undifferentiated picture. Many nuances that exist in people's minds, cannot be expressed by this method of inquiry.

A more varied picture

Your answers to the above questions can be compared to those given by persons in any arbitrarily chosen group. From experience in conducting workshops with groups over the past years, it appears that the range of answers have an enormous spread.

In answer to the first question: How many persons in the UK right now are aged over 65 years? the answers range from 20 to 80 per cent. The average is about 40 per cent.

In answer to the second question: How many persons aged over 65 live in residential care homes? the answers range from 5 to 90 per cent. The average is above 50 per cent.

In answer to the third question: How many of those aged over 65 live so independently that they barely need any help? the answers range from 10 to 90 per cent. The average is just under 50 per cent.

Your answers are likely to fall between the highest and lowest percentages guessed for each answer. Without providing you with the right answers to these three questions, it is already clear that perception about ageing is very varied.

An unrealistic, unfavourable perception

On consideration, what are the real answers to the three questions? Compare your own answers with those below.

At this moment, about 15 per cent of the population is over the age of 65, almost 7 per cent live in residential homes, and about 80 per cent are healthy enough to live independently without significant help from others.

If these answers are compared with the average responses of past groups, a distinct perception of old age is apparent. In general, it appears that the total number of elderly people over 65 years of age and the numbers of elderly people in residential care are largely over-estimated. The numbers of elderly people aged over 65 and living independently are largely underestimated.

Broadly speaking, it appears that at this moment people have a very mixed view of old age, and largely an unfavourable one. The generalised perception is that there are a lot of older persons and that their situation is a rather sombre one. This view could be summarised as follows: they are usually living in residential homes, but some manage at home with/without the help of others.

Even older persons themselves . . .

This view of old age is commonly held among elderly people, especially among those who live near to a residential home. It often seems as if older persons themselves also believe that most old people live in residential care homes.

I remember a single elderly lady. She lived in sheltered housing near a residential home. When she heard that not even 7 per cent of those aged over 65 lived in residential care settings, she was greatly relieved. She concluded that if she didn't want to move to the nearby care home, there clearly were no good arguments for her doing so.

Until then, she considered that her living arrangements had been exceptional, and that sooner or later, she would have to move.

Perceptions about dementia

The fourth and final question in this chapter about concepts and perceptions is: How many people over the age of 65 have dementia right now?

At this moment about 4 to 5 per cent of those aged over 65 suffer from dementia.

Sometimes more, sometimes less

In practice, the estimates (guesses) to the above (fourth) question range from 1 to 80 per cent. The average guess is about 25 per cent.

One person guesses that almost everyone suffers from dementia, another guesses that dementia is a rarity. In reality, the experts can't exactly agree. For diverse reasons, it is very difficult to determine exactly how many persons in the UK at the present time have dementia. Having said that, the figure appears to be in the neighbourhood of about 4 to 5 per cent of all those over the age of 65. (Naturally, the higher the cut-off age, the higher the percentage of persons with dementia. For example, about 12 to 15 per cent of all those aged over 80 have dementia.)

This estimate is much lower than the average guess of about 25 per cent.

A sombre view of old age, without grounds

This overestimation of the numbers of persons with dementia completes our roughly painted picture of those over 65 years of age: there are many; their situation is negatively thought of; they mostly live in residential homes; and a good number of them have dementia!

In fact, the opposite is true: there are not that many old persons (15 per cent of the population); few of them live in residential homes (about 7 per cent of those aged over 65); most can cope well on their own (about 80 per cent of those aged over 65); and a minority of these persons suffer from dementia (about 4 to 5 per cent of those aged over 65). Moreover, for the majority of persons, the first signs of dementia only appear after the age of 80.

The reality is brighter

The reality is more positive than the view of old age held by the majority of persons. In other words, old age is brighter than generally thought. Think of your own situation. But possibly also about: spending the winter months in Spain; starting or continuing studies; doing voluntary work; participating in the many community activities and activities especially for seniors.

Why is the perspective of old age so dark for many? This question begs a more general question. What influences the views, images and perceptions of old age?

Influences on perception and concept formation

Perception is subjective; preconceptions and feelings play a large role in their formation. In the first paragraph of this chapter it was suggested that perception had something to do with the contact that we have with the things or persons about which we have an opinion or view about. Likewise, the perception about old age is influenced by our own contacts with people over the age of 65. If you compare the guesses to the answers with the correct answers, you will see that they have been either overestimated or underestimated. There are several reasons for this. Older persons often find that other older persons look older than they do themselves.

Except for one's own age, four other causes for the great variance in perceptions can be listed. These have to do with information, living environment, family and work.

Information

First, the information with which we are confronted, timely or not, plays a role. This includes information from the media, the newspapers, journals, radio and television. Journalists are not always informed with equal accuracy. The sensational aspects of an event are often given more importance than the background to the event. The reader, listener or TV viewer can be set upon the wrong 'track' as it were. Unpleasant news about abuse in nursing and residential homes undoubtedly colours our view about elderly people who live in these settings. The term 'the greying population' is equally unclearly, if not unjustly used.

To speak about the influence of information on perception is clearly to speak about a vicious circle. Through negative stories about older persons – for example, those stories about their supposed characters, state of health or other attributes – the existing negative images of old age will remain constant, or become even more negative. Old age is less positively presented than is the reality.

Living

The environment in which you live can also influence perception and image formation. To live coincidentally in a neighbourhood where there are all young families, or in a suburb in which the population is mostly elderly, makes a big difference. If you only meet old people in your neighbourhood because there happens to be a residential care home nearby, which is not well linked to other age groups in the neighbourhood, then you will be likely to overestimate the number of persons aged over 65. Presumably, if you live in an area where there is no residential care home, and only rarely meet an older person whilst out shopping, you might think there are fewer elderly people than is the case.

Families

Your own family plays a large part in one's perception of old age. We are all influenced by, for example: the ages of brothers and sisters, parents and grandparents, aunts and uncles; their physical and mental health and the ways in which they cope(d); the extent and intensity of the (past) relationship with these persons; their pleasantness or unpleasantness; their personalities; and their influence and warmth, etc. It is difficult to say exactly what influence all these aspects of families have upon the perception of old age. It is accepted, however, that when asked, many persons list 'family' as an explanation for their particular view about old age. If you used to visit a grandfather or grandmother who was healthy and kind, the chances are that you will have a different image of old age than someone who remembers visiting very frail, dependent grandparents, or, someone whose grandparents had not 'moved along with the times'.

Work

Finally, work is a factor influencing our perception of old age. Those who have come into contact with many elderly people before their own retirement usually overestimate the numbers of older people around. It also makes a great difference if you experience elderly people as 'wise leaders', or as workers who have 'passed their sell-by date' and are just trying to 'fill in time'. For young persons working in residential care homes, the influence of their work upon their perception of old age is very strong. If they work exclusively with persons with dementia, they often conclude that there are large numbers of elderly people with dementia. If people never encounter elderly persons in their work, it is understandable that they underestimate the number of persons with dementia.

Why write about concepts and perception in this book?

Without making some adjustments to our (usually negative) image of old age and dementia, we will not have a clear, accurate image of old age in this present society. Without making corrections to our own image, whether young or old, we will not have the chance to develop a positive image about our own last 'life-stage'. People can hardly be expected to look forward to their old age as long as their negative perceptions remain. Knowledge about the facts and figures can help to correct these perceptions.

'The greying of the population'

When you ask people what the term 'the greying of the population' means, you will often receive diverse and incorrect answers. People have often received an inadequate or incorrect explanation of the term. 'Greying' refers to the changing constitution of the population, defined by age groups. 'Greying' refers to the expectation that the numbers of persons over the age of 65 will increase, whilst the numbers of younger persons will stagnate or decrease. This usually refers to predictions, for example, that in the next twenty-five years, the 'over 65s' will form a greater proportion of the population.

Double greying

This is also a term sometimes used by the media. It refers to the different age groups within all those over the age of 65. A large increase in the number of persons aged 80 and over is expected. A lower increase is expected for persons aged between 65 and 80. In other words, a particularly large increase in very old persons is expected within the total number of persons aged 65 and over.

Dementia in the residential care home

In closing this chapter, it is worth saying a few words about the occurrence of dementia in residential care homes. If people are asked about the numbers of nursing homes and beds for persons with dementia, they usually think that there are rather a lot.

In a nursing home, there is scarcely 1 bed in 7 allotted for persons with dementia. Most persons with dementia do not live in nursing homes. On the contrary, they live at home, or in residential care homes. There are too few beds available for them and any given person with dementia only has a very limited chance of being admitted to a special EMI care facility. (Day care facilities will not be discussed here.)

Whether or not there should be additional nursing home beds and whether all persons with dementia should be admitted to a home are questions that will not be discussed here. There are also a variety of causes that lead to someone being admitted to a care home. As a rule, it depends upon the resources of home care assistance and the degree of behavioural disturbance.

Ever-increasing numbers of persons with dementia

The above information means simply that, if you were to live in a care home and were to become ill with dementia, it would be difficult to find another specialist care facility for you. It also means that your fellow residents (without dementia), would increasingly be confronted with members of their age group who do have dementia. It is hardly surprising then that in some care homes, there are old persons with dementia who do give us cause for concern.

Knowing how and what to do

Because of such concerns, many care homes have started a variety of 'group activities' for persons with dementia. They range from intensive 'group care' to 'living room projects' and special 'day care'. Separate and extra attention is thus provided for persons with dementia. Instead of leaving people alone in their rooms for large parts of the day, they are cared for in a 'family group'-type setting.

To provide information about dementia to the non-demented elderly residents of a care home is another way to address this concern. In this manner, extra attention is paid to those who are more or less forced to share their environment and life with persons with dementia.

In the following chapter the core questions about dementia will be discussed. The questions: 'What exactly is dementia?' 'How do you recognise it?' and 'Is there nothing that can be done to help it?' will be answered.

3 What does dementia involve?

What is this chapter about?

First, let us pause to consider the behaviour that generally occurs in a person having dementia. We call these the 'symptoms'. Thereafter it is important to recognise that these symptoms can be considered from different angles. Then, we will consider that these symptoms, in turn, have a variety of causes. When these points have been made, we can finally ask the question: 'If these symptoms occur, when are we talking about "dementia"?'

If it has been established that a person has 'dementia', then there are many possible types of dementia he/she could be suffering from. The different types will be briefly discussed. In the following section, the possible causes of dementia will be addressed. If you look at the consequences of having dementia on an affected person him/herself, you will find a number of approaches or methods for communicating with the person. These are all attempts to influence the wellbeing of a person with dementia in a positive way.

Introduction

The Jones's are a couple who have been living in room number 321, on the fourth floor of a care home for four years. Mrs Jones has been forgetful for some time. She presently 'invents' one story after another if someone asks her 'what she has been up to'. In the past few months she has been quite restless. 'She's more fidgety than she has ever been', says her husband. Sometimes she sees things that aren't there (at least, Mr Jones doesn't see what she says she is seeing). She searches for her husband, and also for her parents, although the latter have been dead for a long time.

Everyone who has worked with persons with dementia will recognise the behaviour of Mrs Jones. However, dementia is not the same in everyone. Maybe you know of persons with dementia who behave differently, or even more unusually.

Demented?

It is, of course, strange that Mrs Jones behaves this way. A normal person wouldn't behave like this. It is clear that something unusual is going on. In the past, it might have been said that she was behaving 'childishly' or that she had 'hardening of the arteries' in her brain. Nowadays, we rather hastily speak about 'dementia'. With any term, we should be extremely cautious before deciding when or whether to apply it. Outsiders, usually are far to quick to judge people like Mrs Jones, as soon as they appear to have 'trouble thinking'. One resident in the care home feels sympathy for her, another feels guilty; she 'gets on one person's nerves', whereas she makes another person 'feel helpless'. Still other fellow residents 'feel frightened' around her.

The question that will be considered in this chapter is: 'What is dementia?' In other words, when can we say that someone like Mrs Jones has dementia?

Dementia

To explore the answer to this question further, it is appropriate to explain what we mean by the word 'dementia'. The answer that follows is based on knowledge gained by current research. In the course of this chapter, this definition will be repeated several times, so that different aspects can be clarified. The definition is brief and is as follows:

> The term dementia is used when the behavioural changes are a result of irreversible changes to brain tissue. Damage to or the death of brain tissue, cannot be reversed with the current state of our knowledge.

The behaviour of persons with dementia cannot be explained by the 'condition' of the brain alone. Extra information is needed to determine, for example, the influence of the person's personality and life history. (But that is another story that is discussed in the remainder of the book.) 'Restlessness' in a given gentleman, at specific times of the day, may be better understood if one knows that he was a dairy farmer and always milked the herd at certain times. The 'difficulties' that a female resident exhibits when in the presence of male residents, may be better understood if one knows that she remained single, led a sheltered life and was always a very shy person.

Let us return to Mrs Jones. Imagine that it can be clearly established that her unusual behaviour is due to changes in her brain. We could understand her behaviour even better if we knew more about her life, about what type of person she used to be and the influences and experiences she encountered in life.

Not only symptoms, but also head and heart affected

In almost every textbook and workbook about dementia the same overview can be found. It includes a list of the difficulties in memory, actions, recognition of things, intelligence, insight, continence, reading, arithmetic, writing, language and self-care. It also involves difficulties such as: activity, social decorum, orientation, confusion, delusions and confabulation. Last, suspiciousness, aggression, restlessness, moodiness and overt sadness are included.

These symptoms have not been named in their usual order, but have purposefully been split into three groupings: what happens; how one reacts; and how this feels. The first sequence (from memory to self-care) represents the real 'disturbance', or, for simplicity's sake, the symptoms. The second sequence (from activity to confabulation) describes how persons with dementia react to having dementia. We will refer to these terms as 'consequences'. The third sequence (from suspiciousness to sadness) refers to how it feels to have dementia. These terms will be described as 'affective/emotional reactions' to dementia.

Even if you cannot recognise all of the above descriptions in the person(s) you have experience with, you will probably find that most of them are represented indirectly (i.e. wandering, mixing up day and night, constantly following someone, being frightened and screaming).

Misleading

The misleading aspect about the 'summary of symptoms' contained in many textbooks and workbooks is that they appear to have no relationship with one another. Nothing could be further from the truth. The above-named difficulties do not occur independently of one another, but are closely related. The exact relationship of these disturbances may, however, vary greatly from person to person. This relationship can be better understood if the disturbances are separated into the 'symptoms', 'consequences' and 'affective reactions' to dementia.

An example of the relationship

In the beginning, in the early stage of the dementia process, memory difficulties can cause fear and problems in orientation. If, later on, 'insight' also deteriorates with ongoing memory difficulties, suspiciousness, sadness and confabulation of all kinds may occur as well. Later, when, in addition, speech perception and communication patterns deteriorate, loss of decorum, aggression, restlessness and further disorientation may occur. The relationship of the symptoms to the consequences and reactions is not always as described above. These are merely given to show that all symptoms lead to consequences and affective reactions.

With their whole being

From experience, it seems that people with dementia remain concerned about what happens to them. We could almost use the expressions: 'with heart and soul', 'from their head to their toes', 'with all they have and hold', to describe the nature of their concern. In Chapter 4, the 'consequences' of having dementia will be discussed. In Chapter 5, the 'affective reactions' will be considered, for example, why it is that persons with dementia so often believe that their parents are still alive, although they are long since dead?

To consider two other viewpoints of dementia in addition to the aforementioned, it is necessary to make some additional comments and to summarise the discussion of dementia so far.

Behaviour and feelings: close together

It is important to realise that as time goes by and the dementia process progresses, there is an increasing move from 'consequences' to 'affective reactions'. In the beginning, Mrs Jones reacted more with her head (cognitively, reflectively) than with her feelings. Later, she began to react more with her feelings than with her head. She reacts more as a response to what the dementia 'does to her' than from what she 'thinks about it'. Therefore, behaviour and emotions become increasingly linked as the dementia process continues and is visible – what Mrs Jones says or does is dependent on how she feels. Behaviour and emotions eventually become interchangeable.

Again: differences in symptoms

It must be restated, at the risk of appearing to be overzealous in making the point, that there are as many combinations of dementia symptoms as there are people with dementia. There are also differences in the degree or severity of the symptoms. The rate of progress through the dementia process is also different for individuals.

As already mentioned, one can speak about the presence of 'dementia' when the behaviour is influenced by irreversible changes/damage to brain tissue.

A variety of viewpoints

Imagine that you noticed that a good friend of yours, in our case Mrs Jones, is becoming increasingly forgetful, restless and a bit aggressive. She picks fights with everyone, even with you, although you have tried to prevent this and been pleasant to her. In general, two questions could be asked about her: 'Where is this behaviour coming from?' 'Where is it leading ?' These are two completely different viewpoints. Because this is a book about dementia, the first question involves an interest in the relationship between the brain and behaviour. The second question involves an interest in the effect of her behaviour on herself, her family and the environment.

Professionals call the first question a 'neurobiological' or 'medical' view of dementia. The second view could be called a 'psycho-social' view of dementia. Neither question can usefully exist on its own. In the following chapters, we will expand on the second psycho-social viewpoint – the effect of the dementia on the person him/herself, on the family and the environment. In the remainder of this chapter, we will continue to discuss the medical view of dementia.

Possible causes of the symptoms

Let us return to our forgetful, restless and somewhat aggressive Mrs Jones. Even if she has a different 'cluster' of symptoms, it won't make any difference to the following discussion.

Another point needs to be made. Before it can be concluded that Mrs Jones's behaviour is the result of irreversible brain changes, a detailed personal examination needs to be made. First, it must be determined that the behavioural changes are not due to physical ill health, social or psychological changes, or as a result of causes having nothing to do with changes in the brain. The diagnosis of dementia can only be made after all other causes of the behaviour change have been excluded.

Hereafter follows a global overview of the conditions/causes that must be excluded. Thereafter, it is possible to discuss how it can be established whether Mrs Jones has dementia or not.

Physical changes and their consequences

Most often, the following examples of physical changes are listed. (Note that this is still an example.)

1 sensory changes (deafness)
2 circulation (heart problems)
3 digestion (diabetes)
4 respiration (lung infection)
5 nervous system (dizziness)
6 ambulation/movement (stroke)
7 urinary tract infections (cystitis, kidney infections)
8 tissue growth (brain tumour)
9 poisoning (through medication interactions)

In a previous paragraph the causes of dementia were enumerated. The causes were separated into three groups in order to clarify how a person with dementia stays involved and remains affected by what happens to him or her: symptoms, consequences and affective reactions.

Let's now consider examples of disturbances that also occur in people with dementia, but which in these examples arise from physical changes. To remain manageable, these examples will be limited to the senses, the nervous system and poisoning. It is not difficult to imagine that 'being hard of hearing' can lead to, for example, orientation problems, mistaken insights and suspiciousness. A stroke can result in speech difficulties, difficulties in actions and aggression. An excess of, or, incorrect use of medication can lead to confusion, delusions and apathetic behaviour. In other words, before dementia is blamed for the difficulties exhibited by Mrs Jones, (orientation difficulties, aggression and restlessness), her senses, nervous system and medication regime must be examined and further investigations conducted.

Changes in contacts/relationships and the effects thereof

Physical changes are not the only cause of the symptoms and behaviours seen in dementia. During the passing of time, many things can go wrong in one's 'contact with other persons'. The following domains can be distinguished from one another:

1 (loss of) roles: such as giving up of voluntary work or societal functions, retirement from work or caring;
2 age discrimination: for example, to be discounted or prejudiced against because of one's age;

3   contacts: loss of family, friends and neighbours;
4   living conditions: moving or so many new developments/
    changes in one's environment that one is no longer recognised.

There are of course examples of disturbances that also occur in dementia, but which may surface as a result of social changes.

If someone has to retire from an important societal function, this change can result in inactivity and strong mood changes. It is easy to imagine that the loss of close friends can cause someone to become 'scattered', forgetful and neglectful of their own care. It is also possible to imagine that orientation problems can occur after a move. Persons may become 'quieter' because of the sadness and sorrow that such circumstances can bring. Usually though, there remains an attachment to what has been left behind, for example, the family, neighbours, friends or the neighbourhood.

In such situations, before dementia is diagnosed, orientation difficulties, mood changes, being 'scattered' and forgetful, sadness, role changes, the loss of friends and recent moves must all be investigated.

Changes in the person and the consequences thereof

As well as physical and social changes, older persons can also experience psychological changes. Changes can occur more deeply within the person themselves. Changes such as loneliness and self-neglect after widowhood, a diminished self-image after insecurity or bereavement, the individual manner in which persons cope with their loneliness, progressive ageing, which causes a reduction in the speed at which tasks become accomplished, can all occur. These are just a few examples. They barely represent the many possible changes that can occur deep inside the person.

Let us now consider other examples of disturbances that are also seen in dementia. In these instances, however, they occur as a consequence of psychological changes. Imagine that someone experiences such great difficulties when a partner dies that they increasingly turn inwards on themselves. Through this turning inwards, certain delusions (false notions) can persist or chronic self-neglect can become the norm. If one cannot cope with being alone, one can become even more lonely. It can make one distrustful, even to the extent of thinking that company never comes, or leaves, of their own volition, though their presence is still desired. A reduction in the tempo of living can sometimes cause inaccurate perception of the passing of time and inaccurate perceptions about how long it takes others to do more complex activities. In other words, before dementia is blamed for the problems that Mrs Jones exhibits, grieving behaviour, self-image and ageing difficulties must be examined.

Is Mrs Jones suffering from dementia?

The essence of the explanation given hereafter, is related to the previous paragraphs. One can only start to consider dementia if the previous changes have been eliminated from the assessment, that is, in so far as they are possible to determine. If Mrs Jones's disabilities cannot be attributed to such problems, then there is indeed a reason to suspect irreversible brain changes/damage. In other words, without individual assessment to exclude any possible physical, social and psychological factors that can affect health and behaviour, no diagnosis of dementia can be made. Ideally, a team of health care professionals (including blood and urine testing, physical, neurological, psychiatric examination and neuropsychological testing) should be involved in assessing the cause of Mrs Jones's behaviour change.

If the assessment is carried out in this manner, there are four global tracks through which a diagnosis of dementia could be arrived at. The departure point remains: 'Where is the behaviour change of Mrs Jones (or of your good friend) coming from?' The next examples are fictional and interchangeable with other examples. The purpose is to examine the hasty judgements that such behaviour evokes.

Despite medical treatment

Imagine that no physical or psychological causes for Mrs Jones's behaviour changes can be found. Imagine that the doctor has discovered, for example, wax build-up in the ears, some heart rhythm disturbances and a bladder infection. In this case, dementia can only be carefully considered when the behaviour doesn't change after these conditions are treated: syringing of the ears and medication to stabilise heart rate and antibiotic treatment.

Despite social help

Imagine that no physical or psychological causes for Mrs Jones's behaviour changes have been found. Imagine, however, that socially, she has been found to be very lonely after losing familiar contacts following a move. It is conceivable that Mrs Jones moved from Wiltshire to Kent to be closer to her last remaining family members in her old age. But the move wasn't all that she had hoped for. Her family aren't particularly pleased with her presence and she misses her neighbours. Mrs Jones was more attached to her life in Wiltshire than she had realised. In such a situation, dementia can only be considered if her behaviour does not change despite having received help for her social losses. Perhaps a move back, but more likely, joining in with new activities and building new friendships in Kent will help her to re-establish social contacts.

Despite psychological guidance

Imagine that no physical and social grounds for Mrs Jones's behaviour change have been found. Imagine that psychologically, however, something has come to light. For example, she has neglected most of her self-care after the sudden death of her partner or through fear and insecurity from a negative self-image in her old age. You might think she appears to be somewhat depressed. In this situation dementia can only be considered if Mrs Jones's behaviour does not change after help and counselling, but not while she is receiving active treatment or medication such as antidepressants or bereavement counselling.

The fourth possible indication that the behaviour of Mrs Jones is likely to be caused by dementia occurs if no physical, social or psychological conditions or changes have been found to explain her behaviour changes.

It's not that simple

The type of multidisciplinary assessment (screening) sketched above is not that simple to come by in practice. This is because an exhaustive physical assessment of someone may require additional specialists, for example, internists, and urologists. Sometimes, a geriatrician serves to unite these specialities. In theory, such assessment could be done in any large hospital, nursing home or even at a day clinic. However, not all assessment teams contain these professionals or use the same methods. Different regions have access to different resources. This does not have to pose a problem as long as knowledgeable persons from a number of professions participate in the assessment.

One in five persons is not suffering from dementia

About one person in five of those who are thought to be showing symptoms of dementia, and who undergo care assessment, especially at the earliest possible time, are found not to be suffering from dementia. So you can see how important a careful assessment is. If treatable causes are found for the behaviours that look like dementia (for example, depression, thyroid problems), then these behaviours will disappear. It must be emphasised that dementia is not yet curable, though some treatments are very slowly appearing on the market, Aricept being the most recent one. Once dementia has been diagnosed, it will not go away. Gradually it will only become worse, at least, those are the facts at this time. Researchers are in agreement with one another that 'dementia' is a 'probable' diagnosis. That means that only after the brain has been examined after death can a diagnosis be 100 per cent certain. Only then can the 'suspected, probable' causes be absolutely confirmed.

The causes of the changes to the brain in dementia will be elaborated upon at the end of this chapter. The range of existing methods and approaches to keep the negative consequences of dementia to a minimum are also considered at the conclusion of this chapter.

Types of dementia

To pick up on the thread of this story again, we were looking at the question of how the diagnosis of dementia is made. We saw how professionals carefully consider whether 'dementia' is the source of the difficulties. If, from the assessment it is concluded that Mrs Jones has dementia, in other words, that her behavioural changes are likely to be due to irreversible brain changes, then we have still not finished our investigation.

We haven't mentioned Alzheimer's disease (AD) yet, although we have spoken much about dementia. That is because Alzheimer's disease is only one part of the topic of dementia. There are different types of dementia. Alzheimer's disease is only one of these types. It belongs to the so-called 'primary dementias'. There are also 'secondary dementias'.

Primary dementias

The term 'primary dementias' is taken to mean that irreversible brain damage occurred before other eventual physical problems, or, it can mean that irreversible brain changes exist in the absence of physical problems. In practice, this latter situation is usually found in the young–old, when the dementia process seems to have an 'early onset'.

When one is discussing an organ as complicated as the brain, it is self-evident that even irreversible brain changes can have very different effects. We shall now consider Alzheimer's disease.

Which primary dementia?

In taking into account many other facts and observations, professionals can start to establish which kind of primary dementia is likely to be the cause of the brain changes. What are they taking into consideration?

They can look at how quickly or slowly the symptoms became evident. They can consider which symptoms occurred and in what combination they occurred. 'Where' in the brain the changes happen is important, but also the types of damage that occur is relevant. Careful investigation of 'neurological symptoms' is also made. The 'age of onset' (e.g. age 55 versus age 80) of the symptoms is an important consideration, as is information about whether anyone else in the family has had similar difficulties or a diagnosed dementia.

More than Alzheimer's disease

Depending on the information gained from looking at the above mentioned questions, someone might have Alzheimer's disease or Pick's disease. In other cases, it could be Huntington's chorea, Creutzfeldt–Jacob disease, Schilder's disease and so on. To understand what is meant by Alzheimer's disease in general, it is sufficient to know that a particular protein is deposited in certain areas of the brain. Without going into too much detail, the difference between Pick's disease and Alzheimer's disease lies in different combination and rate of development of the symptoms because of the different regions and types of damage to the brain. Huntington's chorea, in turn, involves a very different type and location of damage. The hereditary nature and type of neurological symptoms help to establish its diagnosis very specifically. It turns out, from the investigations of researchers, that about 60 per cent of all dementia sufferers have Alzheimer's disease. This means that Alzheimer's disease is the most common cause of dementia.

Secondary dementias

Secondary dementias refer to damage in the brain resulting from abnormalities or damage elsewhere in the body, and when it appears that these existing abnormalities are not or no longer treatable. For example, brain changes can occur as a result of Parkinson's disease, prolonged unconsciousness, untreatable heart and circulation problems or after untreatable thyroid conditions. Such brain changes, along with their associated symptoms are referred to as secondary dementia. The brain damage due to 'multi-infarcts', 'mini-strokes', 'cardio-vascular dementia' is considered as secondary dementia.

Earlier, it was stated that careful examination at the earliest stage possible, finds one in every five persons not suffering from 'dementia'. This means that the causes of their problems are 'treatable or curable'. Clearly, if one does not receive early intervention, a secondary dementia could develop. In practice, the immediate family usually does not manage to convince the person in question to get medical assessment and help as early as possible. This tends to happen because the so-called 'patient' doesn't see the use of going for help because 'there's nothing wrong'. On the other hand, in the early stage it is not clearly obvious to all in the immediate environment that 'dementia' might be the problem.

The existence of primary (e.g. Alzheimer's and Pick's diseases), and secondary (e.g. cardio-vascular) dementias often causes problems for 'outsiders' and the fellow care-home residents of persons with dementia. They often don't know what to do when persons with dementia have 'lucid' moments, and may assume that the person is faking their difficulties or 'putting on a show'. This is certainly not the case, especially if a person has cardio-vascular dementia. Large fluctuations in functioning are well known and typical of this type of dementia.

A diagnosis of Pick's disease can be made even when the 'forgetfulness' so typical of Alzheimer's disease is barely noticeable. It is no wonder that persons cannot believe that this could be a 'dementia'.

Pseudo dementia

With the current knowledge available, this term is rather old fashioned and out-of-date. It was used to refer to the period of behavioural changes in a patient when they later went back to normal again. In retrospect, we must conclude that if this happened, the assessment of the person must have been poor, insufficient and incomplete. Otherwise, the physical, social and psychological causes of his or her behaviour changes (symptoms) would have been discovered, or taken into consideration.

In other words, if the term pseudo dementia is used, the chances are great that the person using it has an out-dated or narrow view of the symptoms. In such a situation, the physical, social and psychological causes have been inaccurately eliminated or underestimated.

Medical scientific research

Let us now work out the stage we have reached in considering of the subject of dementia. There is an obvious difference between 'causes of symptoms' and 'causes of dementia'. In the first instance, the important question is: 'Can we speak about dementia in Mrs Jones's case?' As we have already discussed, the answer to this question can be found by a team of professionals conducting a thorough personal assessment and examination.

In the second instance, the question is: 'What is the cause of the brain changes in all those persons, and in Mrs Jones specifically, who have undergone a detailed examination?' The answer to this question has been sought by thorough research for decades. This type of research is called 'neurobiological research'.

Causes of dementia

What causes dementia? What exactly causes the typical types of damage to brain tissue? There are six main 'hypotheses' about the causes of the brain damage. Another way of saying this is that researchers suspect and are searching in six different areas for the answer. These areas include: genetic/hereditary factors, nerve cell growth, neurotransmitters, slow virus diseases, the immune system and poisoning. For the sake of completeness, they will now be described briefly.

Six possible types of causes

Genetic research is undertaken when it is suspected that the brain damage seen in a given type of dementia seems to be hereditary. This cause of the dementia is transmitted to the offspring, and is already present at birth. This is the case in Huntington's chorea, one of the primary dementias. Genetic research has accelerated particularly because of the findings from research into Huntington's chorea.

Nerve cell research has focused on the very exact types and measurements of changes that occur within and outside of the different types of nerve cells in particular parts of the brain. Brain tissue is needed to do such research. This is why families are sometimes asked to give their consent for an autopsy to take place after the person with dementia has died. (A new recent line of research involves trying to make 'nerve growth factors', which are substances that help nerve cells to grow faster, in their efforts to regenerate and repair themselves.)

Neurotransmitters are the chemical substances that enable signals to pass between the countless nerve cells in our brain and body. Dopamine and noradrenalin are two well-known neurotransmitters, but there are many others. Dopamine deficiency is the major problem in Parkinson's disease. In Alzheimer's disease, the production of acetylcholine is diminished, although it is not yet known exactly why this happens.

Other researchers are looking at the possible effects of slow viruses and immune system disturbances as a source of the damage caused in dementia. This line of investigation is justified by the findings that in the final stages of HIV/AIDS, some persons also develop dementia.

Another line of investigation is being taken by researchers looking at whether metals such as zinc and aluminium might be causing a type of 'poisoning' as it were. (However, it is normal to have small amounts of these metals in our bodies.) Work is being done to try to determine if 'damaged cells' bind excessive amounts of metal to themselves, or whether large amounts of these metals cause damage to the cells.

No medical treatment for dementia exists yet

When one considers how complex the brain is, and all of the types of cells and substances it contains, it should be obvious that a solution for dementia will not be 'simple' to find. The chance of finding the causes of dementia are limited, as are the chances of finding treatments. There are no current medicines that can 'cure' dementia. (Some medications in the past years have, at best, been shown to slow the deterioration of dementia for about six months and to slightly improve 'activities of daily living' for a very limited time. They have not been available to everyone and are not licensed for use in all countries.) Any claims you read about describing 'spectacular' recoveries from dementia made by individuals, or 'obvious causes' should be treated with great suspicion.

Mistakes

If your room-mate, neighbour or Mr Jones tells you that his wife has Alzheimer's disease, you should ask where, when and by whom his wife was examined. If his wife was not examined carefully, then chances are he got his idea from the radio, a newspaper or an unreliable source. The trouble is, that once Mr Jones thinks that his wife has dementia, and he then hears, for example, on the radio, that 'zinc' deficiency is the cause, he will likely try to get zinc for her. It would be better for him to go to his doctor and ask for a multidisciplinary assessment for his wife, to see whether she really does have dementia.

Misunderstandings

When people say that Mrs Jones is more demented than Mr Peters, it is usually clear what they mean. However, they are not using the word 'demented' correctly. They probably mean that Mrs Jones is more severely affected or showing more symptoms of her dementia than Mr Peters. The minimal symptoms of Mr Peters might have everything to do with the presence of a severe dementia, and the severe symptoms of Mrs Jones may be temporary and reversible.

Hence, the word 'dementia' has little or nothing to do with the severity of the symptoms. It is a diagnostic term used to indicate that there is a relationship between the symptoms and particular brain changes.

Support for the consequences of dementia

Sometimes the dementia process may be long, in other cases it may be short. A period of 10 years' duration is not exceptional. A large portion of one's life then, is thus affected and cannot be re-lived. As a rule, this part of one's life is not an easy one – not for the person suffering from the dementia, nor their family, nor for the others involved, such as fellow care-home residents.

The medical research to date does not have a lot to offer us in practical terms. This applies to its contributions to personal assessment and screening as well as to the findings of scientific research. Such is the state of things, sad though it is. A remedy is not yet visible on the horizon. Hence, whilst we are waiting and hoping, our attention must be focused on working with the consequences of having dementia.

Consequences for the person with dementia

Whilst the search for the causes and treatment of dementia continues, increasingly more research is looking at the consequences of having a dementia upon the sufferer him/herself and on ways of making life as bearable as possible under the circumstances. This is an important issue, namely: 'In which way can we best help a person with dementia?' 'How can we interact with Mrs Jones so that we have real "contact" with her, or can "reach" her?' 'How can we interact with her so that she feels better as a result of our efforts, and so that we do too?'

These questions cause researchers to look in a number of different directions (as with the causes of dementia). These methods have one common goal: to support and maintain the wellbeing of the person with dementia.

Interpersonal approaches and aids

- using and practising 'memory' tasks (memory training)
- counselling (support groups, having a good listener, psychotherapy)
- looking back upon one's life to put a story together (life review)
- actively and intentionally thinking about the past (reminiscing)

- continually providing reminders about the present situation/reality (reality orientation training)
- acknowledging the feelings of the person versus the facts (the validation approach)
- singing, music, dancing, movement to music (music therapy)
- providing known sensory stimuli such as familiar objects, food, smells, sounds for the person who is no longer speaking clearly (sensory stimulation)
- high-technology sensory stimulation with music, colour, lighting, objects, and a variety of furnishings (*snoezelen*)

During the course of the dementia, different approaches need to be used. Not every method is effective at any given time, or during each stage. In order to select which methods will be most effective, it is helpful to have as much knowledge about a person's life history as possible. This not only means details about their personality, and what happened to them in their life but also information about their 'favourite things', 'dislikes', and their hobbies or avocations.

Consequences of dementia for the family

If you are a non-demented resident of a care home, sometimes you will still end up being involved with the family, spouse or children of the person with dementia. That is why it is also helpful to have some insight into the experience of the family. The family doesn't only battle with innumerable practical issues. To have a dementing spouse, father, mother, brother or sister means to be constantly grieving for the changes in them. This is an additional burden. For some, it isn't a noticeable burden, for others, it is barely endurable. In Chapter 6 of this book, special attention will be given to the topic of families. Often, families are in desperate need of information about dementia. Promoting their understanding can help them to carry their burden, which sometimes goes on for years. In many situations, group therapy is helpful for family members. In support groups (such as those organised by the Alzheimer's Disease and Related Disorders Society), many of which have existed for years already, attention can be given to the emotional process involved in getting over a loss or bereavement. In a few instances, individuals require 'one-to-one' counselling and help, even psychotherapy. This occurs especially if, whilst a person is grieving for a person with dementia, other unresolved issues arise, and/or strong feelings of guilt are felt.

In conclusion

We now know that dementia is considered if Mrs Jones's behaviour changes have occurred as a result of irreversible changes to the brain. This information is useful, but it does not give us a satisfactory way of helping or interacting with her – satisfactory, in the sense that it is gratifying both to her, and to outsiders. Before we can discuss how to interact with a person with dementia, we first have to understand, to the best of our ability, what is happening to a person as they experience dementia.

Memory difficulties are the essence of symptoms that present themselves in dementia. Memory will be the starting point of the discussion in the next chapter. This will help to explain what it means to the person him/herself to have dementia. Those who can imagine what Mrs Jones's world is like are in a better position to try to relate to her.

4 Seeking a handhold

Introduction

How our memory works has a lot to do with how information is processed and the circumstances in which that happens. Information comes to the brain via the bodily senses. In view of this explanation, you will see that you can forget many things without being troubled by the type of memory loss that occurs in dementia.

In this chapter, memory will be described by using a metaphor as a model. A number of concepts will be introduced such as: taking in an impression, imprinting it into memory and expressing this memory. These concepts help us to better understand the consequences of dementia and to better understand the world, as Mrs Jones in our example experiences it, as a result of her forgetfulness. Once you can see what this means for a person with dementia, you are one step along the road of being able to choose the best approach and attitude for caring. This model will become a guide for your interactions.

Watch out for the location

Before delving into an explanation of memory, let us first summarise what we know so far. In the preceding chapter it became clear that the subject of dementia is more complex than it seems at first glance. We must constantly decide what it is exactly that we are discussing and which aspect we are considering. So the question at this point is: 'Where are we now?'

Three aspects of dementia

To answer this question, we need to distinguish between three aspects of dementia. First, the symptoms: the behaviour which you, as an outside observer perceive in a person with dementia. These have already been discussed. Second, the diagnosis: 'How does one determine that dementia really is the problem?' This was also discussed in Chapter 3. Third, the consequences of the symptoms were considered and the emotional/affective reactions to them (these will be discussed in Chapter 5).

This chapter deals with the consequences of the most obvious symptom – forgetfulness. Recall that we said that the person with dementia remains intimately concerned about what happens to him/her, with 'head and heart'. The next example may possibly be familiar to you. It illustrates what is meant by these three separate aspects.

Example: a pain in the knee

Imagine that you have a pain in your knee that just isn't going away and all because of a slight accident with a stepladder. Everybody is providing you with helpful advice. They all tell you exactly what has happened to your knee and what you should be doing to get rid of the pain. Eventually, none the wiser because your pain persists, you end up going to the doctor, orthopaedic specialist, surgeon or physio-therapist. In any event, you have finally decided that you will let a professional sort out what is causing your pain. It could be any number of things: a splinter of bone has slid beneath your knee-cap, you have a large bruise or have torn a ligament, etc. Whatever the case, a diagnosis about the cause of the pain will be made. Imagine the cause is a torn ligament. With a bit of luck you'll soon recover and the pain will cease.

More than the cause of the pain

Knowing the cause of the pain is only one aspect of the problem. Imagine that your bedroom is on the first floor. How often in a day do you go upstairs? Or, what if you usually meet your friends at the community sports centre every week for a good workout? Maybe you enjoy walking, and regularly go for long walks with your partner through the park or countryside. Or, imagine that you love to dance. Perhaps you purposely remain very physically active because you don't like being overweight. (These are just some hypothetical suggestions.) It is precisely these consequences of having a torn liga-ment that affect your daily life and which turns it upside down. With 'head and heart' you continue to be affected by your sore knee, even if you know that eventually it will heal.

The other side of dementia

Let us return to the strange behaviour of Mrs Jones. The symptoms represent the first aspect of her illness; the assessment to determine whether her illness is dementia is the second; the realisation that Mrs Jones is deeply affected by her forgetfulness is the third. In other words, she simultaneously tries to cope with her memory problems. Her memory disorder influences her life and her 'spirits'. What has happened to her, and continues to happen to her, continuously influences her existence. It affects her deeply – perhaps more than we will ever be able to imagine.

Awareness context

It is possible that you don't know Mrs Jones very well. Maybe she's doing everything possible to disguise what she herself has already long been aware of. Maybe she acts as if nothing is the matter, although from time to time it drives her to despair. Maybe it makes her very angry or sad every time she realises that she has forgotten where she wanted to go. Maybe she feels ashamed in your presence. Therefore, she does have a certain insight into her own situation.

There are very few arguments to suggest that persons with dementia do not react to what happens to them, let alone wouldn't be able to feel that strange things are happening to them. Hence, we can speak about an 'awareness', similar to that in patients who know/feel that they are going to die. This is what will be referred to as 'awareness context'. The provision of (greater or lesser amounts of) information to a person about what is happening to them influences their behaviour. Observing 'memory' in great detail gives us information about the 'awareness context' of persons with dementia. This is how the consequences of memory difficulties become noticeable to outsiders.

A practical model

Memory can be explained in any number of ways, with varying assumptions and schemes. The model chosen here has been useful in teaching about dementia for many years. To some extent, it opens one's eyes and offers a 'handle' for understanding what is happening to Mrs Jones when her memory functioning 'leaves something to be desired'. It is a simple information-processing model.

Sensory information

Information coming in through the senses ends up in the memory. Throughout life, all kinds of information comes into the brain from the outside. This happens through sight, hearing, touch, smell, taste and kinaesthesis (the awareness of how one's body is moving). Finally, after traversing thousands of nerve cells, this sensory information arrives at the brain, which is a part of the nervous system. Exactly how this process works will not be discussed here. What is important is that you are aware that these six different types of sensory information have different ranges. Simplistically speaking, what you hear comes 'from further away' than what you taste. The range of the information, from seeing to tasting, diminishes. In other words, to transmit information through your senses of touch, smell and taste, you literally have to stand closer to someone than to see or hear them. We will return to this point later on, because it will become clear that sometimes touching and body contact between the carer and person with dementia is necessary for a number of reasons. It is not a whim or fancy on either person's part.

Impressions, imprints, and expressions

Imagine that Mrs Jones is able to remember or recognise information, something she once heard, saw, touched, smelt, tasted or felt. Perhaps her memory is of her wedding day. She *expresses* something which once made an *impression* on her and was *imprinted into* her memory. It would be impossible for her to remember if this had not taken place. She can only recall what she heard, saw and so on, if this information was saved in her memory.

An information-processing view of memory, as opposed to a 'storage' view of memory, consists of three phases. Information from outside is first taken in as an *impression*, then *imprinted into* memory before it can be *retrieved for expression* (recalled as a memory). In other words, information must be gathered or assimilated, then stored and finally, reproduced.

Ever forgotten anything?

Every person forgets something sometime, both large things and small things. Aside from the perhaps frustrating or dramatic consequences of such an occasional instance of forgetting, one doesn't usually worry about it more than is necessary. Try for a moment to remember an instance where your memory failed you. If I were to ask you to find a good excuse for your forgetfulness, which one would you come up with?

Valid excuses

A few of the many excuses for forgetting will be summarised next (without our even striving to make an exhaustive list). Possibly the excuse that you just thought up will be listed among them.

You were (much) too busy.
You had too little information
You had too much information at the same time.
Your attention was focused on something else.
You were accidentally distracted by someone / something else.
It was (much) too long ago.
It didn't interest you.
Something just happened to have interfered with your good intentions (unforeseen circumstances or a sudden event).
You didn't like it.
It wasn't important to you.
You didn't really pay attention.
You were too emotional at the time.
You were in a rush.
You couldn't 'get a handle on it'
There were no resources or study aids to help you.
You couldn't concentrate.
You were very tired.
And so on. . . .

Individual memories

These justifiable excuses can be taken as factors that negatively affect memory, or at any rate, information processing. Not all these factors influence memory the same way in all persons. One person is more affected by one factor than the other. This means that, apart from processes that are more or less the same in everyone, forming impressions, imprinting and expression is different for everyone. One person can process more information simultaneously than another. What is interesting for one person is not so for another. Some are more affected by fatigue than others. Some can concentrate more easily than others, and so on. We thus have very individual memories.

Incidentally, it is the above excuses (also called external factors), that memory training courses teach you to become aware of and keep under control.

The influence of excuses

These factors, which can influence each stage of information processing, actually produce a sort of block. They block the process of taking in impressions, imprinting them into memory and the expression of what you remembered (took in through your senses).

If you are in a situation where there is a lot of activity going on (information coming into the senses) at the same time, for example, you are at a party in a small room, the abundance of activity will certainly block some of your impressions of the information. When you are tired, the imprinting of the information is more difficult. If you are on the street and meet someone whose name escapes you, then something is wrong with the retrieval and/or expression of their name. Naturally you know what the person's name is, it's just that at this very moment, today of all days, you can't get it. Quite certainly you did make an impression and imprint of their name previously.

It is well known that the more (and the more easily) a new situation reminds you of a past situation, the more the stimuli in the new situation correspond with those of the past one. Recall of impressions of the past is easier in the new situation. Also, information that has been imprinted with a great appreciation for the 'meaning', is more deeply imprinted into memory and more easily recalled, than information that is superficially imprinted.

A unique memory

Every person is different. What is important for one person, is not always important for another. Generalisation is impossible. In the following section however, I will generalise in order to draw some broad guidelines and principles. This model makes seven assertions about information processing. You can think of these assertions as 'intelligent guesses' about how memory works. They will give you a certain insight into a number of the behaviours that persons with dementia show. In order to help the clarity of the explanation they will be expressed in quantitative terms (as numbers). In reality, these explanations are about the quality of the information being processed in memory.

Seven assertions about memory

First, the seven assertions will be briefly described. Thereafter, each will be dealt with in more detail. With the help of examples you will see that a number of practical 'handles' for interacting with persons with dementia will be offered.

Some handles require insight into the consequences of certain memory impairments for the person with dementia. And that is the purpose of this chapter – to provide suggestions about interacting and caring for someone, based on an idea about what is happening within the person. At the end of this chapter, all seven assertions will be repeated, together with the 'handles' for interaction.

The seven assertions in quick overview

1   All factors that can negatively affect the process of making impressions, imprinting them into memory and expressing (recalling) them in ordinary persons can also affect persons with dementia.
2   As time goes on, fewer imprints are made of new impressions.
3   As one ages, the total number of imprints ever made are reduced.
4   The older someone becomes, the less information they can simultaneously process (i.e. take in as impressions and imprint into memory).
5   The process of impression formation, imprinting and expression is favourably influenced when multiple senses are used together.
6   Recognition of imprints is easier than the retrieval of imprints.
7   The preceding assertions differ for each sense.

Our excuses are also theirs

The first assertion about memory is: all factors that can negatively affect the process of taking in impressions, imprinting them into memory and expressing (recalling) them in ordinary persons can also affect persons with dementia.

To be completely clear: the factors that might make some of you feel uneasy about your memory are naturally not the causes of dementia. The important thing to recognise is that, as a rule, people with dementia pay more attention to those things that interest them or are important to them at any given moment than those things that seem uninteresting or irrelevant. Just like you, they can be distracted, have a lesser or greater concentration upon something and be subject to their emotions. Not only that, persons with dementia can naturally also become tired in situations where they find themselves confronted with too much information at the same time. Sometimes it is very busy in a home or care home, in the activity room or at mealtimes. In a care home, they may see many different faces and these faces change during the course of the day. Just like you, persons with dementia can have 'too much on their mind', 'not be there with their thoughts', or 'be continually distracted'. You might find yourself being cared for by someone with a soft, lovely face that moves you deeply or by someone who is short-tempered and hasty, who, without meaning to, because of her haste, hurts you by knocking your well-hidden mole. Such interactions can stick in the memories of both ordinary persons and persons with dementia.

How do we keep track?

Memory in persons with dementia can be extra negatively influenced by the factors already mentioned. What is important is that you realise this, and take it into consideration when caring for them. How? By more or less interacting with them in the way that you yourself would wish to be dealt with.

You can do this by not failing the person with dementia when they find themselves in noisy and busy situations. Try to reduce the noise or help them to a quieter area. Make sure you make a clear and good impression upon them. Take note of their interests. Don't visit them with too many people at the same time, and don't try to do too many things at the same time. Ensure that there are as few distractions as possible. Reduce your speed of speaking (and perhaps moving) somewhat, so they can follow you better. And so forth.

In short, you want to take into account all of the same factors that play a role in affecting your own memory functioning in daily life.

Continually less imprints made

The second assertion about memory was: 'As time goes on, fewer imprints of new impressions are made.' See Figure 1.

How can you imagine this? You know that this refers to imprints of information coming to us from our senses (hearing, seeing, etc.). Remember that the model (which is illustrated by the graph in

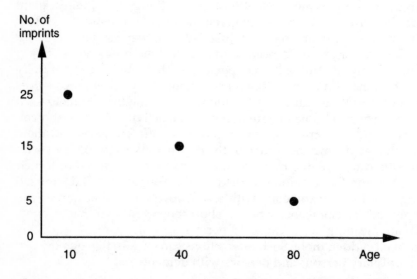

Figure 1 A hypothetical model of memory showing that the number of 'imprints' made (in memory) of a given 'impression', decreases with age

Figure 1) is only giving you a picture or idea about what might be happening to memory in people with dementia. It is just one way of expressing it. How that process really works physiologically in the nervous system and brain is not precisely known and will not be discussed here. Exactly how the previously named factors can negatively influence the making of impressions, imprinting into memory and expression (recall) will not be discussed here either.

Imagine yourself as a 10-year-old forming all sorts of new impressions about the world in a certain situation. Of these impressions, many more than a single imprint is made, let us say, perhaps about twenty-five. However, in middle age, exposed to a similar situation, fewer imprints are made, perhaps about fifteen. Similar impressions at the age of 80 would mean even fewer imprints made, perhaps about five. In other words, as one ages, fewer imprints are made of new impressions.

Let us look at the graph in Figure 1 again. The three points already marked show the number of imprints made as one gets older. If we now connect them with a straight line, you will see that the line slopes downwards. If this line is continued, it will touch (intersect with) the horizontal line (horizontal axis) where the three ages have arbitrarily been marked. This intersection point is very important and is shown in Figure 2.

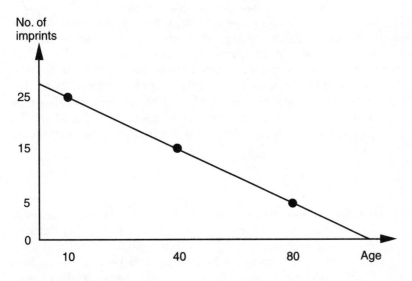

Figure 2 A hypothetical model of memory, showing that at a certain point in very old age, no more 'imprints' of an 'impression' are made.

No more imprints made of impressions

The downward sloping line in Figure 2 shows that with time, fewer imprints are made of impressions. From the point where the sloping line touches the horizontal line, no more imprints are made of the impressions. If you should live to a ripe old age and stay healthy, you will never reach this point. The point in time when no more imprints are made would be at your death. However, during the course of dementia, persons will pass this point eventually, some earlier than others. These persons continue to live but don't make imprints of their impressions any more. This is a dramatic moment has far-reaching consequences for their experiential world.

In the following paragraphs, a few examples of such far-reaching consequences for Mrs Jones will be given. These can of course be matched by examples from your own experiences. It will become clear that dementia 'seems' to begin at this important intersection point. (What dementia is and how it is diagnosed was discussed in the preceding chapter.)

A new face

> Mrs Jones, who just happened to have got out of bed on the wrong side today (and who doesn't want anyone bothering her just now), goes to open the door when she hears the doorbell ring. It's the new nurse. But she doesn't know this. She opens the door, but just a crack. She doesn't like the look of this face, and because she isn't in a good mood, quickly shuts the door again. The new nurse isn't going to take this, waits a while and rings the doorbell again. This scene repeats itself five more times. Even if this situation would continue to repeat itself for the entire morning, for Mrs Jones, the nurse's face might continue to look 'new' each time. Without being able to make an imprint of this new impression (the new nurse), Mrs Jones may never realise that each time it is the same nurse at the door. By the end of the morning Mrs Jones is very tired (not surprisingly) but she has no idea why.

A strange room

By the time someone has been placed in a care home, it usually means that the dementia process has progressed noticeably further. At some point, a person with dementia (now resident) will wake up in a bedroom that looks completely strange and new to them. Mrs Jones wakes up each morning in the same room, that is, in the eyes of her carers! But, for Mrs Jones, no imprints of the impressions of the bedroom have been made. Each morning again, Mrs Jones has no idea where she is.

In Chapter 5 we will see how Mrs Jones remains involved 'with her heart' to what is happening to her. We will see that certain 'strange' experiences can lead to all kinds of emotional/affective reactions.

Haven't had a cup of tea yet

Mrs Jones is sitting in the activity room of the care home. She is sitting in the front row of chairs. She likes to play bingo, but especially likes winning. It gives her a pleasant kind of tension, a pleasurable thrill. She just enjoyed a lovely cup of tea. Suddenly, loud laughing can be heard near the entrance of the room, to the left of her seat. It catches her attention. She turns her head and looks in that direction. Her empty tea cup is no longer in view now. When she returns her gaze to the number card, she sees that her cup is empty. But the teacup of the lady sitting next to her isn't. Indignantly, she exclaims that she hasn't had any tea yet.

Because Mrs Jones cannot make imprints of new impressions (especially when she's distracted and her own empty cup keeps disappearing from her field of view), she could keep on drinking cups of tea. She would have the unpleasant feeling though that she kept being missed out when the tea was being poured. Later, she would make it to the toilet, just in time . . . it seemed to come on so urgently!

Ice-cold hands

Bert works as a care assistant in a home. He has a soft spot for Mrs Jones. In any case, he's always very concerned about her, especially when she's sad. He's not shy about holding her hand. One morning, he's sitting next to her, and realises that she has ice-cold hands. Before he has a chance to tell her how surprised he is that she's so cold, he's called to help elsewhere. When he returns he says to Mrs Jones: 'My, your hands were ever so cold!' Mrs Jones looks at him with astonishment. What is this 'young pup' sitting next to her going on about?

Now that she cannot make imprints of new impressions, she cannot remember that he had briefly held her hand only moments ago.

How does one keep contact?

We mentioned that although persons with dementia do not make imprints of new impressions, they continue to live. That raises the question: 'How, under such circumstances, does one keep in contact with them?' The answer arises from the examples given. Whatever you talk about with a person with dementia must last long enough for them to experience it. In other words, make sure that everything they are taking in through their senses is as clear as possible. As long as you are both looking at a blue sky and clouds, you can talk about it. 'My goodness, can you see that large cloud over there?' As long as you are listening to an operetta together you can say: 'Doesn't that music make you feel cheerful?' But if you turn your back to the window, or wait till the record is finished, and say to Mrs Jones 'That sure was a large cloud', or, 'What did you think about the merry waltz?' then she won't know what you're talking about. In this last example, you are returning to the subject and are using the past tense in your speech. While you are both experiencing it together you can use the present tense. This is also true for smelling and tasting. As long as Mrs Jones is busy eating some cake, you can talk to her about it. Thereafter you cannot. Now let us return to the example of ice-cold hands.

Again: her ice-cold hands

Naturally, Bert couldn't help it that he was called away. But if he had realised that Mrs Jones couldn't make imprints of impressions, he would have handled the conversation differently on his return. He wouldn't have started speaking to her again about it. Or, he would have felt her hands again, would have kept holding them and would have said: 'Gosh, what cold hands you have!' There is a good chance that she may have answered: 'Your hands are really warm!'

As long as something can be sensed or felt, you can easily continue to talk about it. When the stimulus is gone, or cannot be seen in the visual field, then it is outside the experiential world of the person with dementia. In that case, Bert's question will fall amiss. To return to something that is already past, when Mrs Jones hasn't been able to make any imprints of it, is pointless.

One last example will be given to illustrate how important the perception of sensory information (stimuli) is, in order to have/keep contact with the person with dementia.

Parting

Mr Jones often visits his wife in the care home. But, one of the things he finds difficult to deal with is that his wife gets in such a state when he needs to go home and has to leave her there. Sometimes, it bothers him so much he can't even sleep. What is happening? Every time when he indicates that he has to leave, his wife becomes restless. She wants to go with him. Sometimes, she becomes 'panicky' or sad. At the door, as he's about to leave, she grabs hold of him tightly. Sometimes she bursts into tears. His heart breaks at these moments. He's not sure what he should do – stay longer or go home. At night time, he can't sleep because he has made imprints of these impressions. He keeps seeing his wife in front of him. She is holding him tightly and wants to go home.

What happens, then, in such situations? In short, the following. As soon as her husband cannot be seen at the door, in the lift or on the staircase, Mrs Jones turns around and as it were starts to turn over what's happened during the day in her mind. A little while later she's sitting at the table laughing, or walking with a fellow resident, arm in arm down the corridor. She says, winking to the nurse, 'My husband? I haven't heard anything from him yet. It's about time he put in an appearance!' In other words, as soon as her husband is out of her visual field, it's as if he's never been there at all. She cannot make imprints of impressions. She does not even 'know' that she was sad when he left. But he does. No wonder he can't sleep. His wife hasn't been troubled at all, at least, not by his apparent absence.

Had Mr Jones returned after a few minutes, to secretly look around the corner and to check on his wife, he would have witnessed a scene that would have helped him to sleep. He would have seen that Mrs Jones was laughing and walking arm in arm down the hallway with another lady. In short, you must ensure that the person whom you are speaking about remains present by being tangible to the person with dementia. This is the second 'handle' that gives a handhold for interacting with a person with dementia.

But also remember the converse. When something seen, triggers feelings of fear, insecurity or discomfort, remove the 'thing' from the visual field, and these feelings will disappear also. Think about an object in the room, or a shadow on the wall. Sometimes, a fellow resident resembles someone the person with dementia knew and disliked in the past. Their panic will only stop, or they will only become restful again, when that 'former disliked acquaintance' has gone.

For Mr Jones it is difficult to assimilate that the memory impairments of his wife mean both that he is in the process of 'disappearing

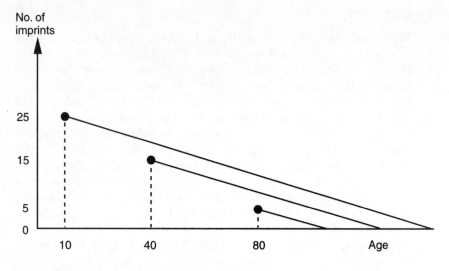

Figure 3 A hypothetical model of memory, showing that the *total* number of imprints made of a given impression also decreases with age

from her life' and separating from her 'in the process of becoming a widower'. This problem will be addressed in Chapters 6 and 16.

Increasingly fewer imprints made of a given impression

The third assertion is that as one ages, the total number of imprints 'ever made' of something, are reduced. See Figure 3.

How can one imagine this? Recall that we are discussing sensory 'impressions' that are being imprinted into our memory from our senses (hearing, seeing, feeling, smelling and tasting). This includes images, ideas, or 'a feeling about' what is happening in the world around oneself. It is not 'reality'.

Let us return to the explanation of the second assertion about memory. We assumed that when you were a child, in middle age and in old age – you made 25, 15 and 5 imprints respectively, of each new impression. This third assertion suggests that, somehow, the total number of impressions ever made is reduced. Fewer imprints of a given impression remain in old age than were made in total. You can see in Figure 3 that from the three points plotted, three downward-sloping lines have been drawn. They intersect with the horizontal line at three different points in old age. Figure 4 shows a line drawn vertically from the first of these new points.

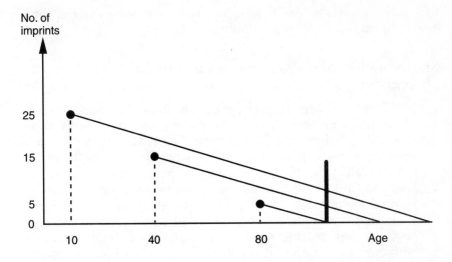

Figure 4 A hypothetical model of memory, showing that in dementia there comes a point where perhaps no more imprints of impressions made after age 80 exist, although memories of middle and early years are still plentiful

No imprints left

The new vertical line cuts through the two top downward-sloping lines at the same time. These downward-sloping lines show that with age, fewer imprints remain of the total original number made. At the intersection points with the horizontal line, there are no more imprints left of 'once-made imprints'. That means that to the left of the intersection point of the new vertical line drawn in Figure 4, no more imprints remain of the most recent memories. This means that there are no more imprints remaining of impressions that were made after the age of 80. You would not be able to remember what had happened after this age.

If you follow the vertical line upwards, you will see that it crosses the second downward-sloping line. It represents the few imprints left from middle age. If you follow the vertical line to the point where it joins the top downward-sloping line, you will see that most imprints remain of the impressions you took in at age of 10.

What is important is this. During the course of dementia, but certainly not in the early stage, this point is reached. Some persons with dementia reach it sooner than others. They continue to live, but eventually retain more imprints of the impressions of their youth than anything thereafter. This has far-reaching consequences for their experiential world, for how they understand what is happening to them now.

Hereafter, a few examples will be given of these consequences as they affect a certain Mrs Peters. You will be able to expand these examples with those from your own experience.

She recognises him when she sees him in the photograph

Mrs Peters has dementia. She turned 85 today. Her son who is in his fifties is visiting. As is usually the case, she doesn't know who this greying man is. He treats her kindly, in a calm and friendly manner. It doesn't matter what he does or tries, she can't recall who he is. Sometimes, he reminds her of her husband. But she still remembers that he isn't around because he died quite young. She's a bit tearful thinking about it again. While the care assistant is helping her to bed, she points to a photo on her bedside table. It is an old photograph of herself with her four children. It is dated, and was taken just in front of her brother's farm in Wiltshire some twenty years ago. The care aid points to the youthful face of her son in the snapshot and asks Mrs Peters who it is. She answers with a combination of pride and regret in her voice. 'Oh, that's Peter. I only had one son.'

Grandchildren?

When no more imprints are made of impressions occurring in the latter years, it is possible that Mrs Peters doesn't recognise her youngest grandchildren any more. When the process has continued longer, she may not even recognise the older grandchildren, even to the point where she doesn't recognise the oldest grandchild whose arrival she greeted with such inwardly contained joy. That little girl made up for so much of the early loss of her husband. When a fellow resident asks Mrs Peters what are the names of her grandchildren, she may burst into laughter denying that she has any grandchildren. 'Are you crazy woman? I've just started courting!'

But exceptions are possible. Recognising and remembering that she has grandchildren is also affected by other influences (factors) related to memory functioning. Perhaps one grandchild makes a stronger impression than another, for example, through their voice, manner of dressing, posture, way of doing things or because of a special bond. One grandchild may be remembered because of this special bond, though the others are forgotten.

Wedded to the first

Whilst this comparison doesn't fit entirely (think back to the influence of many factors acting together), one more example will be given. Imagine that Mrs Peters recently married John after being widowed for thirty years. Let's imagine that since the wedding and everything thereafter, no more imprints of these events have been made. John will never be able to convince her that he is her legally wedded husband, and all the consequences of this wedding are lost to her. Perhaps the time will come when she calls John by her first husband's name, which was William.

In short, be careful to speak more about distant past time than the present to a person with dementia. Reminisce with them. That is the third handle for interaction. It would be better to speak about the First or Second World War than about the Gulf War, the Falklands War, or even Vietnam.

If you knew your fellow resident in the past, you have a great advantage. You can start a conversation up more easily because you already know so much about this person. If this isn't the case, then it's more difficult. Perhaps you could ask family or friends something about their past. If you want to reminisce with persons with dementia, which is usually a very pleasurable activity, then you'll have to find out something about their past.

This causes an extra problem for members of the nursing staff in a care home. They should be as familiar with some of the details of the early life history of the residents, as the back of their hand. They should know the life course or life history of each person. They should be 'in the know' about Mrs Peters' life. They should know who William was and when he died. Such information can be absent because of supposed 'privacy' issues, or because no one alive knows it. At present, noting life history information from family members of a person with dementia is more commonly done in nursing homes than in residential/care homes The truth is that it is needed everywhere.

History and being human

When an individual's life history is missing, you (or care aids and nurses) can make use of the local history of the time period to find out what happened when Mrs Jones and Mrs Peters were younger. When the individual history, and also the general history of the person is missing, keep trying to use general 'life themes' to have conversations (such as emotional events, friendship, becoming a grandparent, youth, work, war and peace, vacations, pets, gardening, even intimacy).

Little simultaneous information

The fourth assertion is: the older someone becomes the less information they can process at the same time (simultaneously).

How can you imagine this? Another term that gives a similar idea
is 'memory capacity'. This is the maximum information (hearing,
sight, smell, feeling, taste and touch) that can be imprinted and
expressed. With age, memory capacity is reduced. To repeat from
memory the telephone number 6823598271 is very difficult and
almost no one can do it without writing it down in smaller groups of
numbers. Yet, almost everyone can repeat the number 472937 without
error.

Sooner or later, the memory capacity of persons with dementia
becomes very limited. Sometimes they can barely utter a short
phrase, or even one word. Next, we'll look at an example about what
happens when persons with dementia are confronted with too much
information at the same time.

Urinating in the wrong place

You address Mr Rose, a resident with dementia, as you meet him
in the corridor. You were just going to the reception desk. To your
left is a red door. It is the door to the room where the house-
keeping staff keep their personal belongings when they're at
work. You don't know that Mr Rose's memory capacity is 'three'.
That is, that he can barely make three imprints of impressions at
the same time. Mr Rose asks you where the toilet is, saying
imploringly, that 'he needs to go very badly'. You've only been
working in this large care home for a few weeks, and aren't
particularly good yet at finding your way around. But, your brain
is working well and you perceive that his request is urgent. So
you start 'Good day Sir. Do you need the toilet? If you take this
corridor on the right and then go left to the end . . . do you see
where that nurse is walking?' You wave to the nurse because
she's looking in your direction. You think again and then say,
'Where the nurse is standing you have to find the third, no, the
fourth door on the left. It's a red door.'

Before you can add that Mr Rose will find the toilet behind that red
door, you see him opening the red door of the housekeeping store
room and fumble frantically with his zipper. But it's too late.

'Bite-sized portions' of information

It's probably already clear to you what happened. Mr Rose picked up on your last three words 'a red door'. He asked about the toilet, it was urgent. So he takes the first available red door he sees and starts going through the motions required to urinate. What went wrong is that you tried to guide him using too many words. Your good intentions came to nought. With his memory capacity of three words, Mr Rose will have been hearing/processing three words at a time, until you got to the last three. These were the ones he hung on to; the others were already gone so to speak.

Nowhere to get the thread

This is roughly what's happening when a person with dementia speaks, but you haven't got a clue as to what they're talking about. They want to say something, start along one tack, but after a few words have lost the thread of what they wanted to say. But they still continue speaking, and usually associate with the last spoken word. This can continue for quite a while. The final words thus have nothing to do with the first ones. There is no apparent 'rhyme or reason' to the sentence. For the bystander, as well as the person with dementia, the story has become an unintelligible jumble.

A Merry Christmas

In hospitals and nursing homes, also in residential homes, care staff have the inclination to want to make rooms extra pleasant and decorative for festive occasions. There are always a few patients or residents who cannot bear this. Sometimes this is noticeable by the increased use of medication to reduce certain people's restlessness. One possible explanation for this phenomenon is that some persons cannot process very much information at the same time. As long as the decorations are familiar ones that people recognise from their past, nothing much usually goes amiss. But nowadays, times are different, and staff members bring in the most unusual things. If the environment undergoes a substantial metamorphosis, sometimes people can really be put out. It can seem as if these people with dementia don't appreciate all of the efforts of the nursing staff! The fewer major changes that are made and the more recognisable the decorations are (recognisable imprints; see assertion number 3), the less unrest there will be.

Out on a visit

The above also holds true for the last example of the fourth assertion about memory. Try to prevent confrontation with too many imprints at the same time.

> Mrs Peters' daughter remained single. After her engagement broke off when she was aged 30, she continued to live with her parents. Together with her mother, she nursed her sick father. After his death, she remained with her mother. A few years later, after mother started receiving her pension, dementia started to become evident. When the brother saw that caring for mother was getting too much for his sister, he offered to take mother to his own home for a few weeks. This enabled his sister to go on holiday. The brother lived on the east side of the country and had four small, active children. After a few days there, things were already getting out of hand. The move from a familiar, to an unfamiliar setting (to her) was too much for mother.

There were too few recognisable imprints and too many simultaneous impressions. This is how, sometimes, well-intentioned offers of help can lead to disaster.

Avoid situations with too much information/stimulation

The above is true for all of the senses, including hearing. We should thus, literally be more careful about the words we use. We often confront the person with dementia with too many bits of sensory information at the same time. This also happens, unnoticed in a busy lounge or activity room, or even when a group of family members arrive together for a visit. This usually overwhelms the person with dementia. And, as for conversation, we usually talk far too much during visits. This means that most of what we say will bypass the person completely. Whatever you say, it should be done with a minimum of words. Use short sentences and speak slowly and clearly. Only tackle one subject of conversation at a time.

In short, do not use too many words at a time if you really want to say something to a person with dementia. This is the fourth handle to help care interactions. Say as much as you can with the fewest possible words.

Using several senses together

The fifth assertion about memory is: the process of taking in impressions, making imprints of them and expressing them again, is favourably influenced when multiple senses are used together.

This actually occurs quite often. You sometimes recognise images, for example, on the television, which remind you of a long conversation or a particular mood, long ago. Or, perhaps you once had a family picnic in the autumn in the leaf-strewn meadows somewhere. When you've captured this image, you may notice that other images from your childhood start re-surfacing – of sitting in front of a wood fire, etc. That the one memory is linked somehow to the other memory has to do with the fact that the process of taking in impressions is a complex one and that information comes in through several senses. If you want to get someone to express something, either through the recognition or remembering of information, then you will succeed better if you use information from more than one sense. The following example will clarify this.

Toileting rounds

In the previous chapter we saw that incontinence (not having voluntary control over the elimination of urine and/or faeces), can happen to someone with dementia. To prevent urinary and faecal incontinence, 'toileting regimes' are often implemented. That means that nursing staff take people to the toilet at particular times during the day, to prevent them from having 'accidents'. Imagine that it's a very busy day and that the nurse has asked you to help with the toileting rounds.

> It is 11.30 a.m. You want to help Mrs Jones to the toilet, and without thinking you say to her 'Mrs Jones, do you need to use the toilet?' She looks at you blankly. Doesn't she hear you, or doesn't she understand what you are saying to her? Maybe it would be wise to ask again, but also to take her by the arm and walk her to the door of the toilet. When you open the toilet door so that Mrs Jones can see what your intention is, maybe she'll comply. When she smells the characteristic toilet smells, and feels her panties being lowered, she might understand what it is that you are trying to help her with.

Several senses but the same message

The above example is given to help remind us that we usually only 'talk' to people. At a certain point, talking alone doesn't work so well with persons with dementia. You must try to make use of senses other than hearing alone. Automatically, we speak only and forget that we have a veritable 'treasure trove' of gestures available at our disposal. But it isn't always easy. There are naturally messages that can only be expressed in words. But still . . .

Briefly, if you want to ask a person with dementia something, then you must try to 'package' your request using various types of sensory 'channels'. This is the fifth handle to help you care for and interact with a person with dementia. Don't rely just on their hearing; try to use sight, touch, smell, just as in the example above.

Recognition is easier

The sixth assertion about memory is that the 'recognition' of imprints (memories) is easier than the retrieval (recall) of stored imprints. For example, someone asks you what you ate yesterday evening. You don't have to think long, because you can remember it exactly. You might say: 'Tomato soup, roast turkey and baked potatoes, green beans, cranberry sauce and sherry trifle for dessert or pudding.' You can express exactly the imprints that were made about your evening meal.

But imagine that the person asking you the question had exactly the same thing for dinner as you did, only you can't remember exactly. You will take longer to think about the answer. To help you out a bit, he gives you a choice between two words every time. 'Was it vegetable soup or tomato soup?' 'Pork chops or roast turkey?' 'Mashed potatoes or baked potatoes?' 'Carrots or green beans?' 'Sherry trifle or ice-cream?' Each time you make the correct choice. After each item listed, all you have to do is answer with a 'yes' or a 'no'. Remembering information is easier when it is 'recognised' from information presented to you, than if you have to 'recall' it without help. This is also true for persons with dementia. The next example concerns Mrs Peters again.

A day at the zoo

The nurses have known for a long time that Mrs Peters loves animals. She was raised mostly on her grandparents' livestock farm. It was also noticeable how much she identified with the small farm located in the field behind the nursing home. She has a good view of it the whole day long. So it was assumed that she would go along on the little outing to the zoo. At least, if her son would pay the £25. This was an 'added extra', and not included in the price of her care. But her son couldn't exactly see the use of such a trip and didn't want to pay. 'Everything goes straight over the top of her. It would just be throwing money away.' After a great deal of persuasion he finally agreed to pay the money for his mother's trip. 'Just because you keep pestering me you understand. Mother won't take it in the least. It'll be gone immediately.'

The zoo, lovely isn't it!

Because you went along to the zoo, too, you were one of the witnesses as to the predictions the nurses had made. They had told you about how Mrs Peters' son had been a bit difficult to persuade. Mrs Peters had the day of her life. It was almost impossible to get her to go into the bus to return to the home. They had never heard her laughing so much before. When, at about seven in the evening, you were walking Mrs Peters back to her bedroom, arm in arm, just as full of contentment about the day as the nurses were, you bumped into the son. How it was that he had forgotten that today was the day of the outing is a mystery. At that moment, you are feeling solidarity with the nurses – all that fuss about the money for the trip. They were right that a day out at the zoo would be good for his mother. She had a smashing day out. The moment to express satisfaction had arrived.

In a semi-nonchalant way, as if the son standing there didn't have any ears, you address his mother and ask: 'Where did you go today?' The son, and you, prick up your ears. It is very quiet. Mrs Peters is reflecting, looks surprised, then somewhat puzzled. She then begins to speak about all manner of things, except that she went to the zoo today. The son, with a hint of a triumphant tone in his voice says: 'I predicted this, didn't I?'

It's logical that you go to your room feeling somewhat defeated. Your plan of 'showing the son' hadn't been so good after all. The nurses will probably not bother trying to get money out of Mrs Peters' son in the near future. What's more, you even feel a bit 'let down' by Mrs Peters, even though you know she couldn't help it. Later in the evening, the telephone rings. It's the nurse, who saw Mrs Peters answer you in front of her son, and who also saw you retreat like a dog with its tail between its legs. 'You won't believe it. I was just sitting with Mrs Peters as she was watching the television. There was a bit on about the zoo. Some young animal born there today or something. Then a clear picture of a giraffe. All at once she says: "We had such a pleasant day at the zoo today!" Did you think that she would remember it?'

Wrong conclusion

In the first part of this example you are asking Mrs Peters to 'reproduce' (recall without help) what she saw at the zoo today, in other
words, to express the imprints made today. Because she 'apparently'
doesn't know, the quick conclusion is usually drawn that she has
forgotten it. In the second part, it appears that she finally 'recognises'
the 'impressions' that she 'imprinted' today at the zoo. It must be
concluded that she did not forget the visit to the zoo at all.

More forgetful or not?

The same distinction between the reproduction (recall) and recognition of information is also relevant when care-home residents judge
whether someone has 'got worse'. One resident thinks that Mrs
Peters has become more forgetful in the last few months. The other
resident disagrees. Who is right? We can find the solution by asking
them both how they reached their own conclusions. The one resident
says: 'For a whole week at morning tea time I've introduced myself to
her, with both name and surname. She still doesn't know my name
though when I ask her.' The other resident says: 'I help to bring her
from her room to the lounge every morning. When I offer her my
arm, at first she looks a bit surprised. Then I usually start to smile,
and then I can notice that she recognises me.

Make use of recognition

In the last example, both fellow residents of Mrs Peters were right.
The first is correct because she is basing her conclusion on whether
Mrs Peters can reproduce information. The other is right because she
is basing her answer on whether or not Mrs Peters can recognise
information. When you use 'recognition' with persons with
dementia, they appear to 'know' more than you would expect. This is
true for the expression of newly made imprints as well as for the
expression of imprints made of impression formed long ago.

In short, use 'recognition' of information rather than 'reproduction'
to work out what a person with dementia really knows. That is the
sixth handle for helping you to provide optimal care. In practice this
means that when you ask a question, you must provide the correct
answer in your question and let the person agree or disagree with the
answer. Or, you might let them choose between two answers to say
which is the right one. You can do this with language (through
hearing), with photos (through sight), and with smell and touch.

The one sense is not the same as the other

The seventh assertion about memory is: the previous assertions will differ somewhat for each individual sense. What is meant by this? How can you imagine this? What does this mean for a person with dementia?

Applied to the second assertion about memory it means the following. When persons with dementia cannot make imprints of what they hear, perhaps they can still make imprints of what they feel or touch. Imprints might still be made of what they taste. This means generally that persons with dementia are better able to express what they tasted and smelt, than what they saw and heard.

Mrs Jones can more easily remember that the nurse who helped her to get dressed today had a pleasant perfume on, or had bright red hair, than what she said whilst helping her.

When applied to the third assertion about memory it means the following. If, at a certain moment there are no imprints left of what a person heard, it is still possible that there are some imprints of what a person saw. In any event, there will more likely be imprints about what a person smelt, felt or tasted. That means that persons with dementia are more able to make imprints of what they felt (and touched) than what they saw and heard. Hence, it might be better to ask Mrs Jones if she enjoyed the meals whilst visiting at her son's house, than to ask who was present.

Applied to the fourth assertion about memory, this means the following. When the amount of information that a person with dementia hears (and can process) is barely one impression, perhaps two impressions of visual information can be taken in and processed. The memory span for 'smell perception' may be larger than two. That means that persons with dementia can generally make impressions, imprints and express their reaction to what they 'feel' rather than what they 'see' or 'hear'. It would be better to ask Mrs Peters about what she felt during the busy trip than exactly what she saw or heard.

Applied to the sixth assertion about memory: if a person with dementia no longer recognises what she heard, in all likelihood she may still recall what she felt, tasted, or smelt. Generally, persons with dementia are better at recognising what they felt rather than what they saw. Mrs Peters may recognise her son more quickly when she feels the ring on his middle finger than if she just hears his voice.

The errors

The last example doesn't just apply to the seventh assertion about memory. In it are also elements that relate to the other assertions about memory. Therefore, the following paragraph will remind you a little of a story in which you must 'spot the errors'.

> Today isn't just a busy day on the first floor, where most of the residents have dementia. There is a rampant cold going around. Only the head nurse is present. She has managed to get some help finally from a first year NVQ student and a staff member from another floor, but still! At noon the residents eat lunch together in a communal dining room. Four persons need help to eat for a variety of reasons. Mrs Peters is on this floor. She's what staff sometimes refer to as a 'walker or pacer'. She often wanders around aimlessly for hours. She hasn't got a spare ounce of fat on her body. Because the head nurse cannot 'spare any hands' at mealtimes, she asks the student to go and find Mrs Peters and invite her to be seated at the table. The student finds her near the exit and brings her back to the dining room. By now it is midday. She pushes Mrs Peters, chair and all, to the table and says 'Listen Mrs Peters: in half an hour we're all going to have lunch, nice and cosily together.' She is barely on her way to the kitchen to get the food when Mrs Peters has disappeared again. Maybe it would have been better to wait until twenty past twelve, after the table had already been set with plates, cutlery and serviettes before saying to Mrs Peters, 'Look, we're going to be eating in just a few minutes.' It would be even better to wait until twenty to one. Then, everyone would already be eating; with all the sounds and smells of food. If you could get her to try the soup and say, 'Look at you all sitting here enjoying your meal', the chances are that Mrs Peters will remain seated.

Beyond words

To demonstrate to a person with dementia that there is food on the table, and that one eats with one's mouth, is usually far more effective than speaking many words about the future meal to be served. In short, don't use words alone (hearing), in your attempt to make contact with someone. Use images, touch, smell, taste and body movements. That is the seventh handle to help your interactions with persons with dementia.

The seven handles summarised

1   The memory of persons with dementia is adversely affected by the same factors as your own.

2   Check that the things about which you are speaking remain in full view, or within reach of the senses.

3   Speak about the past (reminisce) in preference to the present.

4   Use the fewest number of words to speak about things; speak slowly and clearly.

5   Don't rely on words only to clearly express what message you want to get across, use other sensory channels.

6   Ask questions in such a way that someone can recognise the answer subject, rather than having to retrieve/recall it from memory.

7   Rely increasingly on the other senses to communicate, not just on words.

Seeking a handhold

In this chapter the consequences of memory difficulties were discussed. In this way, we tried to give you an idea about what meaning these consequences have for the person with dementia. In summary, memory difficulties force a person to seek a handhold either in a concretely present reality, or in past memories.

If, as an outsider, you want a person with dementia to understand you, then you must ensure that you remain present 'to their senses'. In other words, they especially need your presence close by. We are literally talking about the close proximity required for social interaction. The distance we are referring to is within one arm's length, within 4 square metres. The further you are beyond this distance, the more a person will lose contact with you, and the more they will lose their handhold on feeling safe, . . . you!

5 In search of safety

Introduction

For a long time it has been thought that the process of dementia occurred 'outside of' the sufferer as it were. Carers were convinced that Mrs Jones 'didn't notice any of it', and that everything was going 'over her head'. She was living happily in her 'own little world'. 'Family would suffer more than the patient'.

That families suffer is beyond dispute. (This will be dealt with in the next chapter.) But the above notions represent 'wishful thinking'. That the person with dementia does not suffer is a notion that must be disputed.

A variety of evidence demonstrates that the person with dementia is inclined to think about and be involved with what is happening to them. There are indications that as with terminally ill persons, and those with some other types of illnesses, persons with dementia, also have an 'awareness context'. For our purposes this means: knowing and feeling that 'something is not right', that 'strange things are happening to you'. It is more than having insight into being ill or having insight into one's own situation. To be in the throes of a dementia process is a very problematic experience for Mrs Jones.

A personal loss

To have dementia is a loss that must be understood as being far from easy. Persons with dementia react to what they experience and feel. This behaviour – certainly a portion of it – we will call 'attachment behaviour'. In this chapter we will show that attachment behaviour can be understood as an expression of the increasing awareness of the need for safety on the part of the person with dementia.

In Chapter 3 we saw that the damage caused by dementia could be categorised into three groups: symptoms; the consequences of the symptoms; and affective reactions thereto. The person with dementia reacts with his/her whole being to what is happening to him/her –

with head and heart. In Chapter 4, we made seven assertions about memory to try to understand the consequences of the memory impairments on the person with dementia. We came to the conclusion that they are constantly looking for 'handholds'. Suggestions for providing them were given. In this chapter we will discuss how these same memory impairments lead to persons with dementia looking for 'safety'.

Background

To better understand the affective reactions to having dementia, we need a theory. In this instance we will use John Bowlby's Attachment Theory. After the Second World War, Bowlby, a family psychiatrist, received an urgent request from both the British government and the World Health Organization to conduct research into the situation of children who had been orphaned during the war. He investigated how best to support these children, and to discover the effects of their loss on their personality and development. This research formed the basis for his Attachment Theory. Using this theory we will be better able to understand the feelings of Mrs Jones. A brief summary of the theory follows.

Attachment behaviour

Attachment behaviour is any behaviour that aims to obtain or keep an 'attachment figure/person' close to oneself. In short, attachment behaviour is 'closeness/proximity-seeking behaviour'. The attachment figure is the person whose presence, either incidentally or continuously, is sought. Within a normal life span many persons can be attachment figures: parents, grandparents, a partner, aunts and uncles, older children – even male and female friends, good acquaintances, neighbours, work colleagues, advisors or carers. Well-known examples of other kinds of attachments are those formed when one has to do a mandatory 'stint in the armed services', or when facing miserable circumstances with other people, such as in wartime. People can also have strong attachments to pets, animals, their beliefs, plans, theories, and so on. We shall show in this chapter how 'remembered parents' serve as attachment figures. A few examples of attachment behaviour follow.

Through the sound barrier

Imagine that we are all young parents of young children. We are walking around a football field, chatting and passing the time as our children are playing with one another somewhere close to the middle of the field. Suddenly, a jet fighter flies overhead above the speed of sound and a loud bang is heard. The children are frightened. We remember the sound from our earlier years.

If we were to watch the children closely, we should observe the following range of behaviours. Some children continue to play on as if nothing had happened. Once in a while they'll exchange glances or a few words with us. There are also children who don't really continue playing as before, because they are continually keeping track of us. They are closely monitoring our presence by watching and listening. Some children are beginning to walk back and forth between us and the middle of the field. Others follow us and keep touching us. The pleasant chatting among the parents comes to an end. There are also children who will cling to us tightly. There may even be a child who will also start to call out, cry or yell.

Thunderstorms

According to Bowlby, you could call the behaviour of the above-mentioned children 'attachment behaviour'. These are many different expressions of attachment behaviour and also differences in the intensity of expression. In bad thunderstorms people also often 'seek out' other people. This is also 'closeness/proximity-seeking behaviour'. Often, in a bad storm during the night, sensible parents allow their children to get out of bed and sit around the kitchen table with a comforting drink.

The San Francisco Earthquake

Almost everyone remembers the 1988 San Francisco earthquake, especially the graphic scenes of the devastation shown on television. One powerful image that stays embedded in one's memory is that of the collapsed portion of the motorway that ran through the middle of the city. When the earthquake took place, a number of children's parties and activities were in progress. Nearly as many fathers as children were walking around, trying to record these events for posterity with their video cameras with the result that there are many amateur video tapes recording the behaviour of children in these circumstances of panic and bedlam. As well as the exact moment of the quake, the events preceding and following the quake were also captured on film. It was clearly visible that most children reacted by immediately clinging on to the adults that were closest to them. Bowlby would call this attachment behaviour or proximity-seeking behaviour.

An unknown visitor

When a stranger visits a family with young children, attachment behaviour is sometimes evident. As a rule, children are not usually bothered by the presence of a stranger. The ice is usually broken quickly. When this isn't the case, one can hardly force a child to make the acquaintance of the stranger in question. Left to themselves, sooner or later most children will usually 'brave an encounter' with the new visitor. Sometimes, however, there is absolutely no question of the child wanting to meet the visitor. The child remains near the parent(s) and where they go, the child goes also. In this situation you may sometimes see the child behave as follows.

The young child (barely) dares to come near the visitor, but only as long as the parent is there. While the child can see and hear the parent, he eventually dares to approach the stranger. Imagine that at a certain point, the parent leaves the room to fetch some refreshments or to go to the toilet. In doing so, the parent disappears from the 'experiential world' (the visual field) of the child. If the child has almost reached his goal of approaching the visitor and looks around once more for reassurance from the parent, who is no longer there, then all hell breaks loose. Full-blown panic sets in.

The behaviour of the child in this situation is a good example of what is known as 'explorative behaviour' and 'attachment behaviour'. A child will not learn or explore the environment fully if he feels unsafe. Whether a child feels safe or not is often dependent on the behaviour of the parents.

From the cradle to the grave

According to Bowlby, attachment behaviour is instinctive. That means that it is just as human as eating, drinking and sexuality. It also has a certain survival value to it. Of great importance is Bowlby's contention that people exhibit attachment behaviour as long as they live. To seek the closeness of others is not only the privilege of a child. It is behaviour that, irrespective of age, is human. From the cradle to the grave, people are capable of exhibiting attachment behaviour. This is not typical of any particular age, but of particular circumstances or situations in life. As such, attachment behaviour remains potentially active throughout life. What circumstances, according to Bowlby, could evoke such behaviour?

In which circumstances?

In circumstances such as those listed below, attachment behaviour usually occurs. This means that people in similar circumstances often display closeness/proximity-seeking behaviour. This list is, of course, incomplete and countless examples could be added:

- when people receive a huge, sudden shock, many will call someone's name out loud;
- during a thunder storm;
- in the presence of strong, sudden movements.

Abrupt movements

Let us consider the last item in the list. In the previous chapter we saw that people with dementia sooner or later can no longer make imprints of their impressions. Hence, the importance of staying in their visual field. Therefore, when you approach someone from behind or from the side, even if you do this very carefully, you may provoke a startled reaction when you enter their visual field. To give people with dementia a handhold, you should first try to ensure that they can hear you and see you before coming up close to them. This will reduce the abruptness of your 'sudden appearance' and, importantly, the feelings that can accompany this.

For some people with dementia, who need a great deal of help in getting washed and dressed in the morning, the routine can be full of such abrupt movements. In these instances, if they behave aggressively, it is probably nothing more than experiencing too many unpleasant feelings at the same time in a situation that they can no longer comprehend. Perhaps you may have heard someone shouting and complaining when a nurse is trying to help them with morning care.

In a wheelchair through space

Sometimes I forget about these abrupt movements when I bring a person in a wheelchair to visit me in my office. Mostly, however, I lay my hand on their shoulder and tell them as often as possible that I am right behind them. Imagine how it feels to sit in a wheelchair, without being able to make imprints of the impressions you receive. Your body is moving through space without you guiding it, or knowing from where or to where you are moving. That situation causes continuous small or large shock reactions.

In a strange city

It is not only shock, fear or abrupt movement that can activate attachment behaviour. Unfamiliar situations can also provoke this behaviour. Think back to a holiday. When you arrive for the first time in a new place, you usually feel less comfortable than you do after being there for a few days That uncomfortable feeling gradually diminishes as one becomes more familiar with the environment. A person with dementia who arrives in an unknown place, and who cannot make imprints of impressions, in theory, will remain uncomfortable and restless.

Tired on holiday

Between about six and half past seven in the evening is a time of great commotion in most families. It is rush hour. When father and mother are tired, numerous small irritations are not hard to come by and it's easy to quarrel about something. This can also happen, *en route* to a far-off holiday destination by car. Imagine the following scenario.

> Apart from the fact that you're all closely packed together, you are also tired. This is the ideal situation in which you begin to irritate one another to the point of quarrelling.

What is actually happening, with the children messing about in the back of the car, is this. Two people are tired and demonstrating attachment (proximity-seeking) behaviour. But their proximity-seeking behaviour is not being responded to because neither of them have the energy to do so. In this instance, unanswered, unreturned attachment behaviour continues to exist. To become angry is one way to react to this. In Chapters 6 and 15, we shall see that aggression is a way of coping with loss and that this behaviour usually passes.

Attachment figures

These examples illustrate not only under which circumstances attachment behaviour can occur, but also what can happen when the behaviour is not answered. We have already seen that someone who responds to another's 'closeness seeking' can be called an 'attachment figure'. Their behaviour, 'the answer to the invitation', is very important. If this person is unreachable, if they don't react or if they aren't accessible, this, in the first instance causes the attachment-seeking behaviour to escalate. Examples of such escalation include: continued searching behaviour; loud crying; and more 'calling-out' types of behaviour. Eventually, any or all of the behaviours seen in the grieving process (shock, denial, anger/aggression, bargaining, despair, sorrow) may be displayed. The opposite is also possible. When an attachment figure responds satisfactorily to the proximity-seeking behaviour, the result is immediately noticeable. The person becomes restful.

In short, when people feel frightened, unsafe and insecure, they usually search for safety in the closeness of others. They demonstrate proximity-seeking behaviour – attachment behaviour. According to Bowlby, the behaviours in the above-mentioned situations become stronger if you are alone, or, if you feel alone.

So much for an introduction to Bowlby's Attachment Theory. Let us now move towards the conclusion of this chapter, which you may have already foreseen. Certain symptoms observed in persons with dementia can be better understood if you are familiar with this theory. Mrs Jones's behaviour can be better understood if you assume that her dementia confronts her with many situations that bring forth feelings of insecurity and fear. Perhaps you understand her better when you can see that she is actively searching for safety. In the last chapter we already saw that she was looking for safety with her 'head'. Perhaps she is also looking for safety with her 'heart'. We will now turn from Bowlby's Attachment Theory to the concrete behaviour of persons with dementia.

Parent fixation

If you have worked with persons with dementia, you will have encountered the following.

They try to leave to go home or want to go home. They want to go to their parents or they just leave/escape. No one can hold them back. They tell you they need (the attention of) their parents. They are worried about their parents, or, they believe themselves to be back in their old family setting. Sometimes they behave exactly according to the expectations of their parent(s). They regularly ask how their parents are or where they are.

This behaviour does not apply to every person. One person displays such behaviour more strongly than another and some persons not at all. It can also vary greatly – in the morning it happens, in the afternoon it does not; today it happens, but tomorrow it does not. Sometimes you only realise that this is happening if you ask people with dementia about their parents. In other words, sooner or later, people with dementia assume that their parents are still alive although this isn't so. This behaviour is termed 'parent fixation'.

Parent orientation

Sometimes, older persons who do not have dementia may exhibit 'parent fixation'. It may happen for just a brief moment or period of time. We will return to this later in the chapter. On the other hand, most of them will say, as young orphans regularly do, that they need to think about their parents regularly. Some of them become very emotional when they think about their parents. We call this behaviour 'parent orientation'. This means, thinking about parents, but being aware whilst doing so that they are dead. In speaking with persons in the early stage of dementia, it appears that many do not, or rarely, exhibit 'parent fixation'. However, they often do show 'parent orientation'. They say that they think about their parents regularly, and also that they miss them enormously. Often they burst into tears when confiding this.

Intermezzo

The first aim of this chapter is to show that the theme of 'parents' in the experiential world of older persons (whether they have dementia or not) clearly tells us something about how they are feeling in their present circumstances. The second aim of this chapter is to show that both parent orientation and parent fixation can occur as a result of feeling frightened and unsafe. Both can then be viewed as attachment behaviour, as a form of proximity-seeking behaviour, through which feelings of safety might be achieved. The third aim of this chapter is to provide three explanations that might help to prevent parent fixation in old persons with dementia. Using these, it may also be possible to work out what you can still meaningfully do in your interactions with them. As in the previous chapter, in which assertions about memory were made, the following ideas will also provide you with additional handholds for helping persons with dementia.

Before seeking explanations for parent fixation, we need to look at concepts of both parent orientation and parent fixation in a fuller context. In the first instance this can be done by recounting the experiences and things that people with dementia have told us themselves. The first few examples come from persons in residential care homes. Thereafter the examples come from persons being seen in outpatient clinics and residents in nursing homes.

Examples from residents in care homes

Mrs Woolich thinks about her parents sometimes, but not daily. She really thinks more about her youth than about her parents.

She'd rather talk about the present than her youth. After all, she tells you that she lives in the present. Mrs Daniels readily acknowledges that she thinks about her parents at least once each day. Mrs Carter admits that she constantly thinks about her mother. Whenever the subject of conversation turns to her mother, she begins to cry almost immediately. Mrs Bush often thinks about her parents, especially her father, she says. When she speaks about him, she gets a lump in her throat. The older she gets, the more she thinks about them. More memories are coming back to her all the time. Mr Adams thinks about his parents daily. He just can't get them out of his thoughts. He admits that he has never previously spoken to anyone about this. Now that he's actually talking about them, his eyes keep filling up.

Examples from patients in the out-patient department

I asked Mrs Raynor to give me a few examples of situations that make her think about her parents. She said: 'A while ago my grandson got married. I thought, "I wish my parents could have seen this." You know, my father was a very jolly sort of man. And there were so many happy people there all together. Sometimes sitting in here, I think, "They all look like my father around here." I also think about him at birthdays and so on. No, I don't really miss my parents. I also don't have any of their photos and things any more. O yes, they come into my mind sometimes when I think: "We didn't use to have this or that . . . for example, such a beautifully built home or so many lovely clothes." '

Mrs Karey says: 'Oh sure, they're in my thoughts once in a while, my parents. It doesn't happen often, only occasionally. Something has to happen for me to start thinking about them. Then I might think, "They should be here to see this." '

Mrs Ives says that she thinks about them frequently: 'I had good parents. I was the oldest of twelve children. It was hard work. But I was always contented. Mother sang a lot. You never forget those things.'

Mr Sweeney remembers that his parents died when he was still a 'youngster'. He thinks it's quite normal that he doesn't think very much about them. 'It's logical if you've always been alone.'

Mrs Dwight answers my question by saying: 'Oh, yes of course. Actually, you always need them for a bit of consolation and to have a little chat to.'

Mrs Rymans says: 'Sir, I always think about them. I really wish they were still here with me. I lived my whole life at home with them. So you know, I was a bit of a spoilt child.'

Mrs Hillary cries when she admits to thinking about her parents. 'I had such good parents. I miss them so. I was really close to mother. Sometimes, it's just as if they are still here. I was always there for them. I wish they were still here.'

Mrs Wilson thinks every day about her parents. 'When I'm in a sad frame of mind I do. Or, sometimes I think: "I wish I could ask my mother's advice about that." You see, I've got her picture at home. Whenever I walk by it, I have the habit of stroking her face. I often think, "I wish I still had her." '

Also Mrs Gwen is well aware that her parents are no longer living. But she often thinks of them. 'That's because in between times I'm alone so much. "Mother, I still wish that I had you", I say out loud when something happens. Or: "Mother, if only you were still around." ' Mrs Gwen is now sobbing loudly. 'I'm not one of those who goes running to the church when things get rough', she adds.

Mr Manley says that he often thinks about his parents. 'But not always. About once a week. Sometimes more intensely than another. There are days when I don't think about them at all. But there are days when . . . '

Examples from patients in a nursing home

Mrs Southfield says that she hasn't got her mother any more but that her father is still alive. According to her, 'He's not doing so well though.' She thinks that's because of his old age. I ask her if she ever thinks about her mother. 'Oh sure, everyday. Sometimes I miss her too. She was very good to us. It's nice to think about her. Actually I'd still like to have her with me always. I miss her a lot.'

Mrs Brown realised intermittently (sometimes and sometimes not) that her parents were dead. Her answer to my question, whether she thinks about them, was very insistent: 'Always. You never lose them. Your parents always stay with you. Until your last breath.'

The first time I asked Mr Knight whether his parents were alive his answer was: 'My father died in 1976. My mother is still alive. We live here together.' The second time I asked him he said: 'My mother is still alive. Keep it a secret though.'

In the medical notes I spotted a note about Mrs Rees, written by an auxiliary nurse: 'Whoever pays her attention to her, she calls them either "Mum" or "Dad". When we don't give her attention she becomes very sad.'

Explanations of parent fixation: first explanation

The first explanation for the occurrence of parent fixation comes from the third assertion about memory in Chapter 4. We say that as age increases, the number of imprints made is reduced. At a certain point, no imprints (of the total number of imprints ever made of an earlier impression) remain.

It is very possible that this process is accelerated, in reverse order. As such, it is possible that there are no imprints left about the death of the parents. If that were the case, then Mrs Jones simply 'doesn't know any better'. 'My parents dead? How dare you suggest such a thing!' You can insist all you like but it won't help. With all the consequences thereof, Mrs Jones will remain restless, sad, afraid and will continue to search for her parents. This is one explanation. However, it doesn't offer much scope for your interaction with Mrs Jones.

On the way to a second explanation of parent orientation

A second way of trying to understand parent fixation is related to the second assertion about memory. We say that during the course of the years, fewer imprints of impressions were made. After a certain moment, no more imprints are made. Let us pause for a moment to think about what it might feel like if you are in this situation. How could a person react emotionally, with their heart instead of their head?

Recalling the examples from Chapter 4, 'a strange face', 'a strange room', 'haven't had any tea', it's possible to assume that the person with dementia ends up in a situation where there is no more continuity. It therefore becomes increasingly difficult to attach oneself to others and to a place. The person with dementia becomes 'displaced'.

Displaced

> At quarter past eight in the evening, in the concert hall, you suddenly realise that it's been an incredible rush to get there on time. You're sitting reflecting and starting to unwind as you listen to the music. At the same time, you are secretly hoping that when you get home tonight, the dishes will be done.

Now choose, just as in the above example, another random moment in time. Because you have imprints of impressions, you remain involved with what has happened before and what is still going to happen. Right now you're not doing anything. However, you can, if you wish, remain concerned with what's just happened and what lies ahead. You experience your own existence within the continuity of past, present and future.

This 'continuity' provides continuous recognition and forms, as it were, the fabric of your life. Without being able to make imprints of impressions, this way of experiencing your existence would be unthinkable. In any given situation, a person with dementia will feel continually less caught up with persons and things. Just like Mrs Jones, a person with dementia cannot become connected, even if he/she would dearly wish to do so. A person with dementia lives in a sort of a 'no man's land'. He/she continuously feels separated from persons and things.

Because of their memory difficulties, as we have already seen, persons with dementia are looking for 'handholds'. Literally as soon as he or she 'lets go' of someone or something, their handhold has vanished. Without being able to make an imprint of the impression just made, a handhold only lasts while it remains present or felt. When the handhold is gone, it's as if it never was there, and the search for a handhold begins anew. At a certain point, even the recognition 'Oh, there's my handhold' is no longer possible. Slowly the person with dementia becomes displaced.

Out of joint – dislocated and disconnected

The sighs of family members, fellow residents, and care staff can be readily understood when people with dementia continually tag along with them, try to latch on in any possible way and don't give them a moment's rest. 'I'm busy with her the whole day long.' 'I get up with her and I go to bed with her.' 'It slowly undermines you.' 'It consumes you completely.' This displacement can be thought of in another way.

If Mrs Jones has to continue living without being able to make imprints of impressions, she will gradually feel more separated, as if she is being abandoned by everyone. She does not recognise anyone any more, even her fellow residents. Increasingly, she feels utterly alone. She feels disconnected. Mrs Jones is becoming increasingly restless because of this unbearable feeling. She goes to stand up and looks worriedly at this man whom she does not always recognise as her husband. He has been sitting faithfully but sorrowfully, next to her. She gets angry and says that she is going to look for her husband. 'How can she get angry with me when I still love her?'

Fear: feeling unsafe

At this point, we are still looking for the second explanation for parent fixation in persons with dementia. The second explanation could be that 'displacement' and 'being disconnected' evokes feelings of fear. In other words: the process of not being able to make imprints of impressions does affect persons with dementia deeply and personally. It's not something that happens 'far away from them' or 'over their heads'. They react emotionally to this process. They feel, (and in my experience a lot longer than we tend to think) that strange things are happening to them. This is why we can speak about them having an 'awareness context', just as we do for persons having other chronic or terminal illnesses. It is possible that persons with dementia who are no longer able to make imprints of impressions start to feel severely 'disconnected'. Just the same as every other person who is confronted with this feeling, they will then become fearful. In the normal course of events, people who feel frightened, start to look for safety.

In search of safety

Whoever feels afraid, will go in search of attachment figures through using attachment/proximity-seeking behaviours. Each person does this in their own manner. Persons with dementia span this emptiness and feeling of being separated. This 'feels like' a life-threatening situation; it is very similar to the grieving process.

As soon as the grieving process has started, we have to consider the behaviour and feelings that occur in it (denial, bewilderment, pretending that nothing is wrong, aggression, sadness, fear and despair). Second, all kinds of factors that influence the grieving process play a role as well. For example, the way in which problems were solved (coped/dealt with) earlier in a person's life, or, the presence of unresolved grief.

In the next chapter, about how families grieve, both points will be dealt with at length. For the present, we will suggest that each person with dementia works through his/her feelings of fear in an individual way. How this is done depends upon a person's life history and personality.

The second explanation for parent fixation

Persons with dementia are aware that 'something is wrong with them', 'something strange is happening to them' for a lot longer than we have generally supposed. They remain thoroughly concerned with what is happening to them. In the previous pages it was shown that this 'awareness context' activates attachment behaviour, and hence stimulates proximity-seeking behaviour. The second explanation of parent fixation in persons with dementia dovetails in with this.

If the search for an attachment figure is unsuccessful, dementia sufferers can reach back into their memories for persons who assumed this role in their early attachment experiences. Usually these memories of attachment figures are of parents. But the search for attachment figures will never produce a lasting result when no imprints of impressions are made any more. Two examples follow.

Mrs Battersby

> Mrs Battersby said to me suddenly during a visit, 'Mother and father are still alive, Sir. We still live together here at home. Father is a barber, you must know him eh? He's in his nineties though. Mother is in her late eighties.' Because Mrs Battersby had always proudly told me that she was in her nineties, I asked something I normally never do. I asked her how old she was. When she replied that she was ninety, I agreed that ninety was indeed very old and that her father must be about one hundred and ten.
>
> With a quiet but positive tone, she answered that naturally that he could never have become that old, and indeed that he had never become that old, but, that he was still alive. 'Mother too, as a matter of fact', she added still positively. I was quiet for a moment. Thereafter I moved the table that was between us aside and I pulled my chair up close to hers. I looked into her eyes and took her hands in mine. I said that I had the impression that she was sometimes sad. She agreed. 'Yes' she said, 'I'm full of sadness.' I

asked her what she felt sad about. Immediately she began to cry and said 'Father isn't here any more and I miss him so.'

Mr Fox

During the course of a talk with Mr Fox, a close contact developed between us. He continuously sought to be close to me and kept holding on to me more tightly. To begin with, he supposed that his parents were still alive. He told me that they were doing well. 'They are both still in fine fettle. I still see them every week whether I really can manage it or not.' At a certain point he told me that his mother was his favourite parent, and thereupon he begins to cry. 'I used to go out with her every day. I always went to her with all my problems. Father never seemed to take much notice of things in the family.' Later, in answering my question as to whether or not he is happy, Mr Fox answers: 'Sometimes yes, sometimes no. I think about mother from time to time, and about everything she had to go through, especially with father.' Towards the end of the conversation, when I tried to comfort him because he had become sad, he told me with certainty that his mother and father are both dead. 'They've both passed away.'

Attachment figures

In both examples, to begin with, we see the presence of parent fixation that finally makes room for the acknowledgement that the parents truly have died. This 'turn about' comes when 'proximity/closeness-giving' behaviour is provided, or when proximity-seeking behaviour is responded to. At the start of the conversations, both Mrs Battersby and Mr Fox 'hold fast to' their parents as it were. Towards the end they let go, and hold on to the comfort that is offered to them from close by.

In other words, if, during your contact with a person with dementia you behave like an attachment figure, sometimes parent fixation can disappear long enough for them to acknowledge that their parents are dead. During that brief moment the person with dementia can briefly come to rest. This is how you can have great significance for them.

When no imprints of impressions are made any more, it means the following. When you disappear from the experiential/visual field of Mrs Jones, her parent fixation will return. Not only the parent fixation, but all of the behaviours that go along with it. This is therefore an emotional explanation about why parent fixation occurs. When a person is frightened and cannot find handholds for safety nearby, they return to feelings of safety in their memories. From the perspective of care-giving, this explanation is a practical one, although it can only ever offer temporary help. (It allows us to plan interventions to help persons with dementia feel safer at times. It means that carers must see the person's 'need for closeness' as a desperate plea rather than as a nuisance behaviour.)

The third explanation for parent fixation

A third way to explain why parent fixation can occur comes from listening to what older persons themselves tell you when you speak to them at length about their parent orientation. We've seen that, just like everyone else, older persons (must) think about their parents. In reality, it regularly occurs that older persons say that they miss their parents. They will usually tell you of their own accord if this is the case. It seems to be related to talking about the smaller and larger losses in one's life. As such, both parent orientation and parent fixation can be understood as 'proximity-seeking behaviour' that occurs in situations that cause feelings of fear (feeling unsafe) to arise.

It also appears that parent orientation is most intense when the feelings of loss at the parent's death are strongly present. Finally, it appears that old persons who show a great degree of parent orientation sometimes have the feeling that their parents are still alive. This seems to happen especially during those times when no attachment figures are present in present life. In other words, older persons may sometimes exhibit parent fixation when they are experiencing especially difficult moments and literally no one is present to support them.

For example:

> Mrs Adrians needs to be admitted to the hospital immediately. Her husband has passed away, her neighbour is out, her oldest daughter is on holiday and most of the nursing staff have gone home already. At such a moment, Mrs Adrians wants her parents so badly that she can, as it were, feel them around her. If you, or the other members of staff at the hospital can understand her behaviour, and can make her feel secure enough, the feeling of her parents being 'close by' will disappear. In this situation, what you have done will have a lasting effect because Mrs Adrians does not have dementia and can still make imprints of impressions. She will remember what you did for her.

This view of parent fixation offers a more permanent perspective for working with persons with dementia. This perspective points to grieving behaviours.

A short look back

The theme of 'parents' in the experiential world of older persons, whether they have dementia or not, seems to make a clear point about how persons feel at a certain point in time. Both parent orientation and parent fixation can be 'proximity-seeking' behaviour, which is a way of trying to obtain a feeling of safety in fearful moments. Three explanations for parent fixation in persons with dementia can be given. It is up to you to work out which of the three explanations could be most likely in a given setting, so that you can choose how best to help a person. Just as with the assertions about memory, the explanations for parent fixation also provide us with three handholds to help provide optimal care.

Three handholds for caring

If Mrs Jones or another person with dementia comes towards you wanting to go home, frightened, with restless eyes, perhaps asking you where their parents are, hanging on to you tightly, you cannot be sure precisely what the problem is. It is certainly not wise to say at the outset 'Surely you must know that your parents have long since passed away.' Instead, consider for a moment what the person is feeling. Since her behaviour could be proximity/closeness-seeking behaviour, this need might be answered with a comforting, nurturing type of response.

In general, you will know instinctively how to do that. You know from your own experiences exactly what it feels like when someone 'feels safe' for you. You also know how to give someone this feeling. Usually we all know from experience how to put someone at ease and give them a feeling of trust in you.

Almost everyone has their own word to describe such behaviour. Some call it 'caring', others, call it 'putting someone at ease'. What one person calls 'being warm', another would call 'comforting'. One person calls it about 'supporting someone', whereas another calls it 'offering security', etc. In other words, in the first instance, always try to respond to parent fixation by offering someone a type of 'proximity or closeness behaviour'. Mrs Jones's behaviour could mean that she is seeking safety because she feels as if she's in a sort of 'no man's land' or disconnected. Watch carefully then to see what happens to her behaviour. Three things can happen: the behaviour can disappear, disappear temporarily, or not disappear.

When parent fixation doesn't disappear even with long periods of offering comfort

If Mrs Jones comes to you, wants to go home, looks fearful, is restless, asks you where her parents are, and hangs onto you 'for dear life', your best option is to offer her comfort. If her behaviour doesn't change, even after a long while of trying, in all likelihood the first explanation for parent fixation is most relevant. There are no more imprints of impressions of the death of her parents. She does not remember anything other than that they are still alive.

No matter how much comfort and safety you offer her, Mrs Jones is likely to remain anxious and restless and wanting to go home. She will continue to look for her parents until she is so tired of searching for them and pacing around, that she will almost literally collapse from fatigue. In this case, it is not your manner of interacting with her that has failed to reach her. She has not been able to become attached to you because of her worry about her parents. There is little you can do and you will probably be left with an uncomfortable feeling that does not easily go away.

If parent fixation disappears as long as you are comforting

Mrs Jones comes to you, wants to go home, looks fearful, is restless, asks you where her parents are and hangs on to you 'for dear life'. It's possible that if you comfort her, her parent fixation behaviour will disappear for a while. It will return when you leave. If this is the case then the second explanation for parent fixation is the most likely one. There are no more imprints being made of impressions. Without having an attachment figure around from whom she can get a feeling of safety and security, Mrs Jones will feel frightened and unsafe and think that her parents are still alive. When you make her feel safe, she 'lets go of' her parents and feels at ease for a while, just as in the examples of Mrs Battersby and Mr Fox.

The safety that you display helps Mrs Jones to feel/know she is safe. Her fear disappears and she no longer wants to go home to her parents. She doesn't ask after them any more. She might even tell you that 'they've passed away'. Or, she might admit that she misses them a lot. But as soon as you disappear from her visual/experiential field, she'll begin to look for her parents again. As long as Mrs Jones can hear, see, feel or sense you, she is 'reachable' to you for these short periods of time. Such interactions usually leave one feeling very satisfied. You are functioning as an attachment figure while she can sense you with her.

When parent fixation disappears for longer than the time you spend comforting someone

Mrs Jones comes to you, wants to go home, looks fearful, is restless, asks you where her parents are, and hangs onto you 'for dear life'. When you comfort her, her parent fixation behaviour stops and really disappears. If her restless behaviour does not return, even though you have gone off to do other work, then the third explanation for parent fixation is the most likely one – grieving behaviour. Evidently some imprints of impressions are still being made, but, because of circumstances Mrs Jones feels as though she has been abandoned by everyone. She was so longing for her parents that it was just 'as if' they were with her. Comforting will help Mrs Jones because it will give her the feeling of care and safety that she needs. Her fear and restlessness and parent fixation will disappear 'like snow in the sunshine', because she trusts you. She doesn't need her parents any more, she doesn't need to go home because she can remember your presence, even later on. What you do is precious. You are, and remain 'within reach', even if you disappear from her visual/experiential field. She knows that you will return. You are functioning as more than a person who has offered momentary comfort, but as an 'attachment figure who can be remembered'. That is a wonderful feeling.

Parent fixation which should disappear but doesn't

Sometimes, parent fixation remains even if the first explanation is not the reason. The fact that the parent fixation doesn't go away has nothing to do with the explanation that 'no more imprints of impressions are being made'. It seems as if the second explanation, in conjunction with a person's life history and personality come into play.

The life history

No single form of closeness, no action of comfort can help someone who no longer knows what safety means. It is plausible that some persons, also persons with dementia, no longer trust, or want to trust in anyone again because of traumatic things that have happened during their lives (war, incest, violence). It is as if they have deliberately forgotten what safety is. Even when you behave in the safest, most comforting way, this person will not trust you. You will be left with a very unpleasant feeling of not having been able to 'reach' this person. This is not an easy feeling to get over.

Something else can happen which is even more complicated. Not being able to make imprints of impressions also means, as we saw, that a person is left feeling unsafe and fearful. Said another way, the person with dementia is then confronted with a situation that represents/feels like a 'loss'. He needs to work through that loss, whether he likes it or not. It is possible therefore that, in some persons with dementia, unresolved losses are activated through feeling unsafe. Old feelings of being abandoned, terrified, lonely, abandoned, not listened to, etc., can resurface when no more imprints of impressions are made. These could be such things as: the intense shock of never seeing your favourite sister again because she didn't come home from school one day or said goodbye to you; the loss of your first child and the subsequent years of mental anguish; being unjustly laid off work and all the long years of unemployment thereafter.

Interpreter's note

There are rare case histories of persons who have been helped by intensive long-term care plans.

> One lady cried almost all day long, calling out for her mother, 'Where are you mummy?' and 'Why don't you come mummy?' (Because of this constant crying, no other residents wanted to sit near to this lady because she upset everyone around her. She was never able to answer fellow residents when they asked her what was the matter and why was she so upset. In spite of the valiant efforts of several kindly residents to comfort her, she never stopped crying in their presence.)
>
> After trying to obtain some life history information about this lady, an important fact came to light. Her mother had died in a fire at the neighbour's house while trying to help them. The lady in this example had been 7 years old at the time. Staff guessed that, in going back to her memories of youth to seek safety, she had instead returned to a crisis memory.
>
> Staff decided to give up their coffee breaks, in turn, and sit with this lady instead. At first, they sat next to her and held her hand. After several days, when the lady was used to the intervals of close contact, they put their arm around her, slowly starting to make rocking movements and humming lullabies to her. Several days later, the lady stopped crying during some of these brief periods of intense contact. After several months, this lady stopped calling out for her mother as much, and also started to look for her children. Eventually, the crying stopped for most of the day, although she remained disoriented in time. When her constant crying stopped, it was possible to seat her next to other residents and encourage her to be present at activities. She did

not want to join in actively, but seemed to be pleased to be present in a quiet way.

It must be noted that some members of staff did not see the purpose in doing this and it was difficult to obtain everyone's co-operation at first. The result, in this instance was well worth the try.

The personality

No form of closeness or comfort helps when the person with dementia is asking for more safety than any person can provide. It means that the loss of such closeness/comfort in life has been a very personal experience. What is a small loss for one person may be an enormous one to another. For one person, something that hardly represents a loss is a monumental event for another. One person is utterly 'precise and conscientious about every detail in life', another, just 'seems to sail through everything'. The one is 'nit picking', the other is 'lackadaisical'. It's possible that a person with dementia who was a former civil servant, will be more bothered by his memory lapses and errors than someone who did a less exacting sort of job. In this instance, you could offer the first gentleman all the comfort and safety you know how to give, but for this former civil servant it will never be enough. Asking him to feel safe while he is painfully aware of his errors will be asking too much. With this gentleman also, you will be left with an unpleasant feeling of not being able to 'reach' him.

Summary

Persons with dementia look for 'safety'. This can be in the form of attachment figures, but also through 'parent orientation' and/or 'parent fixation'. While these behaviours are related to a person's life history and personality, they also say something about how a person is feeling at a given moment. They point to a loss experience and/or feelings of fear (feeling unsafe). Both parent orientation and parent fixation can be seen as attachment behaviours, as types of prox-imity/closeness-seeking behaviour. 'What you experience' and 'who you are' influences how you work through losses and grief. This sometimes means that people with dementia can experience a re-surfacing of old painful memories (unresolved losses or grief). Like reminiscing, parent orientation, is a normal behaviour that can also occur in old age. The intensity of this behaviour can increase as a result of a current loss experience, or, can reactivate an earlier loss. Occasionally, parent fixation also occurs in older persons who do not have dementia.

Parent orientation also occurs in the first stage of dementia. This happens, for example, when the process of making imprints of impressions which feel 'unsafe' now, is still functioning reasonably (as well as other memory functions). In such a situation, there must be 'additional feelings of fear' that are contributing to the parent orientation. Missing one's parents commonly occurs then. In the early stage of dementia, parent fixation can also occur in moments when other forms of attachment behaviour are going unrecognised or are left unanswered. Up to this stage, parent fixation, in theory, can be alleviated. That means that it is possible during your interactions with someone who has dementia, to make them feel safe and calm.

In the later stages of dementia, parent fixation arises. Whether this behaviour can be alleviated is dependent upon the explanation for the cause of the behaviour. That means that it will not always be possible to help people with dementia to feel safe and become calm again.

At the beginning of this chapter parent fixation was defined as a term that included the following behaviours:

- trying to go home or wanting to go home;
- wanting to go to their parents, or just leaving;
- no one being able to stop or deter them;
- telling others that they need the care and attention of their parents;
- saying that they are worried about their parents;
- thinking that they are back in their old family home;
- sometimes behaving in exact accordance with their parent(s)' wishes;
- sometimes using their parents to threaten staff when attempts are being made to prevent them from leaving by saying, for example, 'If my father knew that you were keeping me here he'd . . .';
- preoccupied in trying to get to their parents during the whole day;
- often asking where their parents are or how they are.

At the end of this chapter it has become clear that parent fixation in dementia can be understood as a kind of attachment behaviour. Yet that doesn't mean that the lack of safety (fear) that persons with dementia experience can only be expressed by parent fixation. Fear can be expressed in many other ways. Look closely for example at all the tightly held handbags, wads of paper tissues and other collected items that persons with dementia sometimes carry with them for hours at a time! Hence, a person with dementia doesn't only speak about their parents if they are feeling frightened and unsafe. Other behaviours can occur as well.

To go along with or to orient to reality?

As we saw, one of the behaviours that was associated with parent fixation was the desire to 'go home'. It doesn't always work when you try to persuade Mrs Jones that her old house isn't her home any more and that she lives here now. In fact, trying to tell her this often makes her more restless. If you can see her behaviour as a possible expression of her feelings of fear, then another perspective for interacting with her arises.

When she exhibits parent fixation (specifically, wanting to go home), you can translate this to mean: 'I don't feel at home (safe) here.' You can then look for possible ways to help her to feel better (more at home) here. Sometimes this will succeed, sometimes it will not.

An old man in a care home, completely spontaneously, told the following story. It provides a good illustration of both ways of interacting with someone who has parent fixation. It especially shows what the effects of these two ways are.

> One evening I heard a clattering sound coming from the room of my neighbour. I always watched out for her, ever since I heard that she had been diagnosed as having dementia. I went to look in the corridor. Sure enough, there she was completely decked out in a thick coat, bags and an umbrella hanging from her arm. It was summer time! It had been a scorching hot day and now it was about midnight. I asked her where in heaven's name she wanted to go to. She said that she was in a hurry to catch the bus to go to her mother. I told her that she was out of her mind, that her mother was long dead, and that she shouldn't make so much of a commotion in the middle of the night because all normal people were sleeping. And all those clothes on in the middle of the summer! She should go back to sleep, I told her. Boy did I get it. I was busy trying to stop her from going the entire night. Never saw my bed.
>
> Another evening it happened again. I told myself that I would handle it differently this time. She had to go to catch the bus to get to her mother again. She was all dressed, packed up and ready to go like the last time. I asked her to wait a moment for me, so that I could get my coat. I gave her my arm and went walking along the corridor with her. As it got darker along the corridor, she became hesitant. I suggested that since it was so dark out, we should turn around, and go home to have a nice cup of tea and a chat. I started turning, she followed. I offered her my arm. She clung onto it for dear life. We had a cup of tea and she calmed down eventually. Then I told her I was so tired I was

going to bed. I told her she looked tired too and suggested she did the same. She agreed and headed for the bedroom. I waited a moment to make sure she didn't come out immediately and then let myself out. The whole thing didn't take half an hour. The next morning I saw her and she acted as if nothing had happened, she never even referred to it!

In closing

Mrs James was diagnosed as being in the early stage of dementia when she was seen at a memory clinic. During her interview with the psychologist, she appeared to clearly understand what was the matter with her. She was very sad about it and cried a great deal. A few months later, I spoke to her niece who was living with her. It appears that Mrs James had told her niece the following: 'I often have the feeling that I want to go home, to my parents. But I know that I live here and that they're dead.' As her dementia progresses there may come a time when Mrs James feels frightened and alone. She may then think about her parents so much, and see them so clearly with 'her mind's eye' (visual memory), that it feels 'as if' they are with her. She may then speak about her parents as if they are alive. This behaviour may stop (temporarily) if you realise she is frightened and lonely and sit with her.

6 Families and a 'missing' person

Introduction

In the last chapter it became clear that the process of dementia can touch persons deeply and emotionally. That is also true for family members, partners and children. There is no measuring stick that can tell us who is suffering most, the person with dementia or their family. Without doubt, the process of dementia is experienced as a heavy burden by family members. The perception of this burden is different for each person however.

Working through the loss is one aspect of the problems that confront a family. Whether the person with dementia should be cared for at home or in a care facility depends upon what burden the carers can 'carry'. This is sometimes referred to as the 'ability to bear' of the family. This varies from person to person.

What is this chapter about?

The purpose of this chapter is primarily to develop an understanding of the emotional situation of the families of persons with dementia. Sometimes the healthy partner is living in a care home. If there are children, they visit. In this chapter a number of factors that affect the 'ability to bear' will be discussed. The loss process/grieving is one of these factors. Thereafter, the behaviours and feelings that occur during the loss process will be discussed so as to help understand them. Such behaviours occur during the various stages of the grieving process and after the person with dementia has died. Thereafter, we will consider what happens when this grieving process is more difficult than usual.

Finally, we will look at the factors which influence why grieving is more difficult for some than for others. The emotional situation that occurs during the grieving process for a person with dementia is a hazy one. Such emotional haziness has an unfavourable influence on the grieving process. Should the spouse of Mrs Jones be treated as a widower or not? Do the children still have a mother or not? The long duration of such 'emotional haziness' usually contributes to the observation that the grieving process of families is more difficult while the person with dementia is alive, than after his/her death.

Practical problems enough

Sooner or later, dementia will mean that a person has difficulty with their memory, actions, recognising normal topics, insight, reading, making calculations, writing, language and self-care. As we saw in the previous chapter, the person with dementia has a certain aware- ness of these changes and reacts to them. On the one hand they may react, with a change in their normal activities, loss of social decorum or manners, disorientation, confusion, confabulation and incorrect ideas about what is happening. On the other hand, they may react with suspiciousness, aggression, restlessness, mood changes and sadness. For example, the disturbances in Mrs Jones could contribute to her seeking for a handhold, and safety. The practical problems that eventually will arise for her husband and children are countless. They can contribute to a great decrease in Mr Jones's 'ability to bear' or cope with the situation, and eventually, also that of his children. Even if a couple live together in a care home, it means that the fellow resi- dents at the home will also experience a challenge to their 'ability to bear' the behaviour of the person with dementia with whom they will be confronted on a daily basis.

How much help does Mrs Jones need, for example, to get dressed and undressed, to eat, and to go to the toilet? Does she immediately forget what was said to her, or, does she remember it for a little while? Is she suspicious and prone to arguing with everyone, or can she sit and have a cup of tea without irritating those around her with inappropriate conversation? Is she constantly outside, walking down the road, or is she easily occupied in her room? Does she wander naked through the corridor by day or night, does she search for her husband continuously or does she sit quietly the whole day long, looking contented? And so on.

The brain damage, and the way in which the person with dementia reacts to having it, are not the only factors that influence behaviour. Other things can make such reactions more or less difficult.

Factors that influence behaviour

When we look at the Jones's, for example, without going into great detail, we see that the following factors are influencing the situation.

How healthy is Mr Jones? Has he had enough information about what is the matter with his wife so that he knows what could happen in the future? How many children are there? How far away do they live? Are they willing to reorganise their lives so that they can be of 'hands-on' assistance to their parents? What is the living situation like? Do they live on a farm with any of their own children living there too? Do they live in a three-room flat? What services are available in the neighbourhood? Is it possible to find other carers or services to help?

Also, what is the relationship of the Jones's like? What sort of relationship do the children have with their parents? What are the relationships like between the children? Can they speak honestly to each other? Can they speak freely with each other and with their father? Do the children have enough information about what exactly is happening to their mother? Does Mr Jones, and each child in turn, receive enough understanding and emotional support for what is happening to them? Do the fellow residents at the care home know exactly what is the matter with Mrs Jones? Do they know about the behaviours of persons with dementia? How tolerant are they of Mrs Jones's behaviour?

And, to end with, how does Mr Jones experience and work through the realisation that his marriage of fifty years is slowly coming to an end in such a manner? Did he ever think that he might lose his wife like this? The same question pertains to the children. How are they working through the fact that they are losing their mother, at least, the mother they were familiar with, because of dementia? Sometimes this question also pertains to fellow residents at a care home. How does one come to terms with the gradual loss of a good friend and neighbour, whom you gradually see becoming a stranger to you?

No situation is the same

All these factors taken together result in the fact that no two situations are similar. In addition, it also needs to be recognised that they are not necessarily experienced or perceived in the same way. Hence, they can acquire a wholly personal meaning.

The things that are the most difficult for Mr Jones to cope with may be a 'piece of cake' for another spouse. One child may depend upon the emotional support of one parent rather than another. One partner can accept practical help to care more easily than another. One parent will expect more help from their child(ren) than another. One person likes living in a small cosy place, another person like lots of empty space. For some, it's not a big deal to start accepting offers of help; for others, it is a huge decision to stop driving the car. In a care home, one resident will be more bothered by Mrs Jones's behaviour than another. One friend, because of her personality and life experience will find it easier to get along with her than another. And so on.

Through our individual make-up of all such factors, we will observe that one person can bear the burden of caring longer than another. The ability of Mr Jones to bear the burden is in part determined by the way he is grieving for the realisation that he is in danger of losing his wife because of her dementia. Slowly he is losing the wife to whom he has been married for so many years and gone through thick and thin with.

Loss

Regardless of their age, every human being sooner or later experiences a small or large loss in their life. For example:

- the death of a loved one or family member
- failing an exam
- losing one's job
- a promised promotion that doesn't materialise
- to be forced to give up sport through injury
- health problems
- moving house or job
- losing irreplaceable personal objects and things
- the sudden move of a child away from home
- losing a race or competition
- separation and divorce
- losing a pet hit by a vehicle, or one that had to be put down
- losing everything in a house fire or through war
- emigrating
- losing a limb
- losing someone close who has just 'gone missing'
- being subjected to violence
- having a terminal illness
- having left your favourite toy behind on vacation
- experiencing the death of friends and acquaintances
- experiencing stillbirth, miscarriage, abortion

Familiar behaviour, familiar feelings

Much is known about how persons generally work through their loss and about the feelings and behaviours that accompany the grieving process. Who doesn't know about tears; the endless reflecting; the stifled anger; the helplessness; the feeling of injustice; the disbelief; the guilt; the relief; an unexpected moment of pleasure that you distrust; the moments when it feels like the person is still lying next to you, when you think you see and hear them; the endless waiting for someone who will not return; the avoidance of conversations and past places because friends serve as reminders of the loss; the grate-fulness for the lasting memories; the feeling of betrayal with a new found love, or the consoling gesture of another? And so forth.

Periods of grieving

Grieving is usually referred to as a 'process'. Sometimes such grieving behaviours are grouped into three stages: protest, despair and detachment. Others have described this process with more stages including: numbness, denial, anger, bargaining, depression/sadness and acceptance. Sometimes feelings of shame, guilt and powerless-ness accompany grieving.

Bowlby, in describing his Attachment Theory, also spoke about a period of 'working through the loss', particularly when a loved one was involved. He distinguished between the following stages: bewil-derment; searching and longing for; anguish and despair; and recovery. (There are other theories about grieving but they all agree that there are a number of stages and emotions that cannot be 'rushed through'.)

In any event, grieving takes time

These short sections that have loss and grieving as their common thread, all clearly show that this process does not usually pass us by, but grabs each of us. Accepting loss does not happen immediately and certainly not 'on command'. Much time is usually required. Many know this through personal experience.

Different traditions

The above-mentioned behaviour and feelings are more or less under-stood as being the normal human reaction to loss. The manner in which they are expressed and become meaningful is less clear. How grieving happened in small village communities in the past often differs drastically from how grieving occurs in large urban centres now. 'Wakes' are becoming a thing of the past for many. The ways in which other cultures grieve, for example, in Muslim and Afro-Caribbean groups, seem to be longer and more emotive than the traditional Anglo-Saxon style of grief. Different communities and ethnic groups have different grieving traditions and cultures. Apart from the following paragraph, this subject will not be covered in any more detail in this book.

Individual grieving culture

In the second half of this century, it has been said that we have seen an 'impoverishment' of our grieving culture. In the past few years we have seen a swing in the other direction again. It is as if people are increasingly and better prepared for some eventualities. Some persons very consciously choose how they want to be buried, the memorials they wish to have and how they will prepare for this. In this new 'personal grieving' climate, more effort is involved in thinking about and working through the loss. This is important. The expression of feelings associated with one loss can also help to resolve past losses. We need to grieve for losses. If we don't in the short term, the grief will come out in the long run. (In this regard, some have commented that a 'farewell ritual' at the time of a divorce could be very healing for everyone concerned – for both partners, the children, the grandparents and friends.)

More than difficult

If the above-mentioned behaviours represent 'normal' grieving, what, then, is 'abnormal' grieving? When is the grief process more difficult than that described above? This is very difficult to determine. Every person is different. Also the depth of feeling over the loss is a very individual one. What matters for one person doesn't necessarily matter for another. For this reason, there is no measuring stick that can indicate when the sadness ought to be 'lightening'. However, there are three signs that are generally associated with abnormal grieving.

First, when there does not appear to be any grieving behaviour when, humanly speaking, one would expect there to be some. Second, when the grieving behaviour occurs much later than one would expect to see it. Third, when the grieving continues over too long a period.

Just as if nothing has happened

Sometimes no grieving behaviour is evident, even where you would certainly expect it. For example, father has died and the children are behaving as if nothing has happened. There is no sign of grief, even when father is brought up in conversation. There is no protest, no anger and even no sense that what has happened is unfair. Their lives continue just as before father's death. In this situation, the often stated comment 'They're really taking it in stride' should be mistrusted. This sometimes signals that things are not well and that the grief is being pushed away and denied.

When it happens later

This is sometimes also called 'delayed grieving'. For example, someone's brother dies. In the first instance it doesn't appear to affect him. Six months later, when the person comes to the family doctor with a whole cluster of vague complaints, it finally dawns on him that he is missing his brother. The grief surfaces later.

When it takes a long time

As we saw, it is impossible to say how long grieving and the feelings associated with grief should last. Every person is different, and one person's loss is not the same as another person's loss. What is 'no big deal' for one person might be an 'outright drama' for someone else. What is meant by 'too long' is, for example, when someone, many years later, still can't understand why a teacher failed him in an important examination or why his boss had to make him redundant. Another example is when someone continues to be overwhelmed and pained many years later when the name of the deceased is mentioned. In other words, abnormal grieving can be seen when someone, years after the event, continues to feel hard done by; when they are still angry and rebellious; or, when tears still well up at the mention of the deceased. Normally these feelings may be present, but their strength diminishes with time if grieving is occurring.

Why is it that grieving is sometimes delayed or postponed for a long time? What makes working through a loss extra complicated? In order to answer these questions we first have to look at what normally influences the grieving process.

What influences the loss process?

The question is which factors influence how people go through the grieving process and what are the feelings and behaviours that are normally associated with it?

We have already seen that grieving doesn't occur only when close relatives and friends have died. It also happens in situations caused by great change such as divorce or moving house. However, for our purposes in this chapter, we will confine the description of the grieving process to the death of a loved one, so that the comparison with dementia can more easily be made.

It's pretty obvious that the grieving process will be influenced by important factors such as: the type of relationship that one had with the deceased, the personality of the person grieving, the circumstances of the death, the intensity of the bond between those grieving and the deceased, how grief was handled during former losses and the clarity of information available about the death of the loved one.

The relationship

Naturally there are always differences in the grieving processes for the loss of a partner, parents, siblings, friends, colleagues, neighbours, etc. These differences in relationship actually play less of a role than the nature of the bond that one had with the person who died. Hence, it can be more difficult to grieve for a neighbour than for a brother. The death of a mother does not always have to hurt less than the loss of a partner or spouse. The living situation of the person grieving also affects grieving. An unmarried daughter who has always lived at home can have more difficulty dealing with the death of her parents than dealing with the loss of her brother who emigrated some years ago.

The personality of the person left behind

People differ widely in their personality, character, temperament and so forth, but this is not the place to enter into a lengthy discussion about types of personality. What is important here is to realise that each person during the course of their life develops their own style to deal with problems, great or small. One person always becomes reflective, another is rendered nearly motionless, another gets angry when something happens. Yet another person tells anyone and everyone, asking questions in search of a quick, practical solution. Some people accept disappointment better than others. Some deny their difficulties and seem to bypass them. Some resort to blaming others. And so forth.

These different ways of coping with problems can intensify or weaken the feelings that occur during the grieving process. Hence, one person will have the tendency to deny loss or gloss over it longer than another. If someone always tended to blame others for things that went wrong, then they will continue to do so. Those who always easily 'burst into tears', will possibly work through their loss faster than those who contain their hurt.

The circumstances of the death

Many things come under this heading. Did you anticipate the death a long time beforehand or did it 'come out of the blue'? Were you able to be present when the person died? Did it happen recently or long ago? Was it a natural death, an accident, a suicide? And so forth. Working through a sudden, unexpected death is usually more difficult than anticipated death. A suicide is usually harder to come to terms with than a natural death.

The intensity of the bond

The intensity of the bond that the 'person left behind' had with the deceased plays a large role in grieving. The personality of the deceased is also important. Generally, the stronger the bond, the larger the loss that must be resolved.

Relationships between persons are continually changing and are therefore complex. It is also important to consider what the two persons went through together, for example, in a long marriage. How often does it happen that as time passes, the original bond between spouses is weakened? Every attempt to describe relationships in broad terms is too crude and imprecise. Here too, it is impossible to cover this subject in greater detail.

Two types of relationship are often used to illustrate the types of relationships that can result in abnormal grieving. They are the 'exclusive' and 'ambivalent' types of relationships. The exclusive type is a bond with the spouse who was so focused upon them that no other relationships were important by comparison. The ambivalent type is contradictory and conflicting; a sort of love/hate relationship.

The exclusive relationship

In the first example, with the passing of time, the death of one of the partners is inevitable. The survivor feels betrayed and abandoned, not being able to live without the other. The death of the partner speeds up the death of the survivor. Some elderly couples are bonded to each other in a very exceptional way, especially if they did not have children. In a number of cases, this is the background to spouses who die quickly one after the other. Without the partner, life loses all meaning. Some couples wish they could die together after a long life together.

The ambivalent relationship

In the second example, the dead partner barely needs to be grieved for at all because of the conflicting emotions that continue to come into play. On the one hand, the remaining spouse needs the deceased; even before they died, life without them was 'unthinkable and fearful'. On the other hand, the surviving spouse misses them 'about as much as a headache', and finds that they are relieved. In reality, they had probably often wished for the death of their spouse. The conflicting feelings may continue for years.

Unresolved old losses and grief

The grieving process can also be complicated by old, unresolved losses and grief. No one can control this. Some persons find themselves grieving for many persons and events in a very short space of time. Others have unresolved losses to deal with because the new loss happened so unexpectedly. The opposite is also true: the better one is able to work through a loss, the better one will be able to deal with new losses. However, the feelings of disappointment, guilt and sorrow felt, are not necessarily lessened.

With your own eyes

How concrete and real the realisation of the loss was is very important. The more uncertain it is, the more difficult it is to believe that it really happened. Some examples of this follow.

> A couple are both involved in a car accident. The one dies immediately, the other is in a coma and only 'comes to' after the funeral. A wife has cancer, but dies earlier than she was expected to. Her best friend is not able to return from her holidays to be present at the cremation or burial.

These examples share the fact that those remaining could not receive concrete information about the death. They didn't actually see the deceased, neither were they present at the funerals. This is usually the traditional start of the grieving process. You don't have to believe because you weren't there. Some persons, against all other evidence, continue to disbelieve for the remainder of their lives. This is the basis for every plea to 'go and see', rather than to give in to the temptation 'not to see', 'so as to be able to remember the deceased the way they were'.

No choice

There isn't always a choice however. There are situations in life when, even if we wanted it, no concrete evidence or participation is possible. Uncertainty is all that remains. War is such a situation. Many soldiers do not return; there is no information about how and where they were killed or whether they were buried. There is no proof that they died at all, except that they did not return. Children who 'go missing' are another example of this. The longer it takes, the more time that passes, the more likely their death seems, but positive proof never comes. Usually parents keep on 'waiting'. Deep within them the flame of hope is still ablaze. There is also the pernicious, devouring uncertainty that is difficult to sustain because it is so diffi-cult to keep alive. This is why 'finding the body' can be such a blessing and a great relief for the family. It is an end to the uncer-tainty. The proof of the (feared) death becomes concrete and the grieving process can start. The family must now accept, there are no ways around the facts.

Definite or not?

The uncertainty is what sometimes makes divorce so difficult. There is a (hoped-for) end to the relationship, but the partner doesn't usually 'vanish'. Sometimes that is a good reason for the other partner to move away.

Such uncertainty, through which persons, even though briefly, sometimes land on the wrong emotional footing, is the essence of the following example.

> A granddaughter couldn't believe her grandmother had died until the identical twin sister of her grandmother had died. While her great aunt was around, in the same places grandmother had been, at church, and at Christmas, it was just 'as though' grandma was still there.

This uncertainty also affects situations where there is 'suspected adultery'. Uncertainty is more difficult to live with than 'knowing the worst' for certain.

Rather they were (really) dead

Sooner or later, the partner and children of a person with dementia long for the real death of their spouse or parent. One will admit this sooner, and with less shame and/or guilt than another. Some deny these feelings because of the severity of guilt and shame they feel at having these thoughts.

In general, there are three reasons for this longing. First, death would end the suffering of their loved one. The wish that the person with dementia was dead represents their wish that the suffering could come to an end. (Recall that in the previous chapter we looked at the nature of this suffering.)

Second, the wish for the sufferer's death would bring an end to the slow, continuous decline of the person and also an end to all of the feelings that are associated with watching this happen. This thought, then, is understandable. It would end the empty feeling that family members get every time the person with dementia does not recognise them, or every time the person with dementia is angry or crying and yet cannot say why they are upset. It would also end the uncertainty and the feelings of powerlessness that arise when they see the despair of the person with dementia.

Third, death would end the uncertainty. It makes the loss of a parent or spouse concrete and definite. Real death ends the slow, uncertain type of death that accompanies dementia. This longing of family members for the death of the person with dementia also represents a wish that their own emotional uncertainty will end with some sort of clarity. It is a wish to know 'where you are at' again.

Present but absent

The factors that affect every loss and grief process are also valid for dementia. It is grief for the type of relationship that one had with the person with dementia; a loss of the person's perceived personality through the behaviours exhibited; the change in circumstances that the dementia has brought about; a loss in the intensity of the bond that was present; and the process of working through the death before it has occurred.

To follow up the last point: it could be that Mr Jones, feels just as much injustice and as insecure now that his wife has dementia as he did when he lost his job during the Depression. What makes the grieving for a person with dementia extra painful is the uncertainty of the loss, and also the uncertainty of the status of the spouse and children as 'the bereaved'. Is the spouse a widower or not? Are the children 'half-orphaned' or not? Is the person with dementia 'still present' or 'somewhat departed'? Spouses of persons with dementia are treated as widows and widowers.

This uncertainty is comparable to the behaviour and feelings that the families of 'missing persons' feel. They experience the absence of the person, although the proof of the absence is missing. With dementia sufferers, they are concretely present, but the proof of their real presence is gradually diminishing. With regard to this uncertainty, coma patients have sometimes been likened to persons with dementia.

Hope and blame

In a normal grieving process, feelings of hope and blame are usually temporary. For both persons with dementia and missing persons, however, they can persist much longer, even against one's better judgement. It is striking when family members, sometimes even years after a person with dementia has been in a nursing home, still experience feelings of crippling guilt. 'Should I have tried longer and harder to keep mother at home?' 'Did I abandon father when he was in the residential home?' 'If I had come more often would he really have needed to come to a nursing home?' 'If only I hadn't become ill when I wasn't coping so well with my spouse at home.' And so forth. To see families, hoping that there might possibly be some small improvement, against all other information given, sometimes right up until the time the person with dementia is dying, is not a rare event. Where there's life there's hope. Some of the press reports about research into dementia are usually brief, to the point of being inaccurate. Such reports only feed this hope.

Not keeping hope alive can be seen as being disloyal

As long as the person with dementia is still living, the spouse usually hasn't got the heart to dispose of their things or to renovate the house to fit his/her new solitary lifestyle, not to mention the thought of moving or divorcing. The thought of such an action is similar to that of emotional murder to outsiders. It is similar to the parents of missing children, who, from the day the child went missing, never alters a thing in the child's bedroom. The child could return at any moment. This is a long wait for a return that is less likely the more time passes. Only when the situation is definite can clearing and redecorating commence, for example, when the missing person is found dead or alive or when the person with dementia has passed away.

A strong bond can be a disadvantage

In general, a strong emotional bond with the person with dementia can help to support the burden of the family in providing care. But it now appears, that in individual cases, things are a lot more subtle and complex. To be able to continue to care for Mrs Jones, the family must have enough reserve to bear the burden of caring. This 'ability to bear' the burden, as we have already seen, depends on many things but is not the only factor required to care. The 'perceived burden' is also a factor. The very same situation can be experienced as a great or small burden by different individuals. What is a small burden from the children's point of view might be an enormous one for Mr Jones – one that he can barely find the strength to deal with.

Hence, it is conceivable that when a weaker emotional bond exists, a carer seeks assistance from home care services or from a neighbour more quickly. Perhaps a very strong emotional bond with Mrs Jones would make it extra difficult for Mr Jones to accept that his wife will not become old with him. His 'perceived loss' would be much greater in this case.

The person with dementia feels 'let down'

In the last chapter we saw that persons with dementia remain some-what aware of what is happening to them. This leads to their seeking handholds and for safety. When they can no longer find this safety, they can feel utterly abandoned, let down, and alone. 'She follows me around the whole day and night!' complains Mr Jones. 'She asks about her husband even though I never leave her side.' Sometimes, with bitterness and tears he adds, 'When I try to tell her that I am her husband, she becomes furious and starts to hit me and tells me to make sure that he returns.'

The carer feels 'let down'

In this chapter it has become clear that Mr Jones, apart from all the practical problems involved in caring for his wife, is also involved in grieving for her. We say that this grief process is generally more diffi-cult than grieving for a death. Assuming the Jones's had a strong relationship with each other, this means that Mr Jones is losing not only his spouse but the friend with whom he has shared the 'ups and downs' of life. He is losing his wife, his support and his refuge. Hence, this is a double loss. He, too, can feel abandoned, let down and alone. He may even feel 'emotionally divorced', though his wife still lives with him and constantly tags along behind him.

Emotionally divorced but living together

In some couples, where one person has dementia, the contact and understanding that used to be between them, slowly dwindles. To the outside world they still appear to be together, but in fact, they do not 'feel' together any more. This feeling of 'togetherness', which is so necessary to survive and overcome a difficult situation, disappears like 'dust in the wind'. This brings both persons into a strange situa-tion. Mr Jones is losing his wife, support and refuge. At the same time Mrs Jones, through the process of dementia is losing her husband, support and refuge.

Absurd situation

When two persons can no longer rely on each other emotionally, when there is no attachment between them any more, they usually separate. At the end of a long life together, there is usually a strong attachment between couples. When one of them then has a dementia, a very sad, absurd situation arises. Both live together although they become emotionally separated. Two persons live under one roof, but they do not rely on each other any more. They are abandoned, together. It is no wonder then that these feelings, in some circumstances, cause persons to react badly towards one another. It can be a 'trench' of fighting, aggression and even violence.

Unclear status

Just as with a 'missing person', families of persons with dementia sometimes cannot prepare or start to grieve. It takes a long time. Residents at the care home do not see Mr Jones as a widower who is grieving, but rather as a married man. With this image of him, they cannot give him the emotional support that he might so badly need. What he misses most, and is searching for, is also not understood. Perhaps he wants a friend, in this, the worst period of his life. If he happens to go into the room of another resident for a visit, he may be perceived as being 'disloyal' to his wife by some.

I remember a spouse whose wife was in a nursing home. Only after a long while could he admit that he enjoyed the company of an older lady who came to his home once a week to help clean. He enjoyed having a coffee with her and some conversation. Nothing more.

Do I still have a wife?

On weekends, a volunteer sits at the reception counter of a care home. He is a retired post office worker. He enjoys talking to people and likes his work. Since his wife died, this job helps to pass the time during the long weekends. Whenever he sees an elderly couple walking through the corridors, a sad feeling overcomes him. He misses his wife. He knows that Mrs Jones has been diagnosed as having dementia. He feels sorry for Mr Jones. Even when he sees the Jones's together he misses his wife. When Mr Jones came to offer him condolences on the death of his wife, he had to swallow hard and be silent for a moment. Then he said to him, 'Thank you, you're lucky you've still got a wife.'

As soon as he can leave his wife for a few minutes, Mr Jones escapes to the toilet and bursts into tears. He doesn't have the feeling that his wife is with him, let alone that he is 'lucky'.

7 Summary of Part I

If I had known that

The impression that people have about old age and dementia is very varied and usually negative. It is generally assumed that 'there are many old persons who usually live in care homes, the majority of whom cannot survive without help, and that many old persons have dementia'.

This impression does not fit the reality, which is more rose coloured. As of 1992, about one in every nine persons is over the age of 65. Most live independently without any significant assistance. Only 7 per cent of these live in residential homes, less than 7 per cent have dementia and usually dementia occurs in persons over the age of 75.

Most people with dementia live at home, some live in residential homes, even fewer live in nursing homes. Compared to years past, a far greater number of elderly persons live in residential homes. A proportion of these residents do have dementia and, for the foreseeable future that will not change.

What it is all about

According to the present state of knowledge, dementia is diagnosed when a number of health care professionals consider that a person's memory difficulties and behavioural changes are caused by irreversible brain damage. When such assessment is undertaken at the earliest stage possible, it appears that one in five persons who present with complaints do not have dementia. This doesn't mean that early assessment can prevent dementia. Dementia can be excluded from other possible causes of that person's difficulties. The remaining four out of the five persons will have dementia caused by 'Alzheimer's disease' or another type of dementia.

The causes of many dementing illnesses are still not known and there is no treatment or cure. Scientifically speaking, the chances of an imminent 'solution' are slight. This is because there appear to be several causes and many different areas of the brain can be affected. For the time being, we will have to accept that people with dementia are with us, and we have to learn to live with them and care for them in the most humane way possible.

Seeking a handhold

Since neither cure nor treatment are possible at the present time, we have to learn to give guidance and appropriate care to persons with dementia. First, we need to understand what is happening to them. We have considered how memory problems affect the day-to-day functioning of a person. It is clear that the cluster of cognitive and memory difficulties drive persons with dementia to seek a handhold in everything that happens around them, and with whoever is in their company.

In order to help a person with dementia to 'find a handhold' you will need to consider the following. Remember that their memory and attention is influenced by the same factors as yours.

- When you speak to the person, be careful to ensure that he or she can see the things that you are describing, otherwise you may lose them in the conversation.
- It is preferable to ask the person to 'recognise' something rather than to 'recall' something without help.
- It is easier for the person to talk about the past, rather than things that are happening now, such as current events.
- The shorter and clearer your sentences are, the better the person will understand them. Don't talk to persons with dementia for too long. They find it very tiring to pay attention for great lengths of time. Try to use as many sensory channels as possible as this will help.

These are a few tips to help you to care for persons with dementia so that they will have a handhold on you and feel that you are near them. Touching, and body contact helps to overcome the losses they feel and they can come to realise that you are really there and that they are not alone.

In search of safety

It is a false notion to think that dementia does not affect the person who is ill. It is untrue to imagine that a person only has some insight into 'what is happening to them' at the beginning of the illness and that it is suddenly gone thereafter. It is more realistic to assume that the person with dementia continues to feel that strange things are happening to him/her longer than we are inclined to believe. Accepting that a certain 'awareness context' exists in dementia allows carers to have some insight into and to find caring ways of dealing with the affective/emotional experiences of sufferers.

Older people as well as young people think about their parents more than 'once in a while'. This behaviour is called 'parent orientation'. Sooner or later, people with dementia begin to think that their deceased parents are alive. (This can happen momentarily even in normal elderly persons.) This behaviour is called 'parent fixation'.

From the perspective of Bowlby's Attachment Theory, parent orientation and parent fixation can both be seen as attachment behaviours, that is, proximity/closeness-seeking behaviour. This is a behaviour that all persons exhibit at all stages in their lives. It is particularly evident when persons start to feel insecure and unsafe. When people with dementia 'want to go home', it can be a signal that they are not feeling secure in their present environment. Hence, their behaviour can be better understood as being normal in an 'abnormal situation', rather than as being 'abnormal' in a normal situation. Persons with dementia are completely absorbed in the 'comings and goings' of life, and with their search for safety.

From your own experience you will probably know exactly what it means to feel unsafe. Hence, you can understand what it is that a person with dementia is searching for, even when he doesn't always know it himself.

If you want to help a person to feel safe (less frightened), then it is best to remain close to them as much as possible. This will satisfy the person's need to find a handhold, and thus safety. Touch and body contact are essential.

In terms of 'having gone missing'

The family members of persons with dementia also have difficulties. They face a legion of practical and emotional problems. Family members are cornered. They slowly have to take leave of their beloved, whether they want to or not. This is a loss and a grieving process that is accompanied by all of the feelings which go with it. What such families go through is somewhat comparable to those families who await news of a 'missing person'.

When someone is missing, we speak about a 'present absence' of the beloved. There are feelings of both hope and guilt. The more time that passes, the greater the chances are that the person has definitely gone. But the definite news that the person is dead doesn't come. With dementia this 'present absence' of the beloved is also a reality. Here, too, feelings of hope and guilt exist for a long time. The length of the person's presence is a contrast to their absence. The loss is not definite as long as the person remains alive.

Other factors such as the closeness of the affective bond between persons also affect the loss and grieving process. The uncertainty of the loss makes grieving for a person extremely difficult. Hence, whether it occurs sooner or later, the family's wish that the person might die, is understandable. This wish would end the uncertainty and all of the emotional upheaval that goes with it. Only when the person with dementia has died can family members re-orientate themselves.

The unknown is unpopular

One of the conclusions we come to in Part I could be that people with dementia behave more or less like displaced persons, as persons who have lost their place and their balance. They often feel that there is no one on whom they can rely; gradually they have fewer memories to fall back on for comfort. It is perhaps like being divorced without separating – a world of increasing mist, on the outside and the inside, estrangement to the largest degree. In this mist we find the person with dementia going around in search of safety and hand-holds. Because the handholds are not always readily available, the person with dementia can feel abandoned, deceived and utterly alone. No wonder that some persons are aggressive, frightened, suspicious and sad.

Demented, but not that crazy

Images and words cannot convey what precisely happens in the experiential world of the person with dementia. We are just beginning to find the words to use to discuss their plight, words that do not imply that it is a disturbed world that is different to ours. This book is an attempt to lay a few foundation stones beneath the new psychology of dementia and to dispel a few of the myths and unhelpful models about dementia. For example: 'He's doing that on purpose.' 'Of course he doesn't know anything about that.' 'What use would it be to give her more attention?' 'You can't reach him.' And so on.

The title of Part I of this book reflects on the one hand that, certainly at the beginning of a dementia process, persons are still well able to indicate how they wish to be approached. On the other hand, the title is meant to indicate that persons with dementia are like normal persons in all aspects of their living. They are persons like you and I. They behave like all persons do in strange situations, and in unsafe conditions. They seek the proximity of others, whether they are in their own home, in a residential care home or in a nursing home. When, try as they will, they cannot find safety and attachment in their environment, they become difficult and demand our attention.

Persons with dementia are not crazy. That is perhaps the most important handhold to remember when you next are in a position to offer your help.

Part II

Dementia in close-up

Caring in practice

Carers, family and the person with dementia

Better insight into 'what is really happening' can lead to the people in their many relationships with one another to 'grow' rather than to be at cross purposes. The following chapters consider a number of themes that can help you to develop your insight into the complex web of relationships that develop around caring for someone.

8 Working with persons with dementia

Case history example

Rita comes to Mrs Dollands' three time a week. Mrs Dollands' children have divided the remainder of her care between them. With this arrangement, she can continue to live at home even though she has dementia. Rita has been coming here for a year as a home help carer. 'I could write a book about it', she says.

There are the repetitive conversations. Mrs Dollands asks when Rita arrives, for example, 'Are you one of mine?' The first time Rita told her that she was a family worker. Mrs Dollands reacted by turning her away, saying that her family was large enough. She already had enough mouths to feed and clothes to mend. She definitely couldn't take in another one. Later, Rita understood her reaction. Mrs Dollands had brought twelve children into the world and had had two miscarriages. She always added the latter. One of her children died at the age of 17 in a car accident. Rita learned this from the children. Mrs Dollands never spoke about that. The children also told Rita that their mother was hard on herself and on others but that she had been a very good mother. She had carefully scrutinised all the friends they had brought home, and later their boyfriends and girlfriends, but, eventually when they chose spouses, each had been accepted as her true sons and daughters.

It was a great big, close family with Mrs Dollands at the centre. With all of the grandchildren, many of whom were grown up, her ability to keep control over them all had lessened somewhat. Hence, it was understandable when she asked Rita, 'Are you one of mine?' Later on, when asked this Rita would say, 'You could say that', or 'I wish I was, because you are the best mother in the whole world.' Then Mrs Dollands would answer 'You keep your compliments to yourself. You don't need to add another feather to my cap because you don't mean a word of it.' But she beamed while saying this. At times like this, Rita could have thrown her arms around her. A month ago Mrs Dollands suddenly asked 'Are you Josephine?' Rita was quite shocked by this. Josephine was the daughter who had been killed in the car accident. She absolutely didn't know how to respond to this.

Another oft-repeated question of Mrs Dollands was: 'Are you married?' Rita had been living with someone for six years but her first inclination was simply to say no, without further explanation. 'That's a pity', said Mrs Dollands. She looked at Rita closely and said, 'You have a very decent, normal face.' With a pat on Rita's, not inconsiderable backside, she said, 'Everything's where it ought to be.' Rita didn't like this particularly. She was overweight although her partner told her she wasn't. The next time that Mrs Dollands asked whether she was married, Rita told her that she was. She couldn't envisage giving her a long explanation about living together. Mrs Dollands looked at her tummy and asked, 'How far along are you?' Rita didn't like that either. 'I might be heavy but I'm not pregnant', she replied. 'Oh, your husband is probably at sea', said Mrs Dollands.

Sometimes nothing went right. Mrs Dollands yelled and swore and made Rita out to be everything imaginable. Rita was happy when she had finished and could shut the door behind her. Another time though, Mrs Dollands was so distant and aloof that Rita was worried about her. At other times Mrs Dollands was very negative about herself. 'They had better get rid of me, put me under the green grass. Then they'll be rid of me.' When she was in such a mood, it was not possible to get her out of it. Because she had had so much perseverance and unstoppable energy, Rita was afraid that if she had such thoughts in her head she might actually harm herself. Sometimes it is difficult for Rita to stop thinking about Mrs. Dollands. Sometimes her partner bangs his fist on the table and says, 'Hey! I'm still here you know!'

Introduction

Home care helpers tell a range of stories about the persons with dementia they help – some nice, some not so nice. But to see only the nice and not so nice side of work lacks a certain reality. 'In the long run most of us find some way to manage both aspects of our work', home helpers often say. Those who don't manage it sooner or later end up looking for other work. What is it that home helpers find both appealing and difficult at the same time?

Difficult things

Persons with dementia can do or say things that helpers find unpleasant and irritating. Home helpers have said the following things.

Irritating behaviours

When persons keep complaining about everything. When they dismiss everything. When they are suspicious and accuse you of theft although you haven't taken anything. When they behave in an ill-mannered or dirty way. When they can't find a shred of patience. When they become aggressive and call you names. When they don't recognise you or think you are someone else. When they unpredictably 'come out of their shell'. When they react little, or don't understand what it is you want them to do. When you see that they are slowly deteriorating and retreating into their own little unreachable world. When they realise that they are deteriorating.

Extreme or unfulfillable requests

When they are contrary and work against you. When they are angry, frightened or sad and you can't help them. When you try so hard to do your best and nothing seems to help them. When they keep complaining. When they keep doing, calling or asking the same thing. When they are restless and keep wanting to go home and are angry because you won't let them go.

Thankless work

When they immediately forget everything you have just done for them. When they dismantle everything in the house. When you cannot 'reach' them any more. When you see how they behave towards their spouse or children who do everything for them. Actually you never see any results of your work. They never 'get better', no matter what you do for them.

Appealing sides of the work

The following appealing sides of working with persons with dementia will be listed, as home helpers have related them.

Thankfulness

When someone just gives you their hand or kisses you. When they smile with satisfaction because you have done something for them. When they tell you private stories about the past and you realise that they feel comfortable with you. When they are thankful for no reason, or for very small things.

Dependency

When you notice that they react to you, when they give in to you. When you are able to do what you need to, and they work along with you because they trust you. When you notice that they like to have you around. They can be so tender sometimes.

Direct and spontaneous

They express themselves exactly the way they feel. They say what they think and are not afraid of body contact. They don't always look for a hidden motive. You can laugh about the smallest things with them. They can be so to the point, opinionated and stubborn sometimes. They forget it when you've done something stupid. It's almost like starting with a clean slate every time.

Surprising and forthright

They say and do such unexpected things, which you really never could have predicted. When they finally take you into their trust, they can show you so much wisdom and insight about living that you are completely taken aback. They accept you without question. They can be very nice, but also critical and sharp. You can't keep them quiet or put words into their mouth.

Finding the balance

Daily confrontation with irritating behaviour, communication problems or unfulfillable requests can make work tiresome and difficult. This can cause home helpers to have a number of emotional reactions. For example, the doubts you have when someone turns their whole room and house upside down; the discouragement when you keep having to say the same thing; impatience when they keep complaining; the powerlessness you feel when they cannot understand what you want from them.

Thankfulness, dependence, honesty, spontaneity and humour are the other side that balance the difficult aspects of this work. This can stimulate many positive feelings to continue your work. For example, self-confidence comes when someone responds and does what you needed them to; you feel warmth when someone comes to you for a cuddle. You can also be deeply touched by the spirit and humour with which someone is desperately trying to 'keep their head above water'. Many of these feelings can be seen in the story about Rita and Mrs Dollands.

In order to be able to sustain working with persons with dementia and still find your job enjoyable, it is important that the carer can recognise both the difficult and pleasant emotional responses in themselves and to accept them. Some workers will be able to balance these feelings in themselves more easily than others. Many things influence how you are able to do this. One person with dementia is very different from another. It makes a great difference whether you are working with someone who constantly tries to leave, keeps being at cross purposes with you and yet often follows you wherever you go, or, whether someone is co-operative, and spends most of their time sitting quietly looking out of the window. One family is more difficult to work with than another, even if you cannot work out exactly why this is so. One spouse feels more threatened by your presence while another literally looks forward to your visits and values your help.

How you feel yourself also affects your work. After several days of work you are more tired, have less patience, or perhaps become irritated more quickly than at the beginning of the week. Your work is also affected by whether you feel alone and unsupported in your work or whether there is a good team behind you when you need them. Do you trust the person who takes over from you? Do they have the same attitude and way of working as you do? Did you get out of bed on the right side today? Your own disposition is not the same everyday.

Insight into relationships

Helpers have to deal with a complicated interplay of relationships and reactions in their work. They are confronted not only with the sufferer's relationship to themselves, but also the sufferer's behaviour towards the family. Also, they have to work with their own feelings and behaviour towards the person with dementia and the family and their feelings about how the family behaves towards the sufferer and towards the helper. Helpers also have to deal with their colleagues, individually and as a team. What happens within these relationships is like the weather, in that it affects other events and relationships. This makes work very changeable and complex. Insight into the diverse patterns and aspects of these relationships is needed to better anticipate and understand the person with dementia, the family, and the ways in which you react to them. The next example will clarify this.

> On a certain day Mrs Rees is constantly 'finding fault' with her husband. The home help takes his side and protects him unconsciously. Mr Rees senses that he can relax more when the home help is there. As a result of this he more readily does what she asks him to do than when his wife makes a request. This can be enough reason for Mrs Rees to start feeling jealous of her home help who is getting along better with her husband than she is. Mrs Rees says to her daughters, 'That girl works far beyond the call of duty' and 'Her eyes are so controlling'. As a result, the daughters start visiting more frequently to see if what mother said is true. The home help feels unnecessarily 'scrutinised' and complains to her colleagues about the interference of one daughter in particular.

If the home help had understood Mrs Rees's 'nit picking' with her husband as an expression of her anger and her powerlessness, then she probably would have reacted differently. Both of these feelings are part of the loss and grieving process. If the home help had given Mrs Rees enough space to vent her feelings for a while and then waited for the ice to break, things might not have become so frustrating. Instead of becoming a rival to Mrs Rees, the home help could have become her 'buddy'.

If the home help had realised that the interference of the daughter was related to the difficulties that Mrs Rees was experiencing with being helped, then she could have handled it more understandingly. She could have spoken about it to the daughter. Her colleagues wouldn't have needed to listen to her complaints, but rather, they could have been asked for their advice about how they would deal with such a situation.

Insight, 'knowing what's going on', thinking about the reason for the behaviours of both Mrs Jones and her family, can make work easier. Insight can lead to the home help being in better control of the situation, having fewer feelings of powerlessness and more self-confidence. Insight can also help one to realise that you need to learn to accept that not everything you will try will be successful.

Better insight into 'what is really happening' can lead to the people in the many relationships with each other 'growing' rather than 'being at cross purposes' with each other. The following chapters in this book will consider a number of themes that can help you to develop your insight.

9 A look at how family members first notice dementia

Introduction

The word dementia is used when there is evidence that the symptoms and behaviour of a person are a result of permanent brain damage. The damage that can occur may sooner or later affect many abilities including: perception, feeling, thinking, motivation, mood, consciousness and even body movements. The most observable symptoms for us, of what is happening in the brain of the person with dementia, are: forgetfulness, communication problems, the increasing dependence on others and later, incontinence. The entire functioning and existence of the sufferer is affected by the dementia. It also affects the functioning of those around them. This includes family (as we will see with Mr Formby in the next example) and also neighbours and fellow residents or patients.

Mr Formby

About three years ago Mr Formby was told by the hospital geriatrician that there was nothing more that could be done for his wife. After extensive assessment, which had included her being seen by a number of specialists, the doctor had spoken honestly to him. His wife had a type of dementia, namely Alzheimer's disease. He wasn't that shocked by the news, because he had half been expecting it. In fact, the discussion with the doctor had given him a certain sense of relief because now he finally knew what was going on. He hadn't dared tell anyone about this feeling of relief yet, not even his children. Of course he was sad and disappointed too, especially because he had hoped for a nice old age together with his wife now that he was a pensioner. Those hopes now lay in ruins.

He had always been fond of writing, as far back as he could remember. He'd written long letters to his children, long poems to them at Christmas time, speeches for their weddings and also more serious poems. Since childhood he had kept a diary, not constantly, but periodically. Since his retirement he had started it again because he had so much more time. This is how it happened that he had, without knowing it, made a record of the behaviour changes of his wife and what he had gone through with her.

Our holiday in Wales

Sunday August 31, 1986: We came home in a relatively good mood from our holiday in Wales. When the children left home, there was no better news I could have given Beth than that we were going to sneak off for a walking holiday in Wales together. But she just couldn't get into the swing of things on this trip. She criticised almost everything and everyone, whether it was the people in our holiday party or the furniture that was in the hotel room in Llandeilo. In the past she had loved the busy atmosphere of the hotel pub, but on this trip she wanted to go to bed early every night. She kept on making mistakes with the names of people in our group. Luckily she made up a load of excuses and stories to get out of it. Her picking fights constantly was the worst thing. She even started on me. I think she was trying to have a go at me because she was jealous.

I haven't got a clue what to make of her moods. No matter what I suggested, she wanted to do the opposite. She said, 'Let's stay put for a change today dear', when that's what we'd done almost every preceding day. I don't know if she realised that she more or less ruined the entire holiday. When we were lying down one night, having gone to bed early, she suddenly burst into tears and cuddled up to me. She was sobbing like a child. I don't know if she is noticing that she is behaving differently than usual. In any event, she never talked about that. She's never been much of a talker. She never says much about what she's thinking either. This afternoon when we got to Swindon she suddenly started beaming. It was just as if she had found herself again. She's already asleep. I think I'll crawl into my nest too. To be honest, I'm knackered.

When Mr Formby wrote this, he was commenting particularly on those behaviours of his wife that were not characteristic. She can no longer adapt easily in unfamiliar situations. She couldn't feel at home in Llandeilo. Her memory is letting her down at times. She appears to be aware of this and hence confabulates so that others won't notice. She has become very critical. She is 'pitting herself against her husband' and tries to minimise the bustle and activity around her. Her mood is very changeable. She gets the 'wrong end of the stick' often and then becomes upset. One evening she cries in front of her husband without explaining what is the matter. It is likely that she is also doing other 'unusual' things that Mr Formby has not yet picked up on. It is also possible that he didn't write about other things because they were too painful.

Symptoms of dementia, even those which start in the early stage, have many consequences. This is also true for Mrs Formby. She has trouble making new imprints (memories) of the many impressions she is assimilating at the same time. Because of her illness she is being confronted with all sorts of changes that affect her ability to perceive, feel, think, want, know, move and react. How persons with dementia are influenced by and react to these changes is usually impossible to predict for outside observers. To do this, you'd have to know the person very well. The unpredictability is related to her personality and the severity of the dementia symptoms. Also, it is related to the individual way in which we express ourselves, and the influence of our life experience and our temperament. This will be covered in more detail at the end of the chapter.

In the early stage of the dementia process, Mrs Formby's world, and how she interacts with it are changing. You could say that it is sometimes becoming very hazy for her. Yet, she still finds enough familiarity and security to 'keep her footing'.

The environment is a large influence. Certainly in the first stage, Mrs Formby will be aware how her husband and others are reacting to the changes in her behaviour. If sometimes she says something silly or 'out of keeping', she will be confronted with how others react to it. Sometimes they will 'gloss over it' understandingly ('Everyone forgets things once in a while!' 'It's due to old age!'). Sometimes they will be angry and punishing ('Then you had better pay more attention!' 'Think of someone else for a bit!'), or even express bewilderment. Others may even confabulate along with her, trying to pretend that they haven't noticed anything unusual at all.

However they react, most observers will not realise early on that 'something' is not quite right. Unusual behaviour is generally seen as 'an exception' and not as a signal that someone is becoming ill. Mr Formby is still reacting in an accepting way with his wife, even though the holiday didn't meet all of his expectations. Perhaps he is an easygoing person who isn't easily bothered by things. In any event, at the time of writing his entry about the holiday he hasn't got a clue about what is happening to his wife. You could say that while Mrs Formby's world is becoming hazy once in a while, Mr Formby's world is still clear. He is, however, noticing that his wife's behaviour is changing but has no notion yet of why this is happening.

If I had only known!

The events in the lives of the Formby family are more or less typical of what is often called the 'crawling start' of the dementia process. This, almost imperceptible, slow start to the illness is what often leads people to assume that neither the person with dementia nor the family are aware of the changes. This is certainly not always the case. The type of damage and its location in the brain can vary greatly. Sometimes enormous and sudden behaviour changes occur that family members cannot deny. Any single behaviour change can occur in any degree of severity. One change might be more severe for a person than another change. For example, to 'suddenly have difficulty in finding your words' might be a more difficult experience for a person who is very talkative than having brief 'memory lapses'. What one person thinks of as a 'miserable, fraudulent change', another might be able to 'take in their stride'.

It is unusual for those close by to consider the possibility that such changes might be due to dementia if the illness has not yet been formally diagnosed. Even outsiders only really start to notice when the symptoms are persistent and other explanations no longer fit. Even if Mr Formby would have been able to recognise his wife's behaviour changes as possibly indicating that she had dementia, it is not at all certain that he would have been able to accept the consequences of such a thought. The same is true for Mrs Formby herself. How would the day have been if Mrs Formby had realised on the first day of her holiday in Wales that her behaviour meant that she had the beginnings of permanent brain damage? It would not have made things any easier for either of them. But, there is also another side to this story.

Since much time is usually lost before a diagnosis is made, valuable time is lost forever. Knowing early on 'that something is happening' and being able to talk about it together could mean that, from the very beginning both persons will understand each other better. They could be better prepared for the difficult times to come. Otherwise, this slow beginning stage could go on for years with its misunderstandings and uncertainties, the time to speak openly lost forever.

If the Formbys had known what was happening, they could have spoken to each other and eventually perhaps been able to support and comfort each other. The reality is that family members often sigh with hindsight saying, 'If only I had known'. They feel guilty when they realise how lonely the person with dementia felt with all their difficulties, when they assumed they were only being angry, lazy, a nuisance, self-absorbed and so forth.

The definite diagnosis

Wednesday March 15, 1989: Tomorrow we have to return to the hospital for the results of the tests that Beth had in the past months. I think that I will hear what I have already been afraid of for some time; that Beth has dementia and that she will only deteriorate. The children are more optimistic than I am. They think that she's not all that bad yet. If only they knew what I've already put up with these past years. She only seems to have become more jealous, and suspicious. She can't find the way home when she's out for a walk, in fact she's lost the moment she gets out onto the street. She sneaks out sometimes. Last week the police officer brought her home and he told me that she was in a terrible panic when he took her by the hand.

There's no rhyme nor reason to her behaviour. Sometimes she sits looking out in front of her, staring and sometimes she's very agitated. Those are the times when she follows me around the whole day. At other times she won't let me near her.

I've taken to locking all of the doors now. I feel like a prisoner trapped in my own home. I get the feeling that she sometimes doesn't know who I am any more. She calls out for me sometimes even when I'm sitting right next to her. That is terrible. I should make a list of all of the questions I'd like to ask the doctor. It can't be that there's nothing he can do. Isn't there anything that would slow down this thing? Perhaps vitamin injections would help. There's a pill that helps memory I think. Maybe we should change our diet. How quickly will she deteriorate? I want to tell the doctor that she'll be cared for at home, no matter how difficult it is. Does it really have to get worse? What do we do if something happens to me? Who will care for her then? I shouldn't think about what will happen if I become ill and die before she does.

Beth has just sat down next to me and told me a story that I cannot follow. She's pulling on my left arm and I'm writing a few words down, carefully, in between. She's looking at me, I can't describe it exactly but it's with a mixture of tenderness and sorrow. It makes me cry. Right now it's as if she really knows who I am. I have to try to persevere.

Regular occurrences of thick mist

Mrs Formby is long past the point where she can confabulate or cleverly circumvent her memory difficulties. What is 'going wrong' now can't be covered up any more. While she still recognises her husband, he will represent the only beacon in her world, which is becoming increasingly strange. When she wants to go out she finds the door locked. When she sometimes does manage to sneak outside, she has no idea why she went or where she is and what she wanted to do. How she got there is another mystery. And that policeman! What has happened to her one child, and to father at his work? When she sees her husband's face sometimes she only recognises him as someone who 'belongs' to her. But who he is exactly she doesn't know. He must be a good man because he puts his arms out to her. That is comforting when you are afraid. To crawl to safety for a few moments with someone who likes you is a fine thing. Sometimes she finds herself walking around an unfamiliar house with a man who is very pleasant. He's busy doing all sorts of things. She walks after him because it is better to be with him than alone. But when he suddenly touches her affectionately, she goes into a panic. She's not at all pleased about that. He's not her husband. She doesn't want any of that. She wants to call out for her father, but spontaneously calls out the name of her husband. Panic stricken, no handhold any more, Mrs Formby is getting lost in a thicker mist.

For Mr Formby the situation is also becoming less certain and sadder. He doesn't know exactly what is happening but knows that something is clearly wrong. His wife continuously puzzles him. His life is gradually being reduced to what is happening in the few cubic metres of his house. He is being shackled to his own home. His wife keeps tying him down more and more. The more questions he asks about the future, the more determined he is to persevere. Mrs Formby is gradually becoming estranged from her husband. She is also threatening to be cut loose from her very life. As Mr Formby becomes increasingly cut off from his wife, he is becoming increasingly isolated. His wife, who is also his friend, is no longer really present. He wants to protect her, but he also loses his temper with her. He feels so let down by her that he could almost harm her.

Yet another stranger

It happens over and over again that spouses do not ask for help until they really cannot cope any more. When a person with dementia lives alone, family, neighbours and others usually alert helping services. Once some help has been set in place, it can aid the spouse in many ways. It can mean help with caring, with the housework and even some time to do other things for him/herself. It can also mean that the spouse has someone to talk to at the time when they feel most alone in life. Receiving help is also an acknowledgement (from others) that the situation is serious, and being taken seriously by the larger environment.

There can also be disadvantages for the spouse in receiving help. It can make him feel as though he isn't coping any more and it indicates that the situation is indeed serious. That means that the deterioration of his wife is being acknowledged and is therefore more visible. The partner cannot deny it any more. It is a clear sign that he/she cannot do all that he/she would wish to alone any more. This is sometimes felt as defeat. As well, it means having to take a total stranger into one's home, family and relationship. For Mrs Formby the home help might be experienced as 'yet another stranger in the house'. And perhaps, there are even more around somewhere. Perhaps, though, she can get along with the home help even better than she can with her own husband. Mr Formby will certainly find this difficult to accept, especially in the beginning.

Vacant

Friday November 20, 1992: It is one year ago precisely since Beth started to go to the day centre at the nursing home. It's not exactly a day to celebrate, but looking back on it, I'm glad that she could go there. Three days a week they pick her up in a mini-bus. They have assured me that when I need to go in for my operation that there will be a respite bed for Beth in the nursing home. It has gone very quickly with Beth. I can hardly follow what she is thinking, seeing and saying any more. It's as if one thing excludes another. What she sees, she wants to touch. What she thinks, she blurts out or wants to do immediately. She grabs onto the door latch, but doesn't seem to understand that you can open the door with it. She doesn't recognise what she's seeing any more. I wonder if she still understands what she is hearing. Sometimes when I'm speaking to her she looks at me in the strangest way.

I nearly went crazy from all of the commotion. At night time she rattled around through the entire house. She couldn't leave anything alone. Whether it was loose or bolted down, she tried to turn everything upside down. Sometimes it was downright dangerous. She sticks everything into her mouth. She'd even drink a whole bottle of dish-washing liquid. That's why I finally asked for day care for her. With or without some help at home, I'd never have lasted. The doctor also prescribed some sleeping tablets to help get her through the night. My life has become more settled now but I have continued to lose Beth more and more. I often think back to our last trip to Wales together when she was acting so oddly and was so jealous. I long for her jealousy sometimes. At least then we were still together. We still went to bed together. There's no chance of that now. I don't know what's come over her. She's become vacant.

When the whole world has become misty

With home help and day care services Mr Formby is just able to manage. His wife's behaviour continues to change. She cannot think beyond the immediate. What she perceives, thinks and feels barely exists for her. Thinking is doing. What she does and says is what she feels. The meaning of what she is seeing and hearing escapes her. She doesn't comprehend what is said to her. She doesn't know what she is seeing. She touches everything. She wants something now, not later. Familiar things have become strange. Everything is like new. There is less for her to get a handhold on when her world continues to change and becomes even stranger to her. The mist is becoming thicker, and it isn't lifting as often. Day and night are not distinguishable. Mrs Formby rummages, wanders around and is restless. She cannot seem to find any rest any more.

Mr Formby is finding it ever more difficult to 'reach' his wife. He still cares for her, but he is losing her. They are still living under the same roof, but not really together. She's around, but he still misses her. Beth is still alive but his wife isn't. Spouses of persons with dementia often feel as though they are widowed. Physically and emotionally they live without their partner, yet the outside world sees them as being together. Mrs Formby has lost her husband and Mr Formby has lost his wife. It's as if she's dissolving in the mist and he knows she's there somewhere, but he just can't find her.

More than insight into the situation

Insight is one of the first things that dementia steals from people, even in the earliest stages. Insight means that you can understand the relationship between things that are happening; that you can understand 'cause and effect'. Insight also means that you can find an explanation, one way or another, to help you to understand or 'get a grip' on a situation. At the beginning of the dementia process, sufferers struggle to find explanations (reasons) for their failing, uncertainty and their feelings of fear (feeling unsafe). The reasons that persons with dementia find do not free them from uncertainty, and do not help them to find a course of action. Rather, these reasons only make their feelings of uncertainty greater.

Some persons with dementia look for reasons outside themselves and become suspicious. No one suffers as much as the person who is suspicious because they see in everything and everyone, a reason for their suspicion. When the person with dementia then tries to blame others, or to protect him/herself, it doesn't help because the feeling of suspicion is still there. Part of the behaviour of Mrs Formby at Llandeilo, for example, her excuses and criticism of her husband, can be seen as her way of trying to 'keep a grip' on the situation. As the dementia progresses, there will come a time when even those attempts can no longer be made.

Others seek the reason for their difficulties in themselves. In everything that happens they see a justification for their own worthlessness. Not infrequently do persons with dementia say, 'I would be better off dead.' In a certain sense this can be seen as an attempt to stay on top of the situation. The dead do not encounter faults or blame any more. In the first stage of dementia especially, we see that persons struggle to keep a hold on their lives. Such attempts may get caught up with strong emotions such as rage, despair and depression. As the illness progresses, the sharper edges of such reactions usually wear away. These attempts to understand, to reflect about the situation and find something to blame, stop.

Experiences with persons with dementia show us that they practically, intuitively sense that strange things are happening. This evokes feelings. Mrs Formby's brain damage, the literal location of the illness, is only one side of the story. The other side of the story is that she is not unaware, but is involved with the effects of this process through to the very core of her being. This isn't only for the first stage, but throughout the dementia process. This awareness that something is wrong will continue to bring with it more feelings of fear.

The involvement of the person with dementia

Insight into the symptoms that are caused by the dementia process can help bystanders, especially close family members to work through the behaviour changes in the person they loved. However, just knowing about such changes doesn't offer enough of a handhold to help with a way that could improve your interactions with the person with dementia. A more helpful guideline is provided by understanding their 'awareness context'. It is assumed that the person remains deeply involved in what is happening to him or her. This involvement lasts longer than we would like to acknowledge. In the first stage, the person with dementia will notice all kinds of changes that he/she has to work through, in their own way. Denial and confabulation are not the only ways that persons use to try to cope with or manage the changes. Sometimes they 'make light' of their errors, uncertainty and their sadness. In this first stage, persons with dementia are experiencing all of the feelings that go with the grieving process. Mrs Formby is affected by what is happening to her. It does not escape her or happen 'outside' of her awareness.

This 'awareness context' of the person with dementia is somewhat different from 'insight'. Insight is what is becoming impaired. No one can rise above their own failing insight. Neither can we perceive our perception. We can, however, try to 'reflect' our perceptions 'off' of whatever insight remains, as long as it is working. (Annie M. G. Schmidt is a children's songwriter in the Netherlands. Her name is a household word there. She once said that she saw a koala bear getting off of a tram. She knew immediately that her eyes were giving her wrong information, even though she thought it was rather 'cute'.)

Unfortunately, when the entire information-processing system is damaged, there are fewer or even no signals at all given to the person that the information is 'incorrect'. The information provided by the ears, eyes and their sense of balance, create a disturbing reality. But that is their reality. It is frightening and unrecognisable and does not offer any handholds. In their own reality the person with dementia feels lost, estranged and displaced.

Involved with one's head and heart

One person with dementia will resign themselves to what is happening and not offer resistance. Another will not accept it under any circumstances. Some refuse every gesture of well-intended help because there is 'nothing the matter'. Others are angry and refuse all attempts to help them receive a proper assessment. Sometimes, suicide is contemplated. At the beginning of the process, persons with dementia are involved 'cognitively' (with their heads) with what is happening to them. Later on they become involved 'emotionally' (with their hearts). They will react as such to what is happening to them. Their growing feelings of fear start to trigger attachment behaviour (proximity/closeness-seeking behaviour). They want to be around their spouse or children, calling for them, phoning them, following them around, latching onto them, by day or by night, going out into the streets to try to return to their parental home.

The involvement of the partner

Mr Formby is busy with all manner of little jobs that need doing around the house. He has to cook and make sure somehow that there are groceries in the house. Organising these practical things isn't the only difficulty. You could say that for a long time already his own life has been 'on hold'. He hasn't done anything with his stamp collection for ages; neither has he played cards with his friends for a long time. The personal life of the spouse can grind to a halt when their partner has dementia, especially if they had a close relationship in the past. When this is so, the partner doesn't 'give in' or 'lose hope' as readily.

The plans that were made for this period of time must be given up, the future perspective has changed radically. Plans for later shrink to perhaps longing for the weekend when a daughter will come to visit, or looking forward to having a coffee with the home helper tomorrow. This is not likely to be the first time that the healthy partner lands up in a 'faith crisis'. Answers to questions about the meaning of life often continue to evade and may drive the healthy partner to despair. He / she is also driven into a grieving process.

The future is 'under pressure', and the past also becomes controversial. Both partners, especially in the beginning, feel responsible for the present situation and try to find blame with themselves. The meaning of their shared life crystallises out of this. The end results of their years together, the fruits of their shared history colour not only this 'loss experience', but also influence the partner's ability to bear the burden of caring.

The life history

It is the personal life history in particular that gives the particular flavour to the way in which persons behave. The seeds of their past stay with them. Home helpers and other carers can often better understand the behaviour of the person with dementia when they have information about what the person has gone through in life. This knowledge often makes it easier to have meaningful contact with them. To clarify why this is so, a small explanation about memory is needed.

How memory works

(Recall that a more detailed explanation of this was given in Chapter 4.) Memory is a result of how information about the world around us is 'processed'. We receive information through our senses (sight, hearing, taste, touch, smell and balance) and emotions (what is happening 'inside' ourselves and others). Memory, seen as an information-processing system works in three phases as it were. First information is received (we take in information as an impression); then it is stored (imprinted into memory); then memory can be recalled or (expressed) when we need to make use of the memories. Even our thoughts, which are not necessarily sensory or emotional, can be processed and stored into memory.

The past may become the present

It is well known that many people with dementia are continually absorbed by the past. That means that they can still recall the past vividly. The information from the past remains accessible the longest.

They sometimes experience the past as the present. The home helper can only start to appreciate Mrs Formby's sudden, repetitious comments about 'Emily', when she knows that this was her first daughter who died after only a few months. That an elderly male person with dementia keeps getting up at dawn and wandering around the streets, becomes more understandable when one knows that he was a farm hand who was always up early to tend to the chores and milk the cows. There are innumerable examples where, the person's behaviour becomes more understandable once life history information has been related to the carer/helper. Without this, it is almost an impossible expectation that outsiders can follow the person with dementia 'into their reality'.

The present can bring back old pain from the past

Seeing and hearing low-flying aircraft going past has brought back memories of the Second World War to many elderly persons. Fear can bring back memories of fearful experiences. Guilt can bring back old memories of guilt, and anchor themselves to the present situation in a full-blown way. This happens to some persons with dementia also.

Persons with dementia slowly lose their bearing on present reality and end up living in an increasingly strange, different reality. This can bring feelings of great fear with it. They can feel utterly alone and abandoned. Sometimes this present fear reawakens old memories of fear. Financial worries seem real again. Punishment awaits them for coming home too late. The death of a parent or spouse isn't in the past, but in the future again. The comrade who died next to you is just being shot again.

Stimulating reminiscences

Although many persons with dementia 'live in the past', they cannot provide 'factual' information about the past when asked. In other words, to actively 'retrieve' information from memory on command, is very difficult for them. It seems to outsiders often as if they don't know any more. It is more helpful for home helpers to start talking generally about aspects of a person's life history. For example, you might talk about the poverty of the Depression years, how large families used to be, father's work, the war, what birth order the person occupied in a family. When you approach reminiscing in this way, there is a much greater chance that the person will be able to speak about themselves. They need a 'handle' in order to be able to retrieve information from their memory. One possible sample way of asking could be, 'There were ten children in your family weren't there? What was that like?' This is a more inviting way of asking the question than simply asking, 'How many children did your parents have?' Ask about how the dishes got done in such a large family; whether clothing was shared; how vegetables and fruit were preserved; whether they remember beating the mats and what was house-keeping like. This will often give persons with dementia a 'handle' onto which they can attach their memories.

Prompting memory in this way, with real life history information is necessary when the person cannot prompt their own memories any more, or when there is no one else around who can do it. Otherwise, your conversations about the past will be exhausted in no time, and you will miss the contact of 'having reached them' that can come about when they do reminisce intensely. Information about someone's 'likes and dislikes', their daily routine, their 'taste' in decor, their religious practices not only makes real contact more possible, but it also helps to make a person feel comfortable and understood.

The personality also plays a role

The personality of a person with dementia affects the behaviours. Personality, in the sense spoken about here means the whole char-acter and idiosyncrasies that distinguish one person from another throughout their life – their 'way of being' that is typical of them. It means the behaviours or posturing that even in the most variable circumstances in life remain constant. It is this that allows us to recog-nise a person often. Family and friends of Mr Formby might say, for example, 'Isn't that just typical of him, to go about it in that way!' Mr Formby might say to the home helper, 'Do you see that? That is Beth all over again, the way she said that.'

You take yourself with you

How persons react to having a dementia is also related to their personality. People are different from one another. They are individ-uals. Some approach every problem energetically, whilst others adopt and keep the ostrich approach. Not everyone is equally comfortable about expressing what they feel when they are grieving or facing serious setbacks. To express themselves emotionally is more difficult for some than for others. Some persons in real need of help would rather fend it off than ask for it from their nearest and dearest. Those who have always reacted aggressively during setbacks or disappoint-ments may react more brusquely towards those in their immediate environment than others.

Mrs Formby will find it more difficult to accept the changes that the dementia has caused if she was an exacting sort of person. If she had had a 'sunny disposition', she will probably react with less diffi-culty. If you feel easily let down by disappointments and are quick to feel the injustice of things, then self-pity and blaming will more likely be the reactions that you have if you are ever confronted with dementia. You bring yourself and all your reactions with you into your old age, healthy or otherwise.

Friends and family members often conclude that dementia sharpens the characteristics that a person already had. Only those who have really known someone can arrive at such a conclusion. The negative characteristics can also become sharpened. Others say that the person with dementia does things that aren't really in keeping with them at all! The self-control is lost and the brakes (which permit social decorum) have been dismantled.

There is no rule saying that a person will change or stay the same. That cannot be predicted. What is someone's real character? Is it what he or she says or does? Is it the way he or she does things? Is it what a person conceals and the way that is done? What is constant in the behaviour of any person? Who knows?

In summary

In this chapter we considered the influence of the dementia process on both the sufferer and their partner. We assumed a certain 'aware-ness context'. That means that persons with dementia remain deeply aware of and affected by what is happening to them, even when their insight and oversight of the situation start to wane. The ways in which persons with dementia seek handholds and search for safety show us that they retain the 'seeds' of their past life history and personality. What they have gone through in life and what type of person they have been, will affect the way in which they react to the dementia process.

10 From working to caring

Case history example

'I can notice that I care about her, in very small things', said Sarah. Sarah's been working with Mrs Sears and her family for about two years now. Mrs Sears has dementia but still lives in her family home with her husband. The couple moved in with Mrs Sears' parents after they were married and never moved out.

'In the beginning I couldn't get used to it, it felt awkward', continues Sarah. 'I had enough trouble just doing the housework. Mr Sears wanted to help with everything, and you have to accept that. But he had "two left hands". When he finally noticed that he wasn't exactly helping me, he'd go and sit behind the table and stare at me. Or else, he'd go and arrange something to do with his wife's clothing, which only made her more uncomfortable.' Sarah admits that she often found her job very difficult.

Mrs Sears kept asking for attention and that kept her from her work. At a certain point, however, Sarah started feeling sorry for Mrs Sears. She started looking at her work very differently then. She remembers that moment well.

> Mrs Sears was coming down the stairs. She teetered on the last step, and only just regained her balance. I was working in the hallway and saw it happening. There, at the bottom of the stairs she looked so helpless. Then, very politely she asked me if I knew where this place was that she was visiting, even though she'd lived here all her life! That melted my heart. She didn't even know she was in her own home any more.

Since then, Sarah didn't only go to the Sears' home to clean, she started to think about Mrs Sears' illness and what it meant for her. Of course, she still made sure that she got things done on time, but something extra had happened. She had become concerned and she cared about them both. Now she understood better what her friend, who worked at a single lady's home, had been talking about. Her friend had told her that sometimes, when the lady came home from the day care centre, she would go and check up on her again quickly. Her client got fish and chips from the cafeteria and brought them home, but never ate it. After a few hours she'd go out again to the cafeteria for more food. During warm weather, Sarah's friend was worried about the danger of food poisoning with all this food standing around going bad.

The purpose of this chapter

In this chapter, the first thing that needs to be mentioned is that helpers and carers usually 'sense' spontaneously what is required of them. After starting out by 'just doing their work', they find after a while that they are also 'caring'. This makes their work have extra worth because of the carefulness, concern and feeling of responsibility that go with it. The behaviour that results is 'caring behaviour'. Accepting the disabilities of the person with dementia opens up the possibility for the home carer to pay attention to the deeper meaning of that person's behaviour. An important point to make here is that the home carer's position is very different from that of the family carers. Thereafter in this chapter it will be seen how caring behaviour can be influenced by someone's own life history, especially their own attachment history. It is very important for the home carer not to become too involved with the care of the person with dementia, and it is essential to maintain some distance. The differences between family carers and home carers will be emphasised. Finally, the difference between 'over-concern' and 'learned helplessness' will be discussed. The carer must be conscious about the motives, incentives and background to his or her own caring behaviour.

A natural reaction

Because of Mrs Sears' restlessness and constant need for attention, Sarah barely even got to start her work. Mrs Sears' behaviour clearly indicates that she is frightened by what is happening to her. Her purposeless wandering about without a 'tow line' or 'anchor' makes her all the more uncertain. A feeling of fear pervades her thoughts and actions. She wants to find safety and does so by staying close to Sarah and asking for her attention. She is demonstrating proximity/closeness-seeking behaviour (attachment behaviour), which is directed at Sarah. In her world of increasing 'mist', it is an understandable behaviour to exhibit.

In normal circumstances, parents and other carers react to such behaviour from a child by providing the proximity or closeness.

When a child cries, calls out or follows a parent, the parents usually react with 'caring behaviour'. The parent might lift the child up, hold him/her close and say soothing words. This exchange between attachment behaviour and caring behaviour is not something that occurs exclusively between a parent and child. It can happen between all persons, regardless of their relationship and age. The caring behaviour of a home carer towards a person with dementia is an answer to their search for a handhold and need for safety. When you wander, you can get lost in the mist. It is so important to find someone – anyone – to hang onto, especially if that person seems to know their way around. Persons with dementia are sometimes 'Grand Masters' in expressing proximity-seeking behaviour.

In Chapter 9, Mr Formby described how his wife suddenly cried and cuddled up close to him. Later, she sometimes flung her arms around his neck, followed him relentlessly, called his name often and hung onto him. Later still, she held onto him or started wandering around looking for him. In this situation, the spouse was writing about the behaviour of his wife. Her behaviour was coloured by the history of their intimacy. This means that the way in which Mrs Formby tried to get close to her husband was the result of the years of interaction and the way they exchanged their feelings. Many carers describe how persons with dementia also display some of these same behaviours towards them. This means that the carer, without even having to think about it, is already answering some of the requests for safety made by the person with dementia.

From working to caring

As a professional carer, your first reason for being in someone's home is to help them with the housework, or to help with the self-care that has become too difficult to manage. You are there to do something. The house, ward or residence has to look tidy. There is a concrete aim to the work that is visible to you and particularly to others. Others, including your supervisor, will judge your performance partly by the visible results. Naturally you also have to interact somewhat with the older persons in whose domain you are working. You must treat them with the friendliness and respect that you were taught both while you were training and in your own home. Often though, you keep looking at the behaviours of these elderly persons with dementia. When you are new to your work, you will naturally form judgements about persons depending on whether they help or hinder you in your efforts to do your work. You interact with them, but perhaps don't really 'reach' them or 'have contact' with them. With time, as we saw with Sarah, the interactions usually intensify. Because Sarah was 'willing and ready', she was able to see Mrs Sears' behaviour in a new light, not just as an expected symptom of someone who had dementia. Sarah started noticing that Mrs Sears was sending out 'distress signals' and that she needed an answer to them. Sarah answered them, not because it was written in her job description, but because her heart told her to.

Caring means that there's more to the work than what's written on paper. Caring behaviour is more than adding up all the mandatory little tasks listed in your job description. Caring is related to the attitude with which these things are done. Caring involves 'being concerned about', 'caring for' and 'feeling responsible for the other person(s) involved in the situation'. The work to be done can no longer be viewed in isolation from the individual/s for whom they are done, but rather with them in mind – the centre of your involvement.

Sarah herself says that there are small ways in which she notices her 'caring' attitude. She said that she had started 'thinking about' Mrs Sears. This continued even when she was no longer with her. Since Sarah started thinking about what's wrong with Mrs Sears, what exactly it is that she can no longer do and what this means to her, Sarah has started feeling responsible for Mrs Sears' wellbeing.

An important aspect of the work that can bring helpers/carers to really 'care' is that acceptance of the disabilities of the person with dementia. Once accepted, the difficulties no longer need to be stumbling blocks. These difficulties include: forgetfulness, diminished ability to maintain cleanliness and grooming, difficulties in doing normal household tasks, not being able to recognise things, reduced insight, incontinence and problems with language, writing and counting. The time for 'fighting against' what someone says or does, has passed. Also the time of 'trying to pretend that everything is still OK really' has passed. That means that the carer can begin to focus on the consequences of the symptoms and their meaning to the person with dementia.

Sarah is concerned about how Mrs Sears is coping with her disabilities. She is less bothered by exactly 'what goes wrong' and more by 'how Mrs Sears reacts' when she notices that she's made a mistake, can't find things or is lost. The focus of Sarah's attention is thus how to handle the person who is upset, rather than how to handle the symptoms that they have. Knowing and accepting the disabilities 'as a given', frees the carer to concentrate on the meaning and function of a person's suspiciousness, aggression, restlessness and particular moods or thoughts.

Helpers/carers and family

Acceptance is a different matter for families than for professional carers. Carers are starting at the very beginning of a new relationship. In contrast, families are confronted with the loss or decline of a previous long-standing relationship. Their loss is the most important focus. The actual disabilities that the person with dementia has, have a very different meaning for the spouse and children involved. They see their spouse, father or mother slowly fading away and there is nothing they can do about it. Whilst carers first notice the particular disabilities a person has, the family are mostly confronted with the consequences of these disabilities – with a loved one who is changing and getting worse because of an illness.

If Sarah has gone out shopping with Mrs Sears, she can tell you exactly which things 'went wrong', but she will be especially pleased to tell you about what 'went right'.

However, Mr Sears reacts to the total situation. He is ashamed of the behaviour of his wife, and would rather avoid confrontations with her disabilities in public. It is a confrontation with his loss. The interaction of spouses and children with the person with dementia always includes elements of their own grieving. When you are still involved with your own pain, it is often very difficult to find a helpful way of dealing with the person's changed behaviours. If Mrs Sears mistakes her husband for her father, then he will be more accepting of her error when he is less grieved by it.

Carers do not experience these difficulties from the outset. They do not need to break any emotional ties with the person, and hence, are often better able to work out the most useful approach in any given situation. Many carers can even determine beforehand the approach that will work best. Often they are more successful than family members. Carers often admit that it would be much harder for them to do their work if they were caring for their own parents or spouse.

The life review

The contact between the carer and the person with dementia is coloured by the personality and life experience of the person. The behaviour that a child uses to show that he or she is feeling unsafe and needs to be with his or her parents is determined mainly by the way in which the parents react to the child's behaviour. This 'safety-seeking behaviour' (proximity/closeness-seeking behaviour) is anchored to the behaviour of a person in the first few years of life. How the parents reacted to this behaviour will continue to affect a person much later on in life. For example, it will influence how emotional bonds with others are made, how, when the child becomes an adult, he or she will express proximity-seeking behaviour, and how he or she will deal with the proximity-seeking behaviour of others. All these interactions are influenced by someone's 'attachment history'. This is true of you, the reader, the person with dementia and the carer.

There are differences in the way in which small children react to seeing their parents again after they have been separated for some time. One child will immediately seek the (old) safety but another child will 'punish' the parents for the separation by refusing to come near them. Yet another child will not know whether he or she can trust them again or not. Such behaviour is again dependent on how the parents in turn react to the behaviour of the children. Were the parents in a position to offer the child the 'wanted' safety at that very moment? Or did the parents only offer the child safety when it suited them, so that the child could never rely upon their comfort?

One person learns to trust in the feeling of comfort produced by the presence of another. Another person has possibly learned not to rely on others because he or she could never rely on 'attachment figures' when he or she felt unsafe. And so we see that some people have lifelong experiences of trusting others while other people are more cautious and in times of need only trust themselves. Thus, some people find it easier to form emotional bonds with new persons than others. In other words, the proximity/closeness-'seeking' behaviour of the person with dementia as well as the proximity/closeness-'giving' behaviour of the carer are both influenced by the experiences that each one has had during their life.

Every person's life is different

Sometimes a carer doesn't answer the closeness-seeking behaviour of a person with dementia with closeness-giving behaviour. This would have been the situation if Sarah had not seized the opportunity to help Mrs Sears when she saw her stumble on the stairs. Also, a person with dementia may not show closeness-seeking behaviour strongly enough for the carer to be able to 'read the signals'. It may sometimes be the case that the person with dementia may not be able to show signs that the 'closeness of the carer' is actually helping them.

Whether and how persons with dementia seek handholds and safety is dependent upon their own life experiences. It depends upon whether they grew up in a family in which affection was easily demonstrated (with touching, kisses and cuddles), or whether they grew up in a family where the atmosphere was less emotional and cooler and family members kept a distance from one another. How carers react to persons with dementia is influenced by exactly the same things.

Naturally, not all behaviour can be attributed to (or blamed upon) early life experiences. Human behaviour continues to be 'formed' in the years thereafter. When children separate from their parents by leaving home, new behaviours are learned. Attachment to others affects our behaviour. In each phase of life, new developments take place. Yet, we often believe that when persons are confronted with situations that cause them to have serious emotional needs (and dementia is one such situation), then to a large extent, they revert back to behaviours learned during their childhood.

Distance

If Mrs Sears' situation had caused Sarah to become completely absorbed even to the extent of thinking about Mrs Sears in her free time, then we could conclude that there was too much closeness-'giving' behaviour on Sarah's part. Sarah would have to keep enough distance to prevent the care of Mrs Sears from overwhelming her. 'Maintaining enough distance' is the opposite of closeness-giving behaviour. 'Distance' is another way of saying 'widening', 'letting go of', 'loosening the reins' or 'leaving'. This is meant both literally and figuratively. You can be very close to someone geographically, but still feel that there is a great distance between you. You can also be far away from someone but still keep them 'close to your heart'. 'Creating distance' is a process of 'withdrawing'. This can only occur if you are ready to look at your own feelings and recognise the potential signals of over-involvement. It helps to meet colleagues, to talk to them about feelings of frustration or to use others as a 'mirror' to 'bounce your feelings off them'.

Accepting the disabilities of the person with dementia is what turns helping into caring. In order to prevent 'over-involvement' to such an extent that your work becomes too much for you, it is important to be able to keep the necessary distance from the person. You may also need to distance yourself from the 'clumsiness' or 'despair' of the person with dementia so that they do not become your own clumsiness or despair. You are not doing this in order to abandon the person, but only to be able to continue to help them to carry their burden. Creating the necessary distance also means that you will not lose your ability to see the humour of certain situations and that you will not feel guilty for doing so. Keeping the necessary distance means that you can draw a line between your own emotions and those of the other person. Without it, it becomes difficult to evaluate situations and to work out the best way to help. Without the necessary distance, caring can become 'over-involvement', 'meddling' and can even result in feelings of 'total helplessness'.

Families and distance

The distance that carers must keep between themselves and the family of the person with dementia is different from the distance they must keep between themselves and the person with dementia. Most carers keep a suitable distance between themselves and the person they are helping to care for, whilst at the same time keeping sufficient emotional involvement. Families are very deeply involved with the person with dementia. They often have great difficulty in 'keeping a suitable distance'. Carers sometimes think that because they themselves have found a way to do this, that families are also able to 'keep a suitable distance'. Hence, carers can underestimate the emotional difficulties that family members are experiencing. To try to keep this in focus, carers should try to imagine how they would react to well-intended help and advice in an intense grieving situation of their own.

Over-concerned

This literally means to have more concern than is necessary. It also means that the 'closeness behaviour' of the carer is not proportional to the closeness-seeking behaviour of the person with dementia. It can mean giving more than you are being asked to, but it can also mean giving without being asked. Sometimes this is done to give yourself peace of mind, 'because if you didn't do this, something would go wrong'. Working under the pressure of time constraints can also do this. For example, you don't wait until the person tries to dress herself, but take over and do it for her. What is called 'learned helplessness' can occur like this. This means that the person with dementia takes less and less responsibility to do what they actually still could do. This is what appears to be so difficult for carers to accept when they see a spouse or child 'doing too much for' the person with dementia. The person then becomes more dependent than is needed. 'Over-concern' can also be tied up with a helper/carer's self-image of caring, that is, the expectations that they have of themselves.

Self-image and caring behaviour

It sometimes happens that people show concern and caring behaviour because it is important to them that others like them and that they are seen as 'being nice'. They think that caring shows their own caring nature, and they are constantly looking for ways to show this. When they do not express caring behaviour, they don't think that they are 'being nice' and they don't like themselves. Often people have experienced that when they were children, their caring behaviours were especially positively rewarded, particularly by their parents. Over-concern is seen when, for example, carers forfeit their entire identity to caring and closeness-giving behaviour. In order to be able to preserve enough self-confidence, carers then have to continue to remain 'over-involved', even when it is unnecessary. It is rather like being a slave to your own caring or exacting nature. It is as though if you couldn't care for someone, you wouldn't have a life. When others don't need your care, you feel discarded.

Strongly 'independent' behaviour can also be an extension of the self-image of carers. This emphasis on assertive behaviour can be to the detriment of caring behaviour. It can lead to exacting, demanding behaviour in oneself and often results in very high expectations of others. This can cause a carer to place too much emphasis on the independence of the person with dementia and make them insensitive to the real needs. The question, 'What is the use of stimulating and encouraging self-care when the carer can't even see the benefits of doing so?' is asked frequently. This then leads to the question, 'Who is actually helped the most, the person with dementia or the carer?' What should one do when a family carer concludes, 'Enough is enough, I'm spent. Let someone else provide care now. I can't any more!'? It is no wonder that sometimes, two individuals who have totally different self-concepts can come into conflict with each other.

Caring behaviour can also be 'forced' as a result of never having received enough caring in the past oneself. A great frustration can be released by doing the opposite. You give what you never received. 'Caring behaviour' can also be rooted in feelings of guilt – towards those whom you feel you deprived of sufficient care. In this instance you are picking up a thread you had let go. In both these instances, the process of working through one's own pain from the past affects the care of another person. It doesn't mean that the carer should change this. What is important is that you have some insight into your own motivation to care and how you are providing care. It can be very functional (to help you to work through past pain) to care because of such feelings.

Powerlessness

Working with people with dementia can evoke feelings of powerlessness and helplessness. Feelings of powerlessness usually result from you trying to do what you can, but you cannot succeed in doing what you want to. It can also be a result of having expectations that are too great, and possibly unrealistic.

Imagine that Sarah isn't able to persuade Mrs Sears to go out for a little walk with her every day. If she has tried all possible ways to persuade her and failed, then it is likely that after a while she would start to feel powerless. You feel powerless when you use all your knowledge and experience and you still do not succeed in getting the person to do what you'd like them to. Powerlessness is an uncomfortable feeling, but it shouldn't shake your self-confidence necessarily. Sarah finally ends up by choosing not to go out for walks with Mrs Sears. To be able to make this decision, she has to be 'sure of herself'. She maintains her self-confidence and is able to continue caring, even though she feels powerless about the walks. Feelings of powerlessness often force us to make choices or to change our expectations.

Helplessness

This is a different feeling from powerlessness. Helplessness often exists because of insufficient knowledge or experience. Imagine that Sarah's supervisor had asked Sarah to go out for a walk with Mrs Sears every day, even if it is only a very short walk. She explains that this is important for to keep Mrs Sears mobile. The trouble is, Sarah doesn't know how to do this, and she is starting to feel helpless. If no one explains to her the possible ways of doing this, and if she doesn't tell anyone about her problem, she'll probably quickly give up. When the feeling of helplessness lasts too long, it can erode one's self-confidence. No one can sustain caring for persons with dementia without having enough self-confidence, or being able to develop it once the work has begun.

If Sarah is given some tips or ideas to try out with Mrs Sears, her feelings of helplessness will probably disappear. This is true even if the ideas don't all work. Gradually she'll start to feel powerless rather than helpless. The advantage of having feelings of powerlessness in a certain situation is knowing what you can attempt to do, using all your knowledge and experience, and if nothing works, then you don't need to undermine your own self-confidence.

Empathy versus sympathy

A feeling of sympathy doesn't have to be a problem, unless it is the only feeling that working with a person with dementia evokes. If it is the only feeling you have for a sufferer, you are functioning 'outside' of their world as it were. Sympathy can be so overwhelming that it can be paralysing. You would be willing to do anything to help someone, but you cannot any more because you are being 'taken over' by only seeing the problematic aspects of the situation. You might also do everything for a person, really 'pulling out all the stops' to help them. However, because of this, you can't always pay close attention to what the person's real needs are. Those who care only out of sympathy, can easily overlook what the sufferer's own wants or needs are.

If Sarah were to care for Mrs Sears out of sympathy, that feeling would overwhelm her to such an extent that she could not 'feel along' with Mrs Sears. She would thus have too little distance. Her caring would fall short of its goal. Empathy is caring, to the extent that one does not become overwhelmed by the situation of feelings for the other. In this way you can continue to care, because you do not drown in the feelings of, or about the other. Empathy keeps enough distance between you and the person with dementia so that you can appreciate your responsibilities to continue helping that person. Sympathy means that you are so emotionally involved in a situation that you cannot sustain the energy to continue caring.

Give and take

When carers feel helpless or are driven by a feeling of sympathy, it is almost impossible for them to look at the attractive aspects of caring for persons with dementia. You cannot enjoy their stories about the past, even when they are not entirely clear, if you have too much sympathy. If Sarah were to only have feelings of helplessness, she would never enjoy the pure emotions that Mrs Sears expresses. She would find it impossible to enjoy her reactions to situations, because she would only be thinking that her knowledge and experience were not enough to help Mrs Sears.

In Chapter 8, other examples of situations that carers found enjoyable were given. It is absolutely necessary to have some positive feelings, to actively counterbalance all the more negative things that the work inevitably brings with it. In order to be able to continue 'giving', you must be 'receiving' something too. It must be a part of your overall development to learn about the positive things that go along with helping/caring for a person with dementia so that you can continue to plod along with contentment.

There are other factors and circumstances that can make it difficult for a person to find a healthy balance between giving and receiving, for example, the relationship between colleagues, or the family of the person with dementia. If Sarah's colleagues keep warning her that she should be careful about the dependent behaviour of Mr and Mrs Sears, then how can Sarah enjoy even a spontaneously given kiss? If the person's family think that Sarah's work is 'to polish and tidy up', and that 'sitting for a few minutes to have a cup of tea and a chat is of no use', then Sarah will not be able to do her work with as much pleasure.

Finally

'A person can only care well for others if they care well for themselves.' This really means that you must be able to be honest about your own abilities and limits, and to accept them. There are no 'hard-and-fast rules' about caring. It is so important for carers to be able to look honestly at their own behaviour and to become conscious of their own motivations to care. Then they need to look at the possible ways to handle and develop these motivations.

11 Adoption

Case history example

Bill works as a nurse in the community. He had worked with Mrs Evans for a long while. Finally, the day she was moved, he went along to accompany Mrs Evans as she was admitted to a nursing home.

> Her daughter and I took her there together. When we left and I waved to her before we turned the corner, it all became too much. I don't know how long I stood there crying. Her daughter was more 'matter of fact' about it than I was. She comforted me more than I did her, even though it must have been a very harrowing day in her life.

Bill continued, saying:

> I used to go to see Mrs Evans when she was still OK. I gave her daily jabs for her diabetes. I saw her slowly deteriorate to the point where she couldn't live at home any more. She often left the gas on and sometimes went out wandering around the streets in her night gown. In the end, I must have gone to check on her at least three times every evening. I made detailed schedules with her daughter, but the nights were the worst. She was alone then and every morning when you came to see her, you just had to hope everything was fine. The day Mrs Evans left her home was the day I thought I had really failed. That feeling went eventually. Now I just feel sympathy for her. Dementia had turned a 'fiery old lady' into a 'dependent little sparrow'. What an end!

For the first six months, especially in the beginning, Bill checked up on Mrs Evans about once a week, paying short visits to the nursing home. He remembers them well.

I just sort of gravitated towards her. I must have been a bit of a headache for my colleagues at the nursing home because I made it my business to find out everything about her. I checked on her clothing and medicine, and took her outside for a little walk as often as possible. I wanted to keep her away from the other persons with dementia.

One day Mrs Evans failed to recognise Bill. At least, she couldn't remember his name although she still treated him as someone she could trust. As time passed, she no longer gave any signs of recognition and sometimes became angry when he tried to be nice to her. That is what affected him the most.

Looking back at things, she deteriorated very quickly. After a few months she became bedridden. A month later she passed away. What helped a lot at that time was the way in which her daughter treated me like 'one of the family', as a kind of brother. We even planned the memorial service together. If the daughter had treated me as an outsider, or had been more distant, I would have found it much more difficult to get over Mrs Evans's death. The fact was very simply that we had a very special bond with each other.

Overview of the chapter

We have already discussed 'closeness', 'attachment' and 'adoption'. In the next part of the chapter we shall consider how carers can recognise the signals of attachment and how they can work with them constructively. How far can carers go? How do persons with dementia signal that carers seem to be going too far? How can carers prevent and deal with this? We shall also consider how the process of 'adoption' by a carer is opposite to the process in which family members are trying to 'take leave of' the person with dementia. This can cause great problems if both the family and the carer feel they are exclusively responsible for the person with dementia. Finally, we shall see how good communication between the family and carers can help both the process of 'adoption' and the process of 'taking leave' of the person. This can help to create a closer, more equal relationship between the family and the carers.

Giving closeness

While some carers can work with persons with dementia without becoming emotionally involved, in most cases an emotional bond exists. When working develops into caring, this usually happens automatically. It mostly happens because carers become literally and figuratively a 'handhold' and an 'orientation point' for the sufferer. Persons with dementia eventually find themselves in a misty world in which they are frightened. Seeking safety is usually answered by carers who provide 'caring behaviour', for example, by staying close to the person, and thus, literally being a 'handhold' for them. In the beginning it is usually enough for the person with dementia to be able to see and hear that the carer is close at hand. Carers are thus giving the message: 'Look and listen, I'm still here with you.' When the person with dementia has the feeling that no one is near, they will usually seek company, start following the carer around and possibly show 'claiming behaviour', which can eventually become irritating. Later, carers appear only to need to use touch and gestures of comfort to settle the person. It is as if carers are giving the message 'Look, you're not alone.'

At the end of the dementia process, sometimes only intense body contact, such as stroking or massaging hands and making the person feel warm and comfortable is effective. The message that carers then give is: 'It is pleasant and safe here.' Even when all these steps have been taken to calm and comfort persons with dementia, they will often continue to feel afraid, lonely or rebellious. They sometimes express this by constantly calling out and yelling.

The less a person can be 'reached', the stronger is their need for the closeness of a carer – that is, if the carer doesn't want to lose that contact. This takes a great deal of emotional investment on the part of the carer, which usually leads to the development of a close bond with the person. Carers have often had the feeling that they have become the 'family' of the person with dementia. If carers feel an emotional bond with someone, they will also need to work through their feelings of loss when this relationship comes to an end. While some carers find the process of grieving so painful that they decide to become less emotionally involved with future sufferers, most carers see the grieving as a natural result of having had a close emotional bond with someone.

Adoption

While family members are taking leave of their beloved as the illness runs its course, carers are usually just beginning to forge a new bond with the person with dementia. Where one person is dismantling a relationship, the other is constructing a new one. While carers don't literally 'adopt' the person with dementia, we can use this word to refer to what often happens between them. Since communication between them is usually at an emotional level, it follows that attachment is usually a natural result of this. In view of the inevitable grieving process that will occur, it is important that carers recognise this bond of attachment and are able to give a name to it. It is an attachment that is deeper than 'merely accepting the person's limitations', having concern, or caring for them. The essence of this concept of adoption is the feeling of 'caring about' that becomes linked to a strong awareness of one's 'context of responsibilities'. The person with dementia starts to affect a part of the life of the carer. Even outside working hours these feelings are significant for the carer. This 'special significance' does not necessarily mean that the carer 'goes to pieces' because of the burden of this relationship. This relationship needs careful and realistic balancing to remain a healthy and useful one for both parties.

Becoming attached to another involves a process

Looking back at things, carers often say that initially there was 'nothing'. There was hardly any sense of involvement, and that sometimes there was even a feeling of dislike. Slowly this changed to a feeling of acceptance. Gradually they became accustomed to a different attitude and changes in expectation because they learned to understand the person with dementia. Finally, a feeling of 'attachment' to the person developed. This feeling sometimes intensified, especially when carers worked closely with members of the family. Such co-operation can be very satisfying; it can give a feeling of belonging and of being meaningful to someone.

What is the cost of attachment? What are the consequences for the carer who does develop an attachment to the person with dementia? Before elaborating on this, let us pause for a few moments and examine the concepts of 'closeness', 'attachment' and 'adoption'.

Closeness

Allowing or permitting closeness is a behaviour. It is something that you choose to do or allow. It is an action. It might be: calling out to someone to let them know that you are around; touching or stroking someone's hand once in a while; silently remaining near the person to listen to them in their sadness; or giving them a big hug when they are frightened. It could be offering consolation, or even standing there quietly for a while without wanting to intervene immediately.

Attachment

Attachment is the result of a process of becoming close. It is the special bond that you have formed and an expression of your feelings for the other person. The words 'attachment' and 'emotional bond' are, for our purposes, synonymous. Giving your 'closeness' and presence to a person is possible without having an emotional bond to another. Having attachment, without giving your 'closeness' or presence to another, is harder to conceive of.

Adoption

Adoption is the process whereby you integrate another (who is no blood relative, and with whom there is no shared history), into your own life. You cannot avoid them, whatever their habits or limitations. This person has become 'yours', regardless of anything else. Adoption means starting to relate to the person 'as though' you have become 'family'. In this sense, our use of the word adoption does not differ from the usual meaning of the word.

Signals of adoption

Different carers have different ways of dealing with this emotional bond. Many do not even realise that a strong attachment exists. Supervisors will have to caution and protect some of the carers regularly, whilst others will keep the 'necessary distance' for themselves.

> When I'm at home I do think about things for a while. Then I put those thoughts away. Home life and work life do need to be separated.

> I just shut the door behind me. No problem. Otherwise I couldn't keep doing this work.

> When I go home to my family I have to let go of my work whether I want to or not.

> I work every day with her. Of course that creates an attachment. In the evenings I do think about everything that has happened that day for quite a while.

> I couldn't bear it – to just go home and leave my client, who follows me around all day long, to fate.

These sentences show that carers are very individual in how they show that they have adopted the person with dementia for whom they work. There are a number of signals that regularly appear in the stories that carers relate about their work.

From the bare essentials to everything

You seem to know a lot about the person. You know a great deal about their life history and exactly how they are now functioning. This person is no longer a stranger, but a 'known' person to you, reliable and even a 'part of yourself'. It also seems that you can easily 'step into their shoes'.

Doing more than you really have to do

You are so concerned that you would be pleased to do everything for them. You do more than you really have to for this person. You give them a higher priority than others, and you start to become anxious about 'little things' that happen to them. You want to do everything as well as you possibly can.

It's not all that bad

Your acceptance of things that others would find insurmountable or unacceptable, can also be a signal. 'There's really no problem here is there?' 'It's not that bad yet.' Sometimes your concern is so strong that you cannot see when the boundary for 'normal behaviour' has been crossed. Sometimes this is a reflection of your difficulty in accepting that the person with dementia is deteriorating. Sometimes, you just don't want to lose them.

Knowing 'what's best'

One signal is having a lot of criticism for the approach and methods of your colleagues. 'They all deal with it the wrong way. I know her better than they do.' Carers are then so concerned about the person with dementia that they no longer have any faith in their colleagues. They are sure that they are the only one who knows the person 'through and through'.

Taking it all home

Even when you are at home, you keep thinking about the person with dementia. You take her home with you in your thoughts. This is true for the unpleasant things as well as the nice ones. You take both the cares and worries home, and also the happy feelings. You enjoyed their stories, or had a good laugh with them.

As we have already said, it is not uncommon for carers to discover, after the fact, that they have an emotional bond with a person with dementia. This usually happens when the person dies, or has to move into residential or nursing home care, or when the carer gets moved to a new posting. This awareness usually becomes evident when the relationship has ended or when the end is in sight. Carers then often realise that the person meant more to them than they had realised. Often this is expressed through 'continuing to care', as Bill did with Mrs Evans.

Adoption usually happens quite naturally on the part of both persons. Younger carers are often wrestling to establish an identity. It can help them to find this when the person with dementia accepts them. For others, such acceptance is almost like having a mirror image, or symbolic presence of their own (grand)parent. Sometimes, small coincidences either help or hinder the relationship between carer and the person with dementia. The tone of a voice, or a particular way of speaking, a posture or gesture, the eye or hair colour – anything can be of extra relevance.

It is noteworthy that carers often feel accepted by those they care for. Somehow, they know what is needed of them, what the goal of the care is. Persons with dementia usually accept the carers unconditionally. Since the person's need for safety is great, carers often turn into 'attachment figures' who help give them a handhold on life, even if, at first, they would have preferred a different carer. Persons with dementia can also very clearly convey that the behaviour of the carer is unpleasant or inattentive. They show this almost immediately. 'You always know where you stand with them.'

How to deal with adoption

In the past, carers would have been cautioned or given a 'rap on the knuckles' if their supervisors had noticed that they were becoming emotionally involved with their clients. It was thought that, above all, no attachment of any sort was useful (and therefore permissible) between carers and clients. Even though the times and the thinking about this matter have greatly changed, carers still have a tendency to feel cautious about the attachment they feel for their clients. 'Be careful! Is it allowed? Is it a good thing?'

Given that carers more or less naturally become attached to those they care for, the relevant question then should be: How far should this attachment go? Where is the limit? This differs from carer to carer. It is very difficult for an outsider to draw the line for them. Experience teaches us that the boundary for attachment has been reached when the carer admits that the emotional bond is becoming a burden, or when it becomes clear that the carer is no longer able to judge the situation clearly any more. This means that the wellbeing of the person with dementia and/or the carer is affected. This might be, say, if the carer cannot notice the deterioration in the person and keeps emphasising the need for independent functioning. In this case, the person with dementia is at risk. The carer's wellbeing has been damaged when family and friends notice that the only thing the carer can talk about is what is happening at work and how things are going with the person they are caring for.

Dealing with the situation

There are two ways that carers can be helped to cross back over to the safe side of the attachment boundary. The carer can develop a routine, based on the previous experience he/she has in caring, and they can talk about the situation with others. In this way the balance between attachment and distance can be maintained. Both ways offer carers a type of counterbalance from becoming 'over-involved.'

Working to a routine plan

The word 'routine' is used when the work has evidently been well practised, i.e. when it is familiar to the person doing it. When carers say that they are getting into a routine, they usually mean this positively. They indicate that the work is going well. They are no longer, as often happens in the beginning, standing around wondering what to do next, or feeling helpless. Routine does indicate a degree of 'automisation' of the work. It means that a carer has worked out 'the best way' to do things.

One psychological advantage of developing a routine is that the carer no longer becomes emotionally 'strangled' by a situation. Although practise can lead to a degree of 'humdrum', this doesn't necessarily have to be negative. Typically, carers have some feelings of mistrust about the situation both when they notice that they are becoming attached to their client, and when they start to feel that work is becoming a bit 'humdrum'. Both things, however, can have positive effects on work. Attachment ensures sufficient concern. Routine offers a sort of counterbalance against over-concern. Without a certain amount of routine, work could not easily be sustained, precisely because of its emotional demands.

Talking about it

Talking about one's work to colleagues, one's own family and good friends is another way to minimise the chances that 'attachment' will become 'over-attachment'. It is important to be able to speak to someone who has had experience with persons with dementia. If your friends and family don't know what it's like, you cannot always rely on their understanding or advice. Some persons indeed have never had experience with a dementia sufferer; others are perhaps frightened of it. They will possibly not even be able to imagine what your concerns are.

Talking about your concerns with others is possibly more easily said than done. For carers working in the community, it may be harder to get together to speak to colleagues, than for those working in residential and nursing home settings. It is easier if you work in a 'team context' because then there are others who take over the caring where you leave off. Some carers live alone so there is no one to 'bounce things off' when they come home. Others step through the door to find their own family needing their attention and so they may not get the chance to talk about their day.

Talking about your work can help you 'to see it in context', to keep it relative to other things in life. Sharing experiences and happenings with others usually leads to a kind of consciousness about what is happening between the carer and the person with dementia. These discussions also help to reveal why a certain client means more to you than another, and how colleagues experience this. Gradually, it may become clear why attachment to someone can become 'a burden', and what to do when you start noticing this. During work meetings these topics should be aired and support should be given and received for setting and maintaining the 'necessary distance'.

Caring for persons, regardless of their age, is usually an emotional experience. This is especially true when the work is long term, and when one has had previous experience. It always affects you whether you like it or not. This is the most important reason for making sure that at 'work meetings' some time is reserved for talking about 'what work does to you'. This wasn't even conceivable some years ago. That carers and clients sometimes had emotional attachments to each other was tolerated, but wasn't actually 'permitted'. Nowadays, with insight and conviction, we honestly acknowledge that it is precisely this bond of attachment that holds the key to the 'quality' of care. This bond can have a two-fold effect though.

The adoption process and the client's family

The adoption process for the carer runs in parallel to the 'taking leave' process for the family. This has consequences for provision of care that both parties give to the person with dementia. So now we need to ask the important question. 'Who determines what is good for the person with dementia?' Both parties often feel responsible for the situation. Without even realising it, carers sometimes take the place of a son, a daughter or a spouse. The family can become jealous of the carer. This can cause tension in the family and even lead to the person with dementia or the carer cutting the family off. It is often

better, then, for family members to truly step back from caring somewhat.

The person with dementia is increasingly less able to express
his/her own needs. Usually, family 'step in' to meet their needs, the
way parents do for young children. Although this sometimes
happens more easily than others, it goes without saying that close
family members feel responsible. From a certain point onwards,
carers also start to be concerned about the needs of the person with
dementia, because they see on a daily basis that the person is
becoming less able to care for him/herself. So many little things need
attention. Carers see that their continuous attention and care is
desperately needed. This means that carers sometimes feel every bit
as responsible for the person with dementia as do the members of the
family.

Responsible together

How both parties deal with this shared responsibility depends on
both their perceptions of the person with dementia and the
'unwritten expectations' that each has of the other. It also depends on
what is considered to be 'one's own' versus 'someone else's' responsibility.

Perceptions and expectations often remain unspoken. Sometimes
we are not even aware that we have them until a certain moment in a
certain situation arises. Even when people are aware of their expectations, they can't necessarily express them. This doesn't need to
present a problem as long as the behaviour of both parties tallies with
the unconscious or unexpressed expectations that undoubtedly exist.
The family will feel at ease when the care given by a carer fits in with
their perception of the care that should be given. When the care that
family members give to the person with dementia fits in with the
expectations that carers have of them, then carers will feel at ease.
Such a situation does not cause friction and neither party is likely to
be critical of the other. On the contrary, there will be a feeling of
'shared care', for which both are responsible. With Bill and Mrs
Evans's daughter, that was undoubtedly the case.

Such an agreement is not always achieved. There can be many
reasons for this. Families and carers do need to talk to each other
because unreal perceptions usually lead to irritation and disappointment.

No 'handing over' of the care

One practical reason why agreement is not often reached, is that
sometimes there is a 'handing over' of care from carers to families. If

no agreement has been made about what is the responsibility of the family and what is the responsibility of the carer, then there is a chance that some things will be done twice and others not at all. Certainly things will happen differently from what each party expects. This can be avoided by initially talking about it and then continuing to talk about it. Many carers relate what is happening to family members by writing things down in a 'logbook' and vice versa. This is a useful aid but more than that, it also helps to create a feeling of joint responsibility.

If things are not clearly agreed, it can happen that family members expect more care than carers can reasonably give. This easily leads to misunderstandings about how much family members are doing, or the attention and attitude that carers have to them. This happens not only at home, but also in residential and nursing home settings. It is helpful for everyone to know, for example, how many visitors the person with dementia has had, when they came, what happened to the person when they said good-bye, or whether there was any difficulty experienced in trying to help the person to get washed and dressed.

Family members often benefit from finding out from carers how they, for example, set a toileting routine, or deal with incontinence or try to stimulate activities, or even finding out what the carer and the person with dementia talk about during their time together.

That such things do not 'get talked about' routinely is not usually a result of unwillingness. It is more a result of a lack of time, or not wanting 'to bother' someone with small details that they may already know. One often hears from both sides 'I didn't want to mention it because it's already so difficult for them and they already try to do so much in such a short time.'

Differences in the emotional bond

Misunderstandings about care can also come about because of the different emotional positions in which the family and the carers find themselves. We saw that earlier. The carer is forming an attachment whilst the family are taking their leave. The intimacy that daily care often requires usually speeds up attachment. The inevitability of loss and the pain of grieving often speeds up the 'letting go' process. If both parties do not recognise this paradox quickly enough, it will certainly affect practical aspects of care and working together.

Jealousy and a sense of failing

You might ask yourself how Bill would have felt if the daughter had not recognised the special bond that he had with Mrs Evans, and had not known what to do with her own feelings. In any given situation, it is not uncommon for family members to feel some jealousy towards the carer. The family might feel that they have failed or that an aspect of caring that was important for them emotionally has been taken away from them. 'I'm their child and I want to keep on caring for my parents' or, 'We promised each other that no matter what happened, we would continue to look after each other.'

What often happens is that feelings of jealousy lead to feelings of mistrust about the carer. This may happen because of old hurts in a family's history. For example, a daughter may still be resentful of the years of 'interference' in her life that a mother caused. For the daughter, it is a bitter pill indeed when she sees the carer getting on so well with her mother.

These feelings can, sometimes in extreme degrees, return when the person with dementia is finally admitted to a residential or nursing care setting. Such a placement is a very concrete change. It reduces the family's need to provide care but also emphasises the deterioration in the person with dementia. Both feelings of relief and of having failed (along with being jealous and suspicious of the care that will be received) are often present. When families appear to be dissatisfied with care, it can be a sign that they are having difficulty in relinquishing the care.

On the other hand, families can also give carers the feeling that they 'can't do anything right' or that they 'can't build an emotional attachment' to the person with dementia because they are always interfering and criticising. One way for carers to remain aware of family's feelings is to make sure that they have enough information about their father, mother or spouse. It is also important to show an awareness of and interest in the problems that the family are facing.

Anyone who has had to help place a person with dementia in a nursing home and has not been able to supply any information about the family of the person will recall that it leaves you feeling very frustrated and concerned. When you are able to pass along all kinds of information, it feels very different indeed. When you have been able to relate someone's likes and dislikes, their habits and norms, you can turn homewards, knowing that you haven't merely 'placed' someone into care, but that you have 'entrusted' them into care.

When family members share information with carers, it usually means that they have 'symbolically' handed over a part of their loved one to you. If carers, with all respect for privacy and the necessary politeness and restraint, take the initiative to speak to family members about the life of the person with dementia, they will often achieve a new degree of trust with them. Families can then begin 'to share' the person they knew, with the carer. This information will help the carer to see the person with dementia in a more detailed way, and help to form the emotional bond.

Who is the person with dementia? Who accepts responsibility for his/her needs? Who determines what is bad or good for them? These questions are never easy to answer. It is clear, however, that it makes a difference whether it is the family or the carer. In the first situation, we would refer to the carer's role as 'filling in' for what family cannot do. In the second situation, the carer's role would be 'taking over' the care.

The person with dementia will benefit most if the family and carer can achieve a close, equal relationship. This would mean that the carer is accepted eventually as a sort of family member who has the best interests of the person at heart. It also means that the family have enough 'room' to hold the position that is their due. The person will benefit from a very close working relationship between family and carer, especially because he/she is so sensitive to disharmony in the atmosphere around them.

Finally

The process of adoption also requires keeping the necessary distance from someone. Whoever becomes attached to a person with dementia and starts to feel 'like one of the family' to them, will sooner or later have to go through the feelings of grief that arise when the relationship ends. Carers who know this beforehand, consciously try to end the relationship appropriately. 'When someone I've cared for dies, I always try to see them. I also go to the funeral or cremation. That's when my work is really finished.' Carers can have as much sadness at the loss of someone they have cared for as family members. A good relationship between carers and family helps both in their grieving. It helps to share pain with someone who understands. It is important to pay enough attention to grieving. Usually carers who have not grieved well for someone previously in their care, do not become attached as easily to their future clients. They keep fearing new loss and pain. It would be good if, when carers were being trained for their work, they were told not only about the process of dementia, but also about the emotional relationships that develop in this work, and that grieving is a part of it. In contrast, it should also be explained that these emotional attachments will not always occur, and can never be 'expected' of carers.

12 Power

Case history example

Francine, her voice sometimes sounding rather indignant said:

> After a lot of luck I finally managed to get in. She usually was still in bed and had barricaded the front door. Then, she didn't want to get dressed! She never knew what she wanted to put on and so we spent forever messing around without ever getting anywhere. Finally, I just used to decide. She had to wear something, especially clean underwear. If she ever wore dirty clothes or smelt, her son would point it out to me. She was so contrary. I couldn't do a thing with her. How did I manage to get her clothes on? You can guess. They say I'm good at inventing stories. If that didn't work, I used a bit of coercion.

Francine can laugh about it now. But when you're right in the middle of it, it isn't very funny. It just so happened that she had been on a course with her colleagues. These colleagues also cared for persons with dementia and they recognised Francine's stories immediately. Even with the best of intentions, you often want someone to do something that they don't feel like doing. 'We will do it in their best interests', we say. 'Come out of bed, eat, walk a little, play a game, watch television', and so forth. In between, it's 'going to the toilet, exercising stiff hands or joints, putting on clothes or taking them off'. Almost everyone seems to have found a way of ploughing through the daily routine. And when 'something' didn't work, which happened regularly, there was a lot of frustration for all parties concerned. This is especially true for the carer who is doing her best to help the person with dementia.

Francine also says that, like her colleagues, she finds it difficult when she has to guess what the person means. 'We decided a while ago, with Mrs Herbert's family, to continue caring for her at home.'

The Herbert family was well known to the Home Care Services. The rapport was good even when her husband was still alive.

> If I helped her, for example, getting her breakfast ready, I never knew what she wanted. I don't know whether she liked it, I mean, whether she felt like eating. Sometimes she just kept her mouth stiffly shut. I couldn't very well pinch her nose to force her to open her mouth. So I waited, tried again, and then, suddenly she sometimes opened her mouth wide open.

Mrs Herbert's children thought that she didn't want to go on any more. They said that since the death of her husband she had given up. The carers amongst themselves, didn't entirely agree.

> She was disappearing right in front of our eyes. I considered it my duty to get enough food into her. In our course they taught us that you can become very weak and feeble from not getting enough fluid. According to me, Mrs Herbert certainly hadn't lost the will to eat. But I'll admit that it continued to be difficult, particularly for her family. When you can't easily use words to speak to the person, how can you figure out what they think and want and mean?

It took a year for Francine to get over her feelings of guilt after Mrs Herbert died. She felt that if she had only tried harder to get the doctor to do something for Mrs Herbert's physical condition, perhaps she would have felt better and started eating again. Then she would likely still have been alive.

The first part of this chapter deals with different types of power. This may help carers to look at which forms they find acceptable, which they choose to use in carrying out their responsibilities and which forms they want to discard from their repertoire. This isn't all that easy to do because some types of power overlap with others. In the next part of the chapter, we shall see how power and powerlessness have a number of similarities. In nature, the law is 'the survival of the fittest'. This usually applies to people as well! That is why feelings of powerlessness sometimes cause a kind of panic reaction. It is necessary to think about how you deal with your own feelings of powerlessness before you can decide what is meant by acceptable and unacceptable forms of power. Finally, we will consider competition for power. This is certainly something that has no place in the caring environment. Competition will not occur if the person with dementia retreats into a shell. However, most persons become more defensive as others try to penetrate their defences. At the end of the chapter there are a few pointers to show how a power struggle can be prevented.

Forms of power

Exercising power over someone is when, without discussing it with the person concerned, another determines how that person should behave or what is going to happen. In the daily care of persons with dementia, there are many hidden 'moments of power'. These include: 'making decisions for another', 'concern', 'patronisation'.

Making decisions for another

For most carers, power is a 'dirty word'. They regularly have 'pangs of conscience' when they have taken decisions for the person with dementia without any prior consultation. This, however, may be a perfectly legitimate thing to do if there are decisions to be made on the client's behalf. Carers then try as best they can to do what they think the person with dementia would have wanted if he/she had been a position to decide. Carers also try to see if the person can still, somehow, express agreement, even when it is not very obvious. In other words, generally, carers try to place themselves in the person's position to the extent it is possible to do so.

One behaviour, many meanings

Mrs Herbert closes her mouth tightly when Francine tries to feed her. What does this mean? Does it mean that she doesn't want to eat right now or not at all? And if she wants to eat an hour later, or perhaps a day later, is that a change in her mood, or is she waiting for a more appetising meal because she dislikes what is being served now? Are her children right, that her tightly closed mouth means that she has given up the desire to live? Perhaps this behaviour has nothing to do with eating, but means: 'Leave me alone until I feel better, I just can't stomach anything right now.' Perhaps it means: 'I'm not saying anything, but I do have an opinion.' Maybe it means: 'I won't open my mouth even if you try to force it open.' It might even mean: 'Over my dead body!' These responses resemble human defensiveness more than a death wish.

Thus, a single gesture can have many meanings. People are complicated. You don't need to have dementia to think or say under you breath: 'I wish I were dead, I don't feel well, I hope I'm not getting sick.' Or, you might think: 'What on earth is that? Do they think that I'm eating that slop? I feel like something tasty.' Carers often pick out messages from among all those confusing little signals, and find that they still cannot work out what is really going on. They cannot get an 'integrated picture'.

Francine believed in Mrs Herbert's vitality, even though she hadn't really got any good evidence for this. The word 'vitality' is often linked with 'cheerfulness' and 'zest for life'. The word implies a sense of 'motivation' and the 'life force'. Carers often feel the presence of such vitality, even during those times when the strength of the person is limited and even when others are in doubt. Then, you could ask yourself, as Francine did about Mrs Herbert: 'Isn't her weakness possibly a result of not drinking enough, instead of it being a conscious choice of not wanting to live?' Perhaps, at the very moment that a drink is being offered to her, Mrs Herbert cannot comprehend the situation. So instead, you try every trick in the book to get her to drink a little more. You might, for example, put a small cup in her hand with only a small amount of tea in it (because of spilling). You then focus your attention on your own drink and keep on speaking about any number of unrelated things. There's a chance that Mrs Herbert will raise her cup to her mouth and take a sip. When's she's placed it on the table, you pour a little more tea into the cup without her noticing. Perhaps, when Mrs Herbert's still asleep in the morning, you take the trouble to make her some porridge with cream instead of milk and extra sugar. You might even try to encourage her to drink. If it doesn't succeed now, then you try again, and again later. This is manipulation. Carers are not manipulating the person as such in these situations, so much as the disabilities of the person.

There are many other examples of using this sort of power – manipulation – ('in the place of the person'). An elderly male person with dementia does not want to get out of bed. Experience has taught you that once he is washed, dressed and seated, ready to eat his breakfast, he is actually in very good spirits. To achieve that, you keep ploughing through the morning routine. You replace, as it were, the man who is enclosed in a shell of uncertainty and confusion, and who, without this shell, would have been in a position to get himself up. Sometimes it helps to ask him, while he's still lying in bed 'Would you like to shave yourself first?' This little question helps to give him a little more confidence. Or perhaps, you might start to prepare a few things whilst standing near him so that he can see what you're doing. Then, you might loosen the covers at the foot of the bed a little and help him to get his slippers on. Some persons with dementia react well to a somewhat slow, gentle, approach. With others, a firm, business-like approach is the best. The point of all this is not to give you a list of techniques or 'tricks', but to show that 'creativity' and the ability to 'give in' to a situation are sometimes necessary to get you over an impasse.

Concern

Acting 'in the place of another' is different from acting as a result of the feelings of concern that you have for a person with dementia. When you care about someone, concern is a natural part of your relationship. In the previous chapter we saw that carers sometimes eventually come to think of the person as one of their own family. The dementia process certainly causes all sorts of reasons for concern. There are many concrete consequences of having this illness. You want to prevent the person from feeling unhappy, unsafe and lost. In Francine's story, there are elements of acting in the place of someone and acting out of concern for that person.

In work and outside work

When you come to think about it, it's not uncommon in families for there to be a great deal of well-intentioned chiding and admonishing going on and also giving advice: 'Don't you think you'd better wear your coat? It's very cold out today you know.' 'Try to stay very calm and composed if the boss starts to bring that up again today. Don't look so gruff.' 'Please use your T-shirt for a polishing cloth from now on. It's so worn you shouldn't be seen wearing it any more.'

Even though you aren't always thanked for making such comments, they are usually made because you feel affection for that person. You try to give positive advice, which isn't always accepted gratefully and acted upon. 'Just get out for a while. Go for a little walk, you'll see it'll do you good.' 'You really should join the choir again. You always got such pleasure from being in it.' Such statements are made because you are concerned about the wellbeing of those to whom you are attached. You make such statements because you have observed that the person is looking rather pale, or appears not to have enough interests outside work, or you suspect that that things are getting on top of them.

The daily work

In the course of one's work with persons with dementia, a certain amount of chiding and reminding is natural. 'You forgot to drink your coffee. It'll get cold and won't be as nice.' Saying this can give a feeling of a 'little informal gathering'. When the person's memory and understanding of language have deteriorated, then the carer will gradually start replacing concern with giving advice, coupled with shorter phrases to provide help. For example: 'Here', whilst pressing the cup carefully into someone's hand, 'drink this before it gets cold.' The concurrent thought might be: 'Good, at least she's got another

125cc of fluid inside her!' There are other examples: 'Come, let's go for a little walk. Look your coat is here already.' You could also say this in the form of a question: 'Do you feel like going for a little walk?' But you are already standing waiting, holding the coat, knowing that the person will forget both the question and the answer very quickly. You know from experience that resistance is more related to the person's momentary mood, rather than their not enjoying a walk once they get outside.

The only difference between this situation and the one at home, is that the reaction will usually be absent. At home you might get, 'Give me a break Mum, don't keep on at me. I'll drink my coffee when I get around to it'. When giving advice to a person with dementia, it is much more difficult to work out whether you have 'done well' or not. If the person enjoyed the walk and became more relaxed and cheerful as a result, it will be apparent that you used your power well. But usually the results of your attempts to help will not be that clearly visible. Many carers are left with niggling feelings of doubt.

Question marks

Wilma works in a residential care setting. She says:

> We have a sort of 'group activities day care' at work for particular residents. Mrs Alberts is one of the persons who would fit in well, but she never wants to come. She prefers to stay alone in her room. The activities co-ordinator keeps telling us that when she's there she loves it, so I should use a bit of 'gentle force' to try to get her there. I just don't like doing this. She's been living alone for years before she came here. Her husband died five years ago. She comes from a large family herself but she only had two children. The one daughter said that she was always a very quiet, private sort of person. She went to birthday parties and things, but was also glad when they were over. That's why I think that Mrs Alberts has the need and right to be alone, even though I see that group activities have their use.

Wilma tried to look at everything when coming to some conclusion about Mrs Alberts. She had spoken to family members about what type of a person their mother was, and what her life had been like. But Wilma continues to have 'little doubts'. She feels guilty when she doesn't bring her to the group activities and when she later finds her relaxed and happy sitting in the group because the activity co-ordinator went to get her instead. 'She doesn't really participate', says Wilma, 'and you can't really see whether she's enjoying herself or not. She's probably doing her best to put up with all those people around her.' Yet the staff working with the group say, 'She enjoys herself all right. She doesn't do anything, but her eyes say it all.'

A warm heart

There is a chance that the next time Wilma just might think to herself, 'Perhaps I'm communicating some of my own uncertainty to Mrs Alberts, and that's why she's reacting as though she doesn't really want to go to the group.' Wilma tries to do what the activity co-ordinator did. She offers Mrs Alberts her arm and says 'Lets go. They've made apple tarts to go with the tea today. Everyone's waiting for us.' Perhaps that went well for Wilma. You can always learn something from someone else. Perhaps it didn't go well for Wilma because that isn't how she usually acts, or she doesn't say the right things, and that, too, can communicate itself. In that case, it would be better if Wilma went to the activity co-ordinator and said, 'In future, would you please get Mrs Alberts? With you, she enjoys going to the group. With me, she seems to want to stay in her room.' We still don't know for sure what Mrs Alberts wants, but now we do know that several persons are seriously thinking about her, and with caring hearts are giving her the best that they can.

Patronisation

However natural concern is in an intimate relationship, it can lead to 'patronisation', which smothers the other person's initiative. Here, the word patronisation is taken to mean the 'juvenilising' of the other person's point of view. It means treating the other person as though they are 'juveniles' or 'minors', and hence, because of their real age, to treat them in a condescending manner. This is a dangerous departure point, because it makes one blind and deaf to the expression of another. Unnoticed and unwittingly, some carers create a tone of care that is offensive and self-righteous. This is sometimes seen, for example, when the person with dementia doesn't immediately understand what is meant, or when the person is not using correct social graces, or perhaps when he/she is constantly 'underfoot'. Everyone knows how you can feel 'belittled' in such circumstances. The person with dementia experiences this in the same way. This feeling can even be strengthened through their 'powerlessness' to do otherwise, or, through 'old pain' (all those past times when you felt your self-worth was questioned).

From the age of majority to being patronised

Wilma assumed that Mrs Alberts has her own will, even though she cannot always express it any more in words. That is why she uses the information she knows about Mrs Alberts' past and her non-verbal signals to try to understand what Mrs Alberts would want now. This means that Wilma treats Mrs Alberts primarily as a person who has reached the 'age of majority'. The step towards treating someone patronisingly is just a very small one though, as Arthur relates:

> Mrs Hurst sometimes refuses to take her medicine. I don't know why. I try to explain to her why she has been prescribed these medicines, but I don't believe that she understands. Now we crush the pills and put them in apple sauce. I say to her, 'Here are your pills', but usually I have already put the spoon in her mouth before she can respond. Sometimes she spits it out. You can't try again after a few minutes because you don't know how much medicine she got. It really is a problem. We've sometimes discussed giving her the medicine secretly in the jam on her bread or in the porridge. But once you start, it's a bit like skating on thin ice, and then you take away someone's total freedom.

Arthur and his colleagues realise the dangers of the situation. The way in which he gives Mrs Hurst her medicine now doesn't please him entirely. In discussing the power issues that have already been mentioned here he says:

> Of course it is manipulating. I don't know whether in similar circumstances she would have refused medication just as often if she didn't have dementia. She has no immediate family and no one knows very much about her. She strikes me as someone who might have been into homeopathic medicine, a vegetarian and a member of the Esperanto Foundation. I have a lot of respect for that. It would be asking too much of me to just let her die by not giving her her 'meds'. Please don't tell me that I'm not respecting her feelings if, because of my own feelings, I can't do that. When it comes down to it, I don't even know what her 'values' are. I just have a hunch about the type of person she was and try to act with respect for that. So, it isn't really patronising when I put her pills in the porridge and say, 'These are your medicines'. But I think it would be if I put the pills in and didn't say anything about it.

Rules and regulations

As much as Arthur knows where to draw the line, it doesn't always work. It is even more annoying that persons with dementia are often submitted to numerous gratuitous rules and regulations. For example: what time they are taken to the toilet, what time meals are served and which day they get bathed. Even things like: 'Now don't try to stand until someone is with you because you know you'll fall!' There are no easy answers to problems such as how you can get persons to stretch their legs as many times a day as possible or get them out of their 'niche' and let them see things from another's perspective or how you can let someone move or walk whenever they get the urge to, without them falling. There are no easy answers or 'failsafe' guidelines. However, the fact that you are wrestling with and thinking about such problems will show in your attitude. You will be less inclined to make rules, than to have 'problems to solve together'.

Making your own decisions is inevitable

The dementia process eventually makes persons with dementia 'dependent' in almost all respects. This includes areas of: hygiene, standing, going somewhere, what to do to fill the day, communication and so forth. This dependence is an inevitability that the carer cannot 'get around'. That means that carers often must make decisions for persons with dementia. Sometimes decisions are made by a multidisciplinary team, or by the team and the family. Sometimes decisions are made in conjunction with the person with dementia, especially when carers understand his/her reactions as those of a person with feelings, desires and needs of their own.

However, there are many decisions that carers make for the person with dementia on a daily basis. Carers have to react to whatever is happening at any given moment. Are clean clothes really necessary today? Does this person need to sit at a separate table for meals because their cursing and calling out are driving everyone else to distraction? Should the chair be placed in such a way that the person cannot get out (because you're too busy for the moment to take them for a walk)? Who needs your conversation most? Is it the wife who is so fed up today that she can barely function, or her husband who is sitting on the couch looking like a statue? Should you try to find some extra time to cut the nails of a lady whose husband is visibly weakening each day under the strain of caring for her?

Posture and attitude

The dependence of the person with dementia forces carers to make decisions. The limits of the abilities of a person with dementia determine which decisions need to be made on his/her behalf. It is difficult to weigh up which decision is the 'right' one. Even when carers think back on decisions they have made for someone, they don't always know if they did the best thing. Sometimes it helps if for one time only (being aware of all of the options), a carer chooses to do something different than they normally would have done. The attitude with which the decision is made and the way the carer implements the decision is very important. What is done in an 'atmosphere of understanding, respect and acceptance' (out of the limitations of the person with dementia and your own), is well done. This is true, even if the next time you might choose to do something else, or do it in a different way. Those things that are not done in this atmosphere, whether this means actively doing something or not doing something, leaves the other person out 'in the cold'.

The tone of the authority

Carers are often aware of *what* they say. However, their position of power is much more affected by *how* they say things. Carers tend to be less aware of this. You could call this the 'tone of the authority'.

'Sir, look at this, you've burnt a hole in the tablecloth. Do you want to set the whole place on fire? Watch what you're doing with that cigarette or you won't be given another.' Something like this is easily said in the chaos of the moment, even when the carer is a humorous, friendly, empathic person. The carer would be shocked if someone told her she was being 'authoritarian'. Yet, her 'tone' towards the man with the cigarette is just that. Where does this tone come from? Perhaps it is a hidden 'personality trait' that surfaced only because of her shock in that situation. Perhaps it is something that she learned from her own 'upbringing and socialisation' and is unaware of it. Possibly it comes from 'self-blame'. She should have been paying more attention and should not have let the situation get out of hand, but she took it out on the person with dementia without being aware of it. Who knows? It is more important to know that when you use such a tone with the person with dementia, he/she will feel belittled, than to know exactly where this tone comes from. It is essential to realise this no matter what kind of chaotic situations are happening around you. Perhaps the following suggestions will help.

Try to listen, at least once a week, to the 'verbal discharging' of others without commenting on it. Listen especially to the tone of voice used. Observe and analyse the reactions of the person who is being addressed and make conclusions about the tone. Thereafter, try to listen to your own 'verbal discharging', and try to come to a conclusion about your own tone of voice.

When you want to draw a person's attention to a particular 'undesired' behaviour, try to use their proper title: 'Mr Brown' or 'Mrs White'. (Do this, even though you might normally call someone by their first name.) Using this title makes it clearer that you are concerned about a behaviour, and not that you are belittling their position.

Imagine that you started out using 'strong' language; it just slipped out because you were so shocked. It is really an expression of your powerlessness. Many persons in such circumstances start by saying things like: 'Good heavens', 'God almighty', 'What on earth', 'Heck, will you look at this?' Try to resist finishing the rest of the sentence; it can be a good way to deal with your feelings of powerlessness. Sometimes they then disappear in the silence thereafter. If you find yourself coming 'undone' and 'balling people out' more often, then you should be asking yourself: 'What else is wrong or bothering me?'

Indifference

When carers use power 'in the place of' or 'out of concern for another' (because of the emotional bond you have with someone), there is a chance that you are increasing the powerlessness of the other. Slowly, behaviours can develop that increase the powerlessness of the person with dementia. In this sense, 'indifference' can also be thought of as 'power' over someone. This occurs, for example, when the person with dementia gets the feeling that nothing that they do or say is being listened to. The opposite to indifference is 'involvement'. The difficulty with the dementia process is that sometimes the many warm instances of 'involvement' are forgotten. You don't get an 'IOU' or 'gift coupon' every time you do something for someone. You must keep investing yourself in them. No one, however, can do this all the time. But it helps to know the things that can break down this investment process. This could prevent a sort of chronic, slow indifference from occurring.

Blunting

Indifference is usually the result of a gradual 'blunting' of a relationship. It can occur when you have felt the same pain over and over again. Your hope has been turned to disappointment so often. Your energy and motivation haven't amounted to anything. Indifference can also result from not looking far enough. Indifference occurs through not pausing long enough and not looking carefully enough at what is happening around you – through limited use of your imagination. Differences have disappeared and you are not able to see slight distinctions any more. You are not able to see the difference between one person and another, and not between one solution and another. For example, you might not be able to notice that, for one person with dementia, it makes a big difference whether his/her glasses have been cleaned or not, and to another it is less important. Or perhaps you might not notice that for one person it is important to keep their own teeth so that they don't have to have dentures, whilst to another, it isn't an issue.

Not that obvious

Anne thinks about such things a lot. She is taking some extra courses about caring. One of the lessons was about 'self-care'. Some of what was taught, she took with a pinch of salt. She liked the part about 'running small errands' and 'running large errands' though. It was a rather childish term for 'urinating' versus 'defecating', but when you thought about it, it wasn't. It is a problem when you need 'to go' urgently, but a relief when you've gone. Without being able 'to go', you wouldn't be comfortable. It can sometimes be a very tiresome process. People check up on 'whether you've done anything' in the commode pan behind you. Carers often say just that: 'Have you done anything yet?' What happens when you don't know any more whether you have or haven't? Anne thinks it is a strange thought, but, if she couldn't 'pass water' herself any more, she'd miss it. She almost can't imagine what it would be like to 'wet herself' without noticing the 'starting' and 'stopping'. And what if she were a person with dementia? What if it was already too difficult 'to get things right'? Anne says she finds it difficult to speak to her colleagues about this. She said the following:

> I go to Mrs Vernon at fixed times to bring her to the toilet. She usually says that she doesn't have to go and tries in every possible way to stop me bringing her. Finally she gives up and tries. When she's been sitting there for a while, something usually happens. I often think that if I just put an adult napkin on her, then she wouldn't have to be 'put out' with my prompting and trying to persuade her so often. I'd still have to change the napkins from time to time. I suppose that would make her even more dependent on me. She wouldn't do anything any more then. She wouldn't pull up her panties or even straighten out her clothes. She still does that now. Sometimes she even says very resolutely, 'Well, that's that then'. My colleagues don't think this

is as important as I do. After being off for a few days, I return to find Mrs Vernon wearing incontinence material. I sometimes wonder why I bother.

What is obvious is often subtle

What Anne keeps coming up against is the 'obvious'. Where she works, incontinence is more the rule than the exception. What most of her colleagues are worried about is that the clothes and bed linens are dry and not smelly.

Many elderly people have dentures. Many people never really get used to them. They become very problematic when the shape of your mouth changes in the latter years. No wonder that in care homes, and sheltered housing, so many meals get left without being touched. No wonder that Mr White leaves his dentures beside his plate while he is eating. He gets told off for this, instead of getting an 'adapted menu' and a small container for his teeth. It is important for carers to realise that there are many causes that lead to indifference. This is why it is essential to have the opportunity to discuss issues and differences of opinion at team meetings with colleagues. Such discussions can help carers to move from the obvious to the more subtle assumptions of caring and how it is best done.

The power of the norm

There is also a type of power which is related to 'the norm', that is, how things are 'normally' or 'usually' done. This is a strong force in residential and nursing homes. There are often firm rules about how to 'keep things running smoothly'. There are rules for residents, and the care staff who take it in shifts to stick to the routine. Norms and rules give us handles for co-operative work in large endeavours, but they can also help us in smaller-scale projects. It isn't wise to keep turning things upside down for the sake of change. Yet this, doesn't mean that the usual way of doing things doesn't need to be examined critically from time to time.

Security and handholds

Norms and routines give us handholds and security. We all need them. There is a lot to be said for keeping to the daily routine for persons with dementia who are still mostly aware of time. That means that for those who are still able to learn and follow the new patterns of a care facility that to have a routine for getting up, washing, getting dressed, having breakfast and then doing an activity, can be a good handhold. To have a routine for eating can help persons relax because they can expect that 'this will happen and then that'. Some routines need to be protected and nurtured so that they don't become 'uncertainties'. Carers cannot just suddenly change something 'willy nilly' because a new idea has just occurred to them, but they do need to look at the small and large routines critically to remain aware of needs and priorities.

In one day care centre, a lot of attention was focused on mealtimes. The persons with dementia always set the table together. Colourful tableware was used to create a more friendly, homelike atmosphere. The carer always asked for a few moments of silence for those who wanted to pray before the meal. He asked this in a standing position because he felt he didn't really belong to the group who were dining, as he wasn't eating with them. Afterwards, he sat with whoever needed a bit of help. Half an hour after the meal had started, a colleague replaced him, so that he could have his meal in the canteen. This was the established routine. (It is interesting to know how this came about. This custom came from the hospital routine where meals for 'the sick' and 'the staff' were strictly separate. This custom, in turn, came from those times when everyone was afraid of 'infection' or 'contamination' from the sick.)

A new colleague started working at the day centre. He had worked in a hospital where staff ate with the patients. He asked why the staff left to eat at the canteen each day and said that he thought it was 'antisocial'. He was presented with several arguments from those who had worked at the day centre for a number of years. 'I couldn't help everyone who needs help if I ate alongside them.' 'I need a half an hour away from it all.' 'I'd never get a chance to eat if I stayed.' 'Don't take this the wrong way, but I wouldn't be able to get a bite down looking at the way some of these people eat.' These were all arguments that were difficult to disagree with. The new colleague did as he was used to doing. A year later, a number of staff had left and new ones arrived. Almost all of them remained at the table to eat alongside the people with dementia. No one remembers exactly how and when this happened. It just seemed that the old arguments had lost their force.

In the previous paragraph it was shown how the obvious, 'the norm', can lead to indifference. This example shows how even 'non-demented' persons find it difficult to change from their 'normal' patterns and will present irrefutable arguments about their rights and behaviours. Sometimes your own behaviour is a result of learned patterns, and not really about what the best way to do something might be.

Powerlessness and power struggles

In this chapter more emphasis has been placed on the carer than on the person with dementia. This isn't surprising. The power that carers have, precisely because persons with dementia are very dependent is not the most important aspect of this chapter. What this chapter is really about is the *powerlessness* of carers, which they will need to accept. Without accepting their limitations, carers cannot handle their power in the most useful, humane way.

As we have already seen in Chapter 9, people with dementia continue to be deeply aware of and affected by their illness for a long period. They show this through their failing attempts to come to grips with their own limitations and through their 'awareness context'. They know that things are not going the way they want them to, and they can be lost even in their own familiar environment. They see strange people who act as though they know everything about them. One carer said, 'Actually it is a relief when persons are still able to "get stroppy" and stand up for themselves, even though I sometimes find them difficult to deal with like that.'

Not tolerating any answering back

Some persons with dementia react to 'trouble' or 'danger' in the same way that carers do. They engage in a confrontation, try to intimidate others and do not give in to their own weakness. Two examples follow.

> Mrs Banting has terrible pain in her feet. No one has been able to do anything for her. She's learned to live with it. When the pain gets very bad, it totally takes over. This happens particularly in the evenings. Instead of lying on her bed, this is precisely when she wants to go and stretch her legs for a bit. She 'bulldozes' over anyone who walks in front of her. She bangs on the doors. Who knows, perhaps she is seeking a release for her pain in this way. Perhaps it is her way of complaining. In any event, she doesn't tolerate anyone speaking to her about her behaviour.

> Mr Smythe is always confused when he tries to get up in the morning after having been in bed the whole night. It's because of his heart. He would be well advised to stand up slowly and to sit for some minutes on the edge of his bed. Out of habit, he jumps up suddenly and wants to get going immediately. He used to be a farm hand. It was a difficult existence but there was a lot of camaraderie. In the evening he often talks about those days and sometimes plays on the harmonica. That's what he used to do

when everyone sat round after work and 'chewed the cud' with each other. In the mornings, however, there's trouble. The 'spunk' is still in Mr Smythe, but so is the feeling of haste and urgency. There's no time for getting washed and the old, vague fear returns. It's not only his heart that cannot take this sudden change, his personality and age are not suited to rushing either. But, it's a result of his whole life's work. This soft-natured man had always had 'to get going and fast of a morning'.

Certain situations are naturally difficult for carers to deal with. Mrs Banting causes people untold grief and Mr Smythe runs the risk that his heart will fail or that he'll fall and break something. Neither of them will tolerate anyone speaking to them about it. How do carers deal with them? What would you do, even when you knew about their physical problems?

It is probably best not to put obstacles in their way or to 'cross' them. If it's possible, try to work out which of the carers has the 'easiest way' or the 'most calming effect' upon them. Usually there is someone who reminds the person with dementia of their own favourite grandchild or child or someone who knows exactly 'which button to press' to get a good response. There must also be the time and place for carers to ask: 'Why is it so important for Mrs Banting to take her walk? Perhaps I should stay out of her way until her mood changes? Can I say, with a sincere face, without making her feel belittled: "Come, let's first go and have a cup of tea?" '

Learning 'on the job'

Carers often learn during their work how to 'get someone onto a different track'. Francine talks about 'little fibs' and 'tricks'. These should, however, never be the main constituent of care. It can happen that someone does what you want just because you asked the opposite. For example, you might say to a lady who is very tired, but who keeps wandering around, 'Why don't you help me polish the windows for a bit?' She answers back, 'Do it yourself – I'm an oldie and I don't have to work any more. I'm going to have myself a nice sit down.' It may work once, but to keep using such a paradoxical approach with someone can only lead to more confusion in the long run.

If carers want to break through the behaviour of the person with dementia (which arises from their feeling of powerlessness), carers will have to learn how to remove some of this feeling. Sometimes this can be done by mirroring (repeating) the same words that the person with dementia is using, and then changing the direction of the conversation a bit. You can also 'offer someone the words' to express something they cannot. The next example shows this.

> Mrs Turner pinches Ann's arm.
> 'Ow! That hurts!' says Ann.
> 'Good!' says Mrs Turner
> 'You meant to do good, eh? says Ann.
> 'No, I don't want to do good', Mrs Turner continues, pressing her fingers deep into Ann's arm again.
> 'Ow! That really hurts me', says Ann.
> 'Pain is good', says Mrs Turner.
> 'Being nice is even better.'
> 'You aren't nice to me because you always walk away from me.'
> 'So you want me to stay with you?'
> 'Yes always.'
> 'I wish I could always keep you with me too because I like you.'

In this way, Ann has made two changes of direction in the conversation. It isn't important that she cannot predict how the conversation will end.

Finally

Carers often don't have to 'do' anything. It can be enough to do nothing except to let the person with dementia know that you can see that they are feeling powerless and frustrated. In this way, neither of you has to embark on a 'pointless battle'.

To learn from your experiences at work you need insight and the courage 'to look into the mirror'. A collegial atmosphere where it is acceptable to speak about behaviour patterns, and even role play if necessary, is actually a necessity.

Experience is the best teacher. Carers don't necessarily need to know beforehand exactly 'what is the best thing to do'. To dare to improvise and look at what happens is how most learning takes place. Accepting one's own powerlessness can help a great deal. It is important for carers to see that usually, when the person with dementia is 'being totally contrary', it is not meant personally. Rather, it can be a response to the whole feeling of not being able to accept becoming increasingly dependent and feeling increasingly frightened. To learn to deal with uncertainty and doubts is, and will remain, an important part of working with people with dementia. It will always remain a challenge.

13 Transference and counter-transference

Case history example

Carla has always worked as a care aid. Because she is a practical and responsible person, she was invited to be the co-ordinator of the 'home care' division. She was good at organising and improvising, but she was especially liked because of the warmth she displayed towards her workers as she helped them in their task of caring for people with dementia. She understood their emotional difficulties. In the beginning, she had a little chat with each of her workers at least once a week. At a certain point, this became too much for her and Carla decided to call monthly meetings.

> Those meetings certainly were well attended. There was always more to discuss than we could deal with at the time. Many things happened at the meetings and everyone benefited a great deal from them. I always felt strengthened and good about them. Looking back, I must say that in my work I felt obliged to sort out the problems that the home carers were having – not only the clients' problems, but also those of the spouses and family of clients. I didn't for one moment stand back and think of myself as a peacekeeper.

After a year, Carla found that the meetings were becoming more of a burden and that she was having difficulty in leading them. She didn't know why and she didn't tell the group how she was feeling. She began to have sleepless nights and at times experienced feelings of apathy. She blamed it on the menopause. When she finally went to see the doctor, he couldn't find any physical reason for her symptoms. He suspected depression. Since Carla knew deep down that 'something else was going on', she agreed to see a psychologist.

> I remember exactly which meeting was 'the final straw' for me. One of the carers had been trying to sort out the disagreements

between a sufferer and his family for a long time. This carer felt powerless and she felt she'd reached the point where she would finally have to accept that she would never be able to help solve these disagreements. When she started to cry, I did too. Not just a little, I couldn't stop.

During her first meeting with the psychologist, group therapy sessions were recommended. Whilst attending group therapy Carla finally discovered which of her experiences and feelings had caused her reactions. One of her daughters, with whom she had now become reconciled, left home suddenly to live in a flat. Carla had found that very difficult to deal with. She apparently hadn't resolved this situation. Carla had never dared to speak to her daughter about what happened because she was afraid of what the consequences would be if they quarrelled again. Carla would go to any lengths to avoid that. Her own father and mother had fought continuously with each other.

It was a revelation for me to see that in my work I was constantly doing anything I could to stop arguments between parents and their children, even through the carers. I was taking on my carer's feelings of powerlessness as my own inability.

Julie, a social worker, was one of the participants in Carla's group therapy sessions. Julie discovered that she had never accepted her parents' divorce. In her work she was constantly trying to mobilise her clients' children in such a way as to postpone having to admit the client into a care facility. This would mean a forced separation of the parents. It could also mean that the spouse might move and the children would be deprived of their family home. Old pain and old fears can get in the way of our work for each of us.

In the first part of this chapter we will consider what is meant by 'transference' and 'counter-transference', and what it means for our work with people with dementia. What the person with dementia and his/her family 'project onto' the carer is called transference. What the carer 'projects onto' the person with dementia and his/her family is counter-transference. The essence of the counter-transference situation is that the professional bond is determined by more than the attributes of the person with dementia. 'Invisible' things are happening in this relationship. In the next part of the chapter, the causes of transference and counter-transference, which results in both carer and client, respectively, falling into other 'roles', will be examined. The most important issue for both parties is that they experience extremely positive and negative effects. For some clients, the carer's presence can lead to transference; for some carers, the client's presence can lead to counter-transference.

Finally, the consequences of counter-transference will be discussed, both the signs that lead to this happening, and how to deal with it. The key negative aspect of both transference and counter-transference is that it can lead to 'not seeing reality'. The positive aspect of counter-transference is that it can lead to great personal growth for the carer, and warm-hearted care for the person with dementia. Preparation and guidance is required so that carers can think about, talk about and recognise their own feelings that they themselves are projecting. Carers need to be able to express the feelings that accompany this whole process to their supervisors and colleagues.

Introduction

In the previous chapters we saw that within the professional work that carers do, a natural emotional bond or attachment often develops between the carer and the client. The person with dementia continues to be involved emotionally with what is happening to them, even as the world around them becomes increasingly unfamiliar. The clients react to this unfamiliar world by developing attachment behaviour or, closeness/proximity-seeking behaviour. As a rule, carers respond almost automatically, by providing their closeness. Carers thus function as beacons and handholds for orientating the person with dementia. 'Working' with persons with dementia thus turns into 'caring' for persons with dementia. Eventually, the professional bond, usually takes on an emotional dimension.

From the carer's point of view this can be seen as a kind of 'adoption process'. Hallmarks of adoption include: the carer integrating the person with dementia into their own existence, feeling like a family member and having strong feelings of responsibility towards the person. This responsibility is the primary force that leads carers into making and taking decisions 'on behalf of the person with dementia'. Apart from the fact that the person with dementia is becoming increasingly dependent on the carer, the reality is that the carer is in 'a position of power'.

Whether the emotional bond between the carer and the person with dementia is an advantage to the carer depends a great deal upon whether the carer is aware of the emotional bond, and knows how to handle his/her own behaviour. As we have already seen, persons with dementia often interpret the present as being the past. This means that unresolved loss from the past can be re-experienced in the dementia process. Carers usually do not know that such 're-experiencing' of the past may happen to a person with dementia, before they start their work. Carers themselves are not 'clean slates' either when they start their work. Each carer has his/her own way of attributing meaning to both the professional relationship and the emotional bond that occurs with the person with dementia and the family. This can lead to unexpected and surprising outcomes. Through examining the concepts of transference and counter-transference, we will try to gain some insight into this.

Transference and counter-transference

What is transference?

Both these terms refer to the professional relationship between a client and a therapist. (They can also describe the relationship between any two individuals.) In such a relationship, the term 'transference' refers to the client falling into old behaviour patterns and conflicts with the new therapist. The new attachment that the client develops with the therapist, hence, is no longer based on reality. The therapist is 'given' an old role from the client's past. The relationship is an 'old relationship in new clothes'. The client's past is colouring the present. The client is 'carrying over' feelings for someone important in their past, and transferring them onto the therapist. This behaviour is also called 'projection'. In a nutshell: the client takes the new professional bond and distorts it by reacting to the therapist in an inappropriate 'old, familiar way'. The client regards the therapist in the role of another, for example, a parent, a lover or as the 'ideal self'. The client projects ideals, dreams and fantasies onto the therapist arising out of their unresolved life experiences. In the unconscious experience of the client, the therapist represents someone else.

What is counter-transference?

As the term already suggests, it is the opposite of transference. Now, it is the therapist who projects another role onto the client and sees them as another. Again, in this situation, the bond that develops between the client and the therapist is not based on reality. The client is given another 'role' unwittingly. The relationship between the client and therapist is coloured by experiences and feelings that the therapist had in another relationship. The therapist is 'carrying over' these feelings for an important person from the past and is transferring them onto the client. In a nutshell, the therapist is taking the new relationship and distorting it by reacting to the client in an inappropriate 'old, familiar way'. The therapist responds to the client in the role of another, for example, a child, lover or spouse. The therapist projects his/her expectations, feelings and experiences onto the client. In the unconscious experience of the therapist, the client represents another.

These concepts can be more complicated than described so far. Not only can other 'roles' and 'persons' be projected onto another but also personal conflicts, fears, needs and stereotypes. These usually relate to the past, but they can also relate to the future. The essence of the concept of counter-transference is that the professional bond between the client and therapist is affected by the current attributes of the present situation, but also by other factors, some of them unconscious.

The care relationship with a person with dementia

In practice, transference and counter-transference does not only affect clients and therapists. It can also affect the participants in professional caring relationships.

Just as in a 'therapeutic relationship' in which there is a distinction between the professional relationship with a client and the emotional experience of this relationship, carers can find themselves in such a two-sided relationship with persons with dementia. Within the professional bond, the actual care carried out for someone is the means whereby a practical goal is reached. For example, providing whatever services are required to keep someone living at home. The other side of this relationship is the mutual experience of this bond: 'Who does this person represent to me?' How, as what, and as whom, is this person 'experienced'? This can be very different from the professional context. This explains how a person with dementia can experience the carer as 'a doting daughter' or as 'the ungrateful son'. The way in which the person with dementia reacts to the carer sometimes brings the carer into a counter-transference situation. The carer might feel this 'parent figure' finally accepting them, or rejecting them again, or appreciating them and setting them up on a pedestal. Hence, old conflicts and losses can be re-experienced within the professional bond. Positive experiences can also resurface, be re-experienced or even resolved. The professional bond can serve a function for the carer in that it can help to develop the life experience and personality of the carer.

Although both situations differ, therapist versus carer, the essence of what is meant by counter-transference/transference remains the same. This means that the professional bond is affected by more than the attributes of the present situation with someone. More is happening than is visible from the outside!

Transference: the carer is seen as someone else

This is when the person with dementia sees the carer as another, with all of the feelings and expectations they had for the 'other'. As a carer you will be representing different 'roles' and 'persons' for each person with dementia. In any event, you are also functioning as an attachment figure, as has already been discussed. That means that your presence is giving someone a handhold and a feeling of safety. Sometimes you will represent a very particular trusted person.

Causes of the projections of persons with dementia

Transference does not occur in every person with dementia (or carer). It depends upon the person. If there is transference, it comes from the person's extremely positive or negative life experiences. This means that the person can mix up the present with the past. With such experiences, the perceptions of the person with dementia can be so 'coloured' that projections occur.

Extremely positive and negative experiences

The involvement of persons with dementia in 'what is happening to them' can cause positive and negative experiences from the past to 'resurface', or be 're-experienced' as it were. This can affect the relationship with the carer in extreme ways. Feelings of 'always having been treated unfairly', 'losing a loved one', 'being abandoned', 'feeling fearful and suspicious', can return. The carer is then placed in the role of, for example, 'an evildoer', 'the black sheep', 'the social misfit' and so forth. But equally probably, the carer could be placed in the role of 'the ideal child', 'an advisor', 'a favourite child', 'a protector' and so forth. It all depends upon the personality of the person with dementia, his/her life experiences and the feelings that the carer evokes from them.

The past and the present are mixed in together

In the situation where 'the past has become the present', transference does not necessarily occur. In the dementia process, 'the past and the present', 'now and long ago', start to overlap and even to coexist somewhat. Since 'new information' is not processed and stored in memory, the person with dementia often cannot 'place' the carer. For example, the way in which a person with dementia 'experiences' a carer can remind him/her of 'father'. The person that the sufferer then sees, 'is father', and not merely someone onto whom the sufferer is projecting unresolved feelings about father. No new meaning is being given to the relationship the person with dementia had with his/her father. When carers are sometimes mistaken for parents, siblings or children, it is a case of 'mistaken identity'.

As we saw in the early chapters of this book, persons with dementia are often looking for their parents. Someone who provides care and comfort can 'feel like a parent' and the person begins to think about his/her parents. Another example is the elderly lady who thinks she is still young and looking after her own children. This can cause her to think that the carer is one of her children. This explains why sometimes carers can partly be the reason for the person with dementia expressing anger, sorrow, happiness, fear or contentment. This is important because it is one way in which the feelings of the person with dementia can have a clear form and expression, rather than remaining vague and 'bottled up'. The carer is the person whose presence allows the person with dementia to express their 'crystallised' feelings.

Although less common than the examples of 'mistaken identity' above, there are situations where persons with dementia do project unresolved feelings from the past onto the present. For example, the lady who remained single, against her wishes, and who now wants to become engaged to her carer, or, the childless lady who now sees the carer as the daughter she secretly wanted.

Not always clear

The behaviour of persons with dementia is coloured by who they have been and what they have experienced in life. The occurrence of carers being 'misidentified', 'given roles' and 'having other identities projected onto them' does not need to be a problem, as long as the carer is aware of this and can understand what is happening. Insight into these situations can prevent discomfort and dissatisfaction. If you know that the person with dementia is rejecting you because he/she thinks you are another person, you don't need to take the blame yourself. Knowledge about the life history and the personality of the person makes it easier for the carer to know who they represent. Sometimes though, even when carers have a great deal of knowledge about the person with dementia, it still isn't entirely clear who they are for the person. Think back to Sarah in Chapter 10. Does Mrs Sears think Sarah is her daughter or someone from whom she is seeking advice? In Chapter 12, is Francine being seen as a deceitful person?

Transference can also occur between family members and carers. Marcia related the following:

> I work for Mrs Noble. Her daughter is always 'visiting' when I'm there. Yet, she keeps complaining to me that she is so busy. I told her that if she's so busy, it isn't necessary for her to take the time to visit when I'm with her mother. She doesn't pay any attention though. She keeps coming over when I'm there, and meddles with and makes comments about everything I do.

The above description doesn't provide us with enough information to know how to interpret this situation. More than one explanation is possible. Let us assume though that transference is occurring. It is possible that Mrs Noble's daughter has all kinds of motives and motivations to visit her mother when the carer is present. The daughter is not aware of these.

For example, she might long for 'exclusive contact with her mother', 'be suspicious of rivalry from the carer', or, 'want to be seen in the role of the ideal daughter'. Any of these might be the real motives for the irksome visits. Perhaps this daughter always felt that her older sister was mother's favourite. Now that the older sister is dead, she has been able to gain some special affection from her mother, but the carer is now perceived as 'getting in the way of' this hard-earned affection. The daughter might be re-playing (projecting) her feelings of jealously towards her older sister onto the carer.

Here are two other examples to consider. Perhaps a client has erotic feelings. He is unaware, however, that he is projecting them constantly onto his carer and behaving inappropriately with her. Perhaps Mrs Southfield starts to treat her husband's carer as one of her own children. (What appears to be transference in a person with dementia is often a conscious process, i.e. a misidentification.)

Counter-transference: when carers see the person with dementia as someone else

The converse of transference also happens to carers. Counter-transference occurs when the carer sees the person with dementia as someone else – more than a client for whom one is concerned. The client can sometimes evoke feelings in a carer, whereby the carer puts them into a different role, with all of the feelings and expectations they have for the 'other' person. Persons with dementia can confront carers with unresolved feelings, or needs. For example, a carer might still be angry with one of their parents who was extremely dominant, or the carer may still be missing a dead grandparent. The age difference can help persons with dementia to play different 'roles'.

Carers sometimes land up in a counter-transference situation right at the beginning of their work. This happens when carers are unaware that they are seeking to accomplish, resolve or settle or even discover. There are unconscious unresolved aspects of their life. Is it possible that a carer, whose mother is dead, projects this relationship with her mother onto the caring for a person with dementia? In her caring, she is unaware that she is doing everything for the person with dementia, not because the person is so very dependent, but because it makes the carer feel better.

Counter-transference processes also happen between the carer and the family of the person with dementia. Carers can have all kinds of ideas, feelings and fantasies which they project onto the family. The behaviour of the spouse, son or daughter of the person can evoke all kinds of reactions from the carers, which are related to the carer's own unresolved life history. Consider the next example. Marcia, the carer in the previously mentioned example, doesn't recognise Mrs Noble's daughter's behaviour as 'transference'. She takes it personally. She reacts out of an unconscious feeling of insecurity, and from the ambition always to want to 'be the best'.

Causes of the projections of carers

There are all kinds of projections, both positive and negative. Carers can have any number of concepts about older persons with regard to their own unresolved conflicts. Carers can see persons with dementia as 'substitutes' for other persons they miss, and even project their fear of losing loved ones, or the loss of their own life, onto them.

Stereotypes of the elderly

Sometimes carers see elderly people as demanding and stubborn. Others see them as kind, dependent, and understanding. When carers approach elderly people with such a 'global impression' (or stereotype), they are reacting to their own notion of 'older person' rather than to each individual old person.

Unresolved conflicts

It is possible for carers to project their unfulfilled wishes from important persons in the past, onto persons with dementia. For example, the 'claiming' behaviour of a person with dementia who is fearful and seeking safety can represent the behaviour of the carer's mother when, after her divorce, mother stiflingly 'clung for dear life' onto her eldest daughter. For another carer, the unexpected demands or swearing of an elderly male client might evoke feelings of the humiliation her father or older brother caused her by being overly authoritarian.

When carers encounter their 'own parents', with whom they had an unpleasant relationship, through the behaviour of a person with dementia, counter-transference can occur. It can occur through very small and subtle behaviours. It can be through the tone of voice, a gesture, an expression or an action or mannerism. In a flash, the unpleasant experiences with the carer's own parents can be re-lived and evoke the old reactions from the carer.

Substitution for something missed

Projections of a 'wished-for relationship' or an 'unfulfilled need to belong to someone', or 'to care for someone' are also possible. Thankfulness for the dependence of the person with dementia, and the stories about the past, can represent the much longed-for presence of a grandparent, spouse or even a child for a carer.

Fear of the loss of loved ones

Projections of 'the anticipated loss of loved ones' and the associated fears can also occur. In caring for an elderly person with dementia, it sometimes occurs to carers for the first time that people are not immortal, and that the lives of their own parents will not continue forever. The carer sometimes realises deeply, for the first time, that they will lose their parents. The visible decline in the person with dementia can confront them with their own mortality.

As well as the projections already mentioned, wherein the carers transfer all facets of their own feelings onto the person with dementia, other unconscious motives can also be transferred. Some carers choose this work 'to repay an old debt', 'to assuage guilt', 'to make good', 'to be appreciated' or 'to prove something to themselves'.

Consequences of projections

Projections influence the behaviour of carers and can unhelpfully influence the 'adoption process'. When carers project their own needs onto persons with dementia, they are reacting first, to their own feelings and needs and not those of the sufferer. The development of the emotional bond between them, and the feelings of responsibility that the carer develops towards the person with dementia can become greatly distorted.

'Fear of losing loved ones' and 'confrontation with one's own mortality', can lead to overprotection of the person with dementia. 'Over-concern' can also result. Such behaviour is testimony to the fear that the carer has about losing his/her own grandparents, or their own death. The carer tries to protect his/her own life, and their loved ones against becoming dependent, deterioration, helplessness and death. The fear of losing loved ones, which is projected onto the person with dementia, can, in extreme cases, lead to irresponsible behaviour on the part of the carer. Some examples are: to keep someone alive at the expense of everything else; to refuse to allow them to be admitted to a nursing home (where the person with dementia would doubtless be better off); to stay with the person with dementia and continue to care intensively for them, even outside work hours. When a carer tries to prevent being confronted by the death of loved ones, or their own death, and works with the person with dementia primarily to prevent such a confrontation, then the carer is seriously harming their perception of reality. In such circumstances, the fact that the person with dementia is indeed dying, and perhaps wants to die, is no longer perceived by the carer. Harm could result if, for example, a carer resisted following an 'agreement' about 'not forcing food any more'.

In the case where the social worker in Carla's group therapy sessions (see the beginning of this chapter) had not resolved her own parents' divorce, there was also evidence of 'irresponsible' behaviour. Against her better judgement, this social worker tried to delay, as long as possible, admitting persons with dementia into care settings. At first glance, that might seem like a reasonable goal. However, when the best interests of the person are not dealt with, or the interests of the spouse, family, neighbours and ancillary carers, irresponsibility and the abuse of power can result.

Projections can also lead to the discourteous treatment of the person with dementia. Unresolved conflicts can result in the carer dismissing or rejecting him/her. The carer may reject the person's 'claiming behaviour' because it represents the stifling interference of their own mother or father. Unresolved conflicts can also cause a carer to 'over-react'. For example, a carer might become angry out of all proportion because the commanding tone of voice of the person with dementia evokes years of pent-up anger towards her dominant father, who issued commands about everything. The carer may even become 'disappointed' in the person (although he/she can do nothing about it), and hence, withhold normal reactions and even needed care.

When 'substitution for a loss' is an unconscious motivational force, it can result in the carer 'hanging onto' the dependence of the person with dementia, which the carer fosters. When the person with dementia doesn't fulfil these expectations, the carer feels disappointed and unappreciated. The carer may, in turn, reject the person.

Projections can result in great personal difficulty for the carer. One carer felt guilty about the way she denied her own grandfather's dementia. This carer was well known for her tremendous 'resilience'. She was always ready to work in the most difficult situation, even with clients who were particularly aggressive. This work made great demands on her, but it helped her to appease her own guilt feelings. When she discovered that her own anger and aggression towards her own grandfather was a result of her ongoing grieving process, she was finally able to let go of her feelings of guilt. She finally understood that her unpleasant behaviour towards her grandfather had been a consequence of her denial that she was 'losing him slowly'. She dismissed the evidence that he had dementia and believed that he no longer cared for her. She felt 'abandoned' by him. Instead of guilt, she now felt appropriate sadness. Finally, she was free to recognise that she loved him very much. She was also able to ask for help more quickly when things were becoming too difficult for her at work. She also started asking to be placed with clients who were less difficult.

Projections do not always cause problems either for the client or the carer. Sometimes carers 'find their own parents with whom they hardly had any relationship', in the behaviour of a client. This makes it pleasant to care for the person. The carer 'does their best' to care well for the person with dementia and to make life pleasant for them.

Signals of counter-transference

How do carers recognise that they are in such a situation, or are close to being in such a situation? The following reactions may point to 'counter-transference': having extreme reactions to someone; when the distinction between work and home life is becoming unclear; when the carer has virtually 'become family' to the person with dementia; and when it takes an exceptional amount of emotional energy to break the emotional bond with a person with dementia. These forms of counter-transference will be discussed now.

Extreme reactions

By extreme reactions, we mean that someone reacts very emotionally to seemingly trivial provocation. These reactions are seen to be extreme by 'an outsider', but also by the carer him/herself. Such reactions might be provoked by the person with dementia, or by the critical reactions of others to the person with dementia (the spouse or children of the sufferer, colleagues, room-mates). The carer may, to her own surprise react angrily to her husband when he cautiously dares to say that he thinks she's 'making too much' of her work with the person with dementia.

The same things are happening at work and in one's private life

When someone experiences the same tensions, conflicts and emotions in their work as they do in daily life, it starts to feel like there is no distinction between work and private life. This person is always encountering the same difficulties. It would be coincidental for work and home life to be so similar. It is more likely that the carer is 'taking him/herself' into both situations and coming up against similar difficulties. An example of this would be if the carer still lives at home with her mother, who is very meddlesome and tiresome. When the carer is at work with Mrs Fisher, a person with dementia, who is prone to following her around, she gets the feeling again that 'she's not being left alone for a minute'. The carer feels in that both her private and work life, she's in the same situation emotionally. She might eventually come to 'hate Mrs Fisher for her meddlesome behaviour'. Mrs Fisher is only seeking safety from anyone and everyone who is around, including her carer, whom she is afraid to let out of her sight.

'Being like' versus 'becoming' family

In Chapter 11 we found that one of the hallmarks of the adoption process is when the carer starts feeling as though the person with dementia has become 'like family' to them. The essence of this matter is the difference between 'being like family' versus the real feeling (and responsibility) of 'being a family member'. Ideally, 'being like family' means that the carer doesn't drown emotionally in the situation, but is able to keep the necessary distance to care, even when the emotional bond with the person with dementia is very close. When this distance no longer exists, carers feel as though they 'are family', instead of feeling 'like family'. This is perhaps the clearest signal of counter-transference.

The end is in sight

Other signals that can indicate that counter-transference is occurring may arise when the emotional bond between carer and the person with dementia is nearing its end. For example, a carer might stop work because of maternity leave, or the person with dementia may need to be admitted to a nursing home. When the bond with the person is laden with the 'extra role', or 'deeper meaning', that the carer has projected onto it, the threat of loss causes great problems for the carer. The carer may do everything to prevent the person with dementia from being admitted to a nursing home or dying. When death occurs anyway, the carer can be left with extreme feelings of having failed. If the person with dementia is admitted to a care home, the carer may continue to give an extreme form of 'continued care'. Recall the example of Bill in Chapter 11.

Personal growth

In the preceding sections, the overall impression has been that counter-transference is generally an experience with many negative aspects. At first glance, it certainly appears that way. Being confronted with sickness, death, old age, dependence, future loss of loved ones is every bit as natural as the attachment and adoption process. These are the 'risks' of the job of caring for persons with dementia. At the same time, these things can lead to enormous personal growth for the carer. These themes will be encountered by everyone sooner or later. Usually, people only discover later in life that their parents 'won't be around forever'. It is common for people not to think about their own mortality until something triggers these thoughts. Carers, however, have the chance to encounter such life themes at a much earlier stage in their lives. If they can be taught to think and speak about these encounters as 'deepening experiences' rather than 'unpleasant confrontations', their own fears will diminish and their appreciation for their work will increase. This often makes carers much more 'mature' than their age cohort members in other lines of work.

Finally

If carers are not aware of transference and counter-transference, problems can arise that compromise their professionalism. Insight into these processes gives carers the chance to identify these conflicts, to deal with them and not to let them affect their work as 'carers'. When carers discuss such themes with each other, they usually discover for themselves what their motivation to care is, and whether there are 'extra roles' involved. Carers can usually understand which situations detract from the care the person with dementia needs and is entitled to. Open discussions with each other can help to gain insight into one's own, and other carer's emotional reactions. This helps to keep carers functioning 'as themselves' without ending up in counter-transference situations.

It is essential that carers are not denied the chance to talk about such issues, whether they occur in one-to-one or in group settings. It is very difficult to care for a person with dementia. It is even more so when the carer only sees 'aspects of themselves', or 'others' in the sufferer, and does not see the person with dementia. The carer must refrain from pre-judging the client and the family, and to keep looking at what is really happening in parts of the relationship 'network' involved. What is this person really feeling, behind their behaviours? How do others react to them? What roles do 'your own past experience' and 'unresolved conflicts' play in how you care for persons with dementia? Looking at these things honestly will help carers to avoid being 'laden down' with feelings that really are not intended personally for them. This frees carers to build genuine relationships with persons with dementia and their families.

14 Intimacy and sexuality

Jenny Turner, care manager of a residential home gives the following account of a situation which that has become increasingly difficult to understand.

Mr Sommer came to live here eighteen months ago. He had apparently experienced mild symptoms of dementia for a few years. While his wife was healthy there weren't any big problems. Then she became ill and later died. That's a year ago now. When she died, his situation turned out to be worse than anyone had imagined. His doctor referred him for assessment and he ended up coming to live here.

In the beginning the carers thought Mr Sommer was a pleasant man. There was something very helpless about him. He absolutely didn't know where he was, but enjoyed everything that happened around him. He needed some help to wash and dress. You had to lay everything out ready for him and remind him in which order to do things. He managed well enough then. Every morning there's a communal breakfast and 'tea break'. He never went there of his own accord, but once someone helped him to get there, he enjoyed himself. We have a number of ladies here who got along well with him. For the rest of the time, he sat alone in his room, didn't read, didn't watch television, didn't walk along the corridors. Because of this, the carers often dropped in to see him for a few moments in his room when they were around.

After a short while, however, there was a change in the carers' relationship with him. They no longer visited him spontaneously any more, and I noticed that they had even become reluctant to help him. At the team meeting, the reason finally emerged. Mr Sommer was sometimes 'too touchy'. He sometimes suddenly grabbed hold of a carer and pulled her towards him. As he was a strong man, it was very difficult to get out of his grasp. At first, carers didn't tell other carers that this was happening. Each carer assumed that she was the only one who had experienced this.

However, Kate, who used to work here, never had any difficulty in helping him. She came from the same village as Mr Sommer and was able to chat freely about the persons they both knew. When he grabbed hold of her, it was to get his balance, or just because there was a sort of trust between them. That was Kate's explanation. She sometimes embraced him, because although he never spoke of his wife and their conversations were always jolly, she had a soft spot for him. As Kate was happy to help him and didn't seem to be bothered by anything, the other carers were reluctant to say that they found Mr Sommer difficult to work with. When the dam finally broke, I heard many more stories and so I decided to speak to him about his behaviour. I told him that although he probably didn't intend it, the carers were not pleased about his 'touching' them. He immediately shouted me down. He said he had never bothered the 'girls'. He knew of men who couldn't keep their hands to themselves, but said he had never been one of them. When I told him that he was doing this, he looked at me perplexed and said that he wouldn't even consider doing such a thing. Had he forgotten, or was Kate's explanation the right one?

A few weeks ago Mr Sommer probably had a stroke. That's why he was being given a bed bath in the morning. Almost no one wanted to help him any more. When his private parts are washed, he gets an erection. Sometimes staff have walked in to see him masturbating. When staff leave, to return later to wash him, things go wrong again. One carer is more 'down to earth' than another, but everyone finds it embarrassing and some carers feel 'used'. Whenever possible, I go to help wash him so that the staff don't feel they are dealing with this situation alone. I can't pretend that I'm role-modelling the right way to deal with this situation because, in truth, I don't know what that is. I'm pretty hard-headed though. He probably doesn't know what he is doing, and its a fairly natural thing. I don't find it very pleasant witnessing it though. I'd rather help clean up someone's bowel movement.

Layout of this chapter

In this chapter we shall look at the perceptions of the person with dementia and the resulting communication. The assumption behind this example is that persons with dementia have the same needs as everyone else. Differences in the way in which they express or meet their needs are related to generational differences, life history and sex.

For many persons with dementia, touch is an important way of communicating. It does not always represent sexual motive or intentions. Carers don't always understand this and are then left to deal with their own confused reactions. The length of time the carer has known the person with dementia plays a role in this as well. Thereafter, the essence of this chapter will be examined – the much-needed, intensive presence of the carer suggests a sort of intimacy, although there may not (yet/ever) be any. This confusion can lead to communication problems and to undesired intimate advances. Finally, we shall examine the ideas that carers have about old age and sexuality. These determine the boundaries of physical intimacy in caring for persons with dementia, and how carers deal with sexual behaviour, 'touching' and other undesired sexual advances and intimacy.

Introduction

As the dementia process progresses, the contact between carer and client becomes more intimate. The diminishing mental abilities of persons with dementia prevent them from expressing themselves and communicating in normal ways. Non-verbal behaviour is increasingly used to indicate what he/she is thinking, meaning and feeling. His/her emotions and behaviour are increasingly prone to being 'at cross purposes'. Not only this. There is also every reason to assume that the person with dementia, just like every other person, needs human tenderness and warmth.

Despite the aforementioned, the person with dementia is less able to conceal this need and usually shows it more directly. When carers encounter this, they assume that the desire for attention and warmth is a request for sexual contact. This perceived request can evoke mixed feelings in them. Contact with clients also becomes more intimate because of their increasing dependence on others, not only for practical help, but especially for emotional support. That is how, whether it is desired or not, carers inevitably end up relating intimately to the person with dementia. This can evoke mixed reactions for persons with dementia also.

In Chapter 9, dementia was described 'from the inside' of the sufferer, in so far as that is possible to do. By going this one step further, by trying to describe dementia as more than 'symptoms', we tried to look at the behaviours of sufferers as having 'meaning and purpose' rather than being 'somehow deranged'. If we assume that persons with dementia are indeed 'affected by and involved with' what is happening to them, then it is essential for the carer to look at the meaning of the person's behaviour. You can do this by trying to imagine what life must be like 'in the person's shoes', but also by realising that the person with dementia, like the carer, is human.

Contact with the outside world

The gradual decrease in the cognitive abilities of persons with dementia makes communication more difficult. When the normal meaning of words has been lost, when some topics are no longer familiar and hence become 'new' to the person with dementia, when he/she is lost in the middle of a sentence and cannot complete it, the 'senses' serve as guides to what is happening. Hands feel objects to discover (again) what it is or what it does. Eyes discover things and places (again) because, like for an explorer for whom everything is new, the person with dementia cannot recognise or 'place' objects around them. Touch, smell and taste are likewise instruments that bring them into contact with the world around them. Senses provide 'handholds'. When a person is less able to rely on 'cognitive abilities', he/she is forced to use senses to perceive the world. Seeing, hearing, feeling, smelling and tasting help the person with dementia to survive. He/she must slowly 'change gear' from a 'verbal' to a 'non-verbal' guidance-system. The person's tenuous thinking abilities gradually force him/her to use 'touch' as a life-saving way of staying in contact with the world.

Need for communication

Even if someone's abilities to achieve 'self-worth, appreciation, love and the feeling of belonging' have disappeared, there will always be a number of basic needs that will not disappear. Not only the physiological needs (such as eating, drinking, sleeping, eliminating, shelter, movement and sexual stimulation), but also the need to 'feel safe and secure'. Persons with dementia will increasingly seek to meet these needs 'non-verbally' as the dementia process progresses. Touch is the best communication tool for doing this.

Every person seeks to fulfil their own basic needs. The means by which needs are realised and, how we regard the needs of others, is determined by our culture, personality, generation, and beliefs. How we realise our basic needs differs from person to person although there are common factors involved. This is true of persons with dementia as well as carers.

Time periods and generations

Persons are the products of the times in which they live. They are subject to the 'spirit of the times' and to the cultural and regional norms and values. Those belonging to a given generation will experience and express their personal needs in a way that is generally in keeping with the 'times and place' in which they lived. As such, views about relationships, dating, married life, homosexuality and masturbation are related to time periods, cultures, beliefs and societies. It used to be 'unseemly' for a girl to 'chat up' a boy in public. Nowadays, women can be much more demonstrative before others accuse them of being 'loose' or 'a whore'. It used to be thought 'unmanly' for a male to openly show his need for affection and warmth. Today, it is more often seen as a 'blessing' if men can show their feelings openly.

It is more common for youngsters nowadays to see their parents 'in their birthday suit' than it ever was in the past. Nudity on television is also more common now than in the past. Naturists (nudists) were rare in the past. Now, a whole branch of the tourist industry caters for them. In the 'older generation of now' there are couples who have never seen each other naked in the light of day, and who will not express affection for each other in any way in front of others. There used to be things one 'ought not talk about'. Nowadays, no one can escape the 'safe sex' campaign and advertisements related to AIDS prevention. In other words, the older generation grew up with different norms and values than the youth of today does. In general, it seems that today's youth are more natural and open about their bodies.

Individual life histories and beliefs

People are also the 'product' of their own individual life history and beliefs. How persons express and fulfil their human needs is not only determined by the family (values) with which one grew up, but also by the spouse/partner chosen in later life. How men and women learn to express their needs for intimacy and their sexual desires is also determined by the way in which the partner deals with them, and, by the way in which the couple communicates with one another about these needs. Everything that happens to a person from childhood to adolescence affects them. If their development was disturbed by, for example, incest, violence or rape, they will probably be less able to react openly to touch or the physical advances of others.

It is not only sexual abuse that adversely affects a persons' emotional (and therefore sexual) expression. Feelings of 'extreme inferiority', 'emotional abandonment' or 'societal segregation' also have adverse effects. Emotional abandonment occurred in some large families and in some very intellectual environments. Examples of those segregated to some degree from society include: priests, nuns, school mistresses, nurses, the 'rich man's son' (who did what he pleased), the poor family's child (who had no time to play because he had to work to help make ends meet). Those with chronic illnesses (e.g., tuberculosis, polio), and those daughters who were expected to remain at home to look after their parents in their old age were also segregated. Such factors play a role in the lives of many people with dementia. Hence, they also affect how persons with dementia interact with carers now.

Male/female differences

It is difficult to estimate the extent to which sex differences determine how certain needs are expressed, in conjunction with the obvious biological differences between the sexes, and the differences in upbringing between males and females. How males versus females were raised is also affected by the time period and culture in which someone grew up. It is often said that for women, having an 'intimate relationship' is a necessary condition for having a satisfying sexual relationship. Others disagree. It is clear, however, that in the older generation, who barely had any concept of contraception (and for whom it was largely taboo), women took larger risks than nowadays. One wonders to what degree the fear of undesired pregnancy was a 'damper' to making love in married life. For many elderly women, undesired pregnancies 'in wedlock' seem to have created defences that are still evident now.

Mrs Dollands, in Chapter 8, implored Rita on a daily basis, 'never to trust a man'. 'They're all rogues and they only want one thing.' For many elderly women, menopause was also a difficult time, even though it came with the relief of not becoming pregnant again. Many women felt worn out, drained, past their 'sell by' date and 'set to one side'. Another saying of Mrs Dollands was: 'Watch out for when you become 36. You'll be traded in for two 18-year-olds then.'

Whether males and females really are different in their affective and sexual needs can no longer be maintained for certain. Perhaps we will only know after a few generations of 'emancipation'. We can say for certain, however, that elderly females of today certainly had a different upbringing from the men of their day.

Reading literature about intimate and sexual relationships also points to sex differences. A female author, describing female sexual feelings, gives a different impression than a male author writing about female sexual feelings. The converse is also true. Male sexuality, described by a female author is different to male sexuality described by a male. Such differences are also visible in care situations. Carers report that elderly ladies generally express more embarrassment and shame at having to wash themselves or to get undressed in the presence of others than elderly males. This is especially true if the carer is male. Male persons with dementia are not usually as self-conscious in the presence of female carers.

Non-verbal communication

Three observations can be made about non-verbal communication. First, as the course of dementia progresses, 'touch' becomes an increasingly important form of communication between carers and persons with dementia. The increasing dependence of persons with dementia leads naturally to carers having to touch them more often. Second, for many persons with dementia, touch will be the key means of communicating. Third, persons with dementia remain 'persons' with the same human needs as anyone else. How they experience their needs is affected by sex differences, time periods and life history. This is also true for the way in which persons with dementia experience how carers 'touch' them. With regard to the practical help persons with dementia need and the efforts to 'reach them', non-verbal communication is often the only way in which a carer can remain in contact. The way in which carers express themselves to a person with dementia through touch, and how they react to being touched are likewise affected by sex, time period and life history, and beliefs. This is why one carer will be very different from another.

Communicating: expressing and interpreting

Every one of us has been involved in a misunderstanding at one time or another. You say something you don't mean, or, what you say is misinterpreted. It's not always easy to express exactly what you want to say in words. Working out what someone else means can be just as difficult. Sometimes the consequences of misunderstandings are not worth bothering about; sometimes they cannot be overlooked. That is perhaps even more strongly true for non-verbal communication in which body language or gestures play a large role. The meaning of touch, or of being touched, is not always immediately clear. Take, for example, someone putting an arm around you when you are crying. Non-verbal communications are just as prone to being misunderstood, if not more so, than are verbal communications.

The meaning of intimacy

The root of the word intimate comes from the Latin word *intimus*. The 'in' part refers to 'the innermost', for example, that which penetrates the defences. It is possible to think of human beings as having layers of 'zones' around them. The outer zone is for superficial contacts, the middle zone is for deeper contacts and then there is the innermost zone, within which there are no defences. This is where your total trust in another comes from. The actual distance in space between persons also plays a role. This can be centimetres, metres, or whatever. 'Closeness in centimetres' doesn't mean 'intimacy'. A doctor may give someone a thorough physical, even internal examination. This all happens at the most superficial level of contact though. While washing a person, a carer will be calm and caring, but not intrusive in contact.

Nowadays, the word 'intimacy' is almost exclusively linked to 'sexuality', especially with regard to unwelcome sexual advances. What is so repellent about this, is not that the advance is at the sexual level, but that it happens with total disregard for the integrity of the other person – his/her boundaries are infringed. Sexual relationships do not necessarily have to be intimate, but when they are, partners will respect each other's safety/comfort zones.

The dementia process can cause the inner and outer zones in a person with dementia to become muddled. This can also happen to the carer who is emotionally involved with a person. Sexual boundaries can become misplaced. When you give a lot of yourself, you may become more vulnerable and defenceless. Even without an intense concern for the other, it is still possible that they suddenly appear within your defence boundaries. Sometimes this happens deliberately, and such behaviour is dishonourable or caddish. But it can also happen accidentally.

When Mr Sommer grabs a carer, what does he mean and why is he doing this? In the story that Kate related, it is clear that there is more than one explanation for this 'grabbing hold of' behaviour: needing support to get his balance; a gesture of affection; an expression of sexual needs, sexual intimation and so forth. What is also evident is that the attitude of each carer is determined by the personal explanation they have and the meaning of the behaviour to them. Things that influence/colour the carers' explanations are, for example, the unexpectedness of the gesture, the strength with which Mr Sommer grabs them and whether or not they know him well. Let us not forget the possibility that perhaps Mr Sommer is mistaking a carer for his wife. Considering this possibility might help a carer understand his behaviour better. In that instance, saying to him, 'Mary would say, "No John, not now John"', might be familiar and more understandable.

The length of the contact

There is something else worth noting. Being unexpectedly 'grabbed hold of', was seen by most carers as 'undesired intimacy'. However, Kate, the carer who knew him longer/better, did not think this. There was a certain intimacy between them because they had grown up in the same village, knew the same people and places. Perhaps this is why she didn't judge his behaviour in the same light as her colleagues. It is, and will remain difficult to determine what a simple gesture means: a handhold when you are unsure of your balance, an advance arising from sexual feelings, the need for tenderness and warmth or an attempt to be close to another human because one is so frightened. Or perhaps it is just the caring situation – being close to someone and being in close physical contact with them might evoke feelings/memories of intimacy. The more that carers work with people with dementia, the better they will be able to judge the reason for the behaviour of any given person. If a carer has just started working with someone, there hasn't been enough time for any emotional attachment to have occurred, let alone intimacy. Every gesture, touch or physical contact made by the person with dementia is more likely to be experienced by the carer as 'undesired intimacy'. In the second part of Jenny's account, sexual behaviour is very clearly evident.

Erection

What meaning do you give to Mr Sommer's erection? Does this happen deliberately, or because of the stimulation of the situation. Are his sexual feelings a result of lying in bed naked and being washed, or, because he needs to urinate? How you will react to this situation depends upon whether or not you think he is responsible for his erection and what your own experiences in this regard are. If this is the first time a carer experiences this situation, it can be highly embarrassing. Don't forget: erections can also 'just happen'. It could be highly untimely and embarrassing for him that someone just happens to be present when this occurs.

Masturbation

Another issue in this story of Mr Sommer is his masturbation. Carers can be left with the feeling that they are being used, or that he is making use of the situation. But another explanation is also possible: when persons have strong sexual feelings or stimulation, masturbation is not uncommon. Perhaps he is doing this out of habit, and because of his dementia, doesn't realise what an awkward situation this is for a carer to confront. Some persons do have sick tendencies to need witnesses for their sexual arousal and actions (exhibitionism). It would seem to be somewhat extreme to think of Mr Sommer in this light. Such tendencies usually occur at a much younger age. There is a greater chance that it is a habit arising from loneliness, boredom or sleeplessness. It might be related to the feeling of being displaced in one's own body (for example, as a result of being half-side paralysed and searching helplessly for something to make you feel that you are still there).

Masturbation occurs in women for all of the same reasons mentioned, but in addition it is also sometimes done to keep warm. Such 'fingering' sometimes becomes a habit that continues day and night. This also makes carers feel very uncomfortable. It looks 'unaesthetic', smells and brings with it feelings of 'shame'. In such situations, it helps if you realise that such sexual behaviours in persons with dementia have nothing to do with you. However, it remains difficult to witness them. Even Jenny, who presumably has a fair bit of life experience, and who thinks of herself as being 'hard headed', doesn't escape feeling uncomfortable. It is possible to pose the question, whether even having to see such things is an infringement of the intimacy and integrity of the carer. You can also pose the question the carer experiences 'counter-transference' of shame for the person with dementia. You have only to hope that you will never be in such a situation yourself.

Desired and undesired intimacy

As a carer you touch the person with dementia whilst bathing, washing, dressing and mobilising and possibly feeding him/her. These many ways of touching may suggest an intimacy that is not (yet) there. One carer said, 'As a carer you touch everything. That sometimes unlocks things in the person with dementia.' New carers sometimes work for persons who are very dependent, and because of such close contact, surprising and difficult situations can arise. This is very difficult for carers when they have not yet had the time to develop feelings of 'closeness and concern' for the person with dementia. Such situations are far more difficult than if a carer sees the dependence of a person with dementia gradually developing. When an emotional bond has developed, it is mutually devastating when a newcomer takes over the care. It is inappropriate for a new carer to 'take over' the behaviours of the old carer (such as the use of the person's nickname). Carers who assume such familiarities do not see that they are rooted in a trusting and long-standing relationship with the person with dementia.

Misunderstandings

In very trusting relationships between carers and persons with dementia, the chance of misunderstanding is greatest. Intensive physical contact can evoke erotic feelings in a carer. They might not even be directed towards the person with dementia, but they can be picked up. Perhaps such feelings are projections of the carers, and possibly it is just a mistake in their 'body chemistry'. Naturally it is also possible for younger persons to fall in love with older persons. In one's professional relationship with a person with dementia, this is not permissible. One's own ability to reason is usually enough to restrain one. It can be very confusing none the less, particularly because feelings are unacceptable for oneself, and in society. You may not even dare to admit them to yourself. That is the difficulty: pushing feelings away and looking for another way out.

Even if carers are not bothered by such confusing feelings and are not demonstrative of them, it is still sometimes possible for persons with dementia to become mixed up about their presence and mistake their intentions. Any action that the carer views differently from the person with dementia can sometimes easily take on sexual connotations, and all of the feelings that go along with this. This is unpleasant for the person with dementia because it usually leads to a 'distancing' on the part of the carer. But not only that. His/her needs for tenderness and safety and longing for human warmth are misunderstood. How, then, are these to be met? Every new attempt to resume contact will quickly strengthen the first interpretation 'of making sexual advances'. While the dementia process is bringing the sufferer into an increasingly 'unsafe' (frightening) world, the opportunities for real human closeness and affection are diminishing. The path to such closeness is being closed off and the mist around the person with dementia becomes thicker while there are fewer chances to reach out and to get a hold of others.

Some persons with dementia have never learned to ask for tenderness in any way, other than through sexually coloured overtones. In such instances, their gestures and actions can only be associated with sexual advances, although the desire and meaning behind it all is quite different. Even when the intention is a sexual one, it can happen because the person with dementia perceives the carer as their spouse or partner. This is not transference, but a case of mistaken identity. It also happens that transference does occur, such as when the person is missing his/her spouse. Feelings of missing and longing for the spouse can be projected onto the carer, but somewhat accidentally in a sexual form. The use of obscene language and actions do not have to lead to misunderstanding. Some behaviour is clearly intolerable and leaves nothing to be assumed.

Obscene language is often used as a compensation for loss of status and feelings of inferiority. Carers who are clearly able to define their own limits and boundaries in such situations are doing well. For most carers, however, such situations remain uncomfortable and intrusive. Sometimes it helps to ignore such behaviour. It always remains important to speak to colleagues about such experiences.

The subject of 'undesired intimacy' is less of a taboo subject than it used to be. Thankfully this is so because societal recognition of such problems is increasing. Consciousness is being raised. There is an impression, however, that the tolerance limits of carers are fairly high. At the beginning of a caring situation, there is a period of 'wait and see' what the person with dementia means exactly. This results in carers being cautious and withholding while they are getting to know the person and the new work setting. When carers get beyond this stage, and especially when they have learned to deal with their own emotions, they are usually able to give the warmth and intimacy that the person is seeking, irrespective of whatever unfortunate means he/she has of expressing these needs.

Within their work, carers often are more open in their behaviour towards persons with dementia than they would be in normal societal interactions. Carers admit that they would be more distant with individuals they encountered, for example, on the bus or train. 'Sometimes I do things with my clients that I would almost never conceive of doing otherwise, like giving someone a hug or a cuddle.'

With whom does the initiative lie?

Carers usually sense whether a person with dementia desires human warmth or sexual gratification, whether a hug or a kiss is being sought. For many carers it makes a big difference who takes the initiative. Some say, 'The more openly and often warmth is asked for, the less I can give.' Often the initiative lies with the carer, for example, stroking someone's arm, or holding their hand. Little opportunity for initiative is left to the person with dementia. This is a pity because many persons can express themselves much better by 'offering' a caress than by 'receiving' one (being caressed). This is true for both young and old persons. One's life history, generation and sex also influence this, but also one's understanding of sexuality and old age.

Old age and sexuality

It is still the norm that children find it difficult to imagine that their parents have sexual relations with each other. Young persons usually imagine that they will have active sexual lives well into their old age though they usually can't imagine the older persons they know being sexually active. 'Older persons don't have sexual feelings anymore.' The film *Love in Later Life* (1982, W. Ouwerkerk), is about a couple Kees (aged 70) and Marre (aged 69). There is one scene in this film that shows the couple naked and making love to each other. Carers generally resist such images. Part of this resistance is explicable. Not everyone finds it easy to watch films with sexual content in the company of others and to speak about this thereafter. (Even here, one could ask whether or not there wasn't an infringement of a person's integrity to request them to watch such a film.)

To watch older persons being sexually intimate can come across as a sort of exhibitionism. This feeling is strongest if your own parents are nearly the same age as the couple in the film and if they always closed their bedroom door to keep the children away from their love life. Most carers have difficulty with images of 'senior romances' and admit that in work settings they silently gloss over the fact that older persons have longings for sexual intimacy. 'The fact that something close and beautiful could happen between two older persons, and that it might not stop with hand-holding is not often considered', said one carer cautiously.

Norms and values

Dealing with sexual feelings is very personal for both carers and persons with dementia. The discussion therefore becomes difficult when it comes down to creating conditions or opportunities for persons with dementia to express sexual behaviour. Carers, persons with dementia, and their spouse and other family members will all have their own norms and values. Families can have different norms than care facilities. Some persons object strongly to persons with dementia forming affectionate relationships with other sufferers. Others sometimes find the rules and regimes of care facilities 'sterile'. Some spouses of persons with dementia feel betrayed when they come to visit and see their partner behaving affectionately towards another resident; others are relieved that at least they have found comfort from someone.

Another issue comes into play here: the existence of 'one's own value system', and 'one's professional norms and values and code of conduct'. Where these are in agreement there is no problem; when they are not, there is conflict. A carer may find the sexual advances of a widowed person with dementia more acceptable than those coming from a married person. Carers who see masturbation as a normal part of sexual activity are less likely to have difficulties in accepting this behaviour in a person with dementia than carers who don't.

Talking about undesired sexual intimacy

Carers are sometimes confronted with advances from persons with dementia that shock them. They must ask themselves whether they 'want to' or 'must' accept them. As carers will not always be able to 'relate to' or 'understand' such behaviours, it is sometimes labelled as 'undesired intimacy', even though it may have an entirely different meaning. Speaking with colleagues is one way of trying to under-stand what the real meaning might be. The following guidelines might be helpful.

Air your feelings first. Talk about them honestly.

Work out which feelings a given situation evokes in you. It can be that you experience a number of different feelings at the same time, and that the same behaviour in a different person does not upset you.

Try to be concrete and to write down as precisely as possible what you are talking about, exactly which behaviours you are referring to.

Try to imagine how the person with dementia feels in these circum-stances; assume that they are aware that 'something is happening to them' because of the dementia process. Their needs for tenderness, safety, handholds, protection and consolation may be affecting their behaviour.

Ask yourself whether/to what extent the person with dementia is projecting these feelings onto you. (That means, to what extent is it possible that the person's personality and life history are causing them to transfer feelings onto you? Or, to what degree does the person with dementia confuse you with other persons from their past, and hence, mistake you for someone else?)

Finally, ask yourself whether you might have any 'counter-transference' towards the person with dementia? (That means, to what extent are you projecting things and feelings from your own personality and life history onto the person with dementia?) Perhaps you see something 'more' or 'other' in the sufferer, than 'a person who needs particular kinds of professional help'. Perhaps the feelings that you have for the client do not tally with a professional relation-ship and societal norms. It could simply be that you find it difficult to express yourself non-verbally and physically towards the person with dementia.

Not every carer can automatically understand and fulfil a client's needs and requests for warmth and safety. Every carer is unique because of their own life history and makeup.

Limits

As a carer you have rights too. You don't have to accept everything. When have the boundaries of your own norms and values been exceeded? When have the scales tipped too far? Generally, it is diffi-cult to say precisely. Every situation is different, and every relationship with a person with dementia is different. Thinking in terms of 'good' versus 'bad' is usually not very useful. It is better to find yourself ready to be honest and open enough to evaluate each situation afresh. It helps to realise that not everything has to be 'mulled over', 'known' or 'become known'. Talking to colleagues, asking them questions and sharing experiences with them can help to clarify your own limits and boundaries.

The 'desired intimacy' of a person with dementia, whether it arises from the need for a handhold, safety or sexual needs, can be experienced by a carer as 'undesired intimacy'. The opposite can also occur. Sometimes, a client's dependency on 'much-needed intimacy' is continually experienced by the carer as 'undesired intimacy'. The annoying thing about this is that the power in a caring situation in not equally distributed. A carer can always 'retract' or 'disengage' from a situation when it becomes unpleasant or too much for them. The person with dementia usually has no choice about the presence of the carer, who might be left with feelings of shame or opposition.

Protection of the person with dementia

Sometimes carers are confronted with the sexual behaviour of the healthy partner towards the person with dementia, or with the sexual behaviour of another, for example, a neighbour, towards a single female person with dementia. The question that arises in such situations is: 'To what extent does the person with dementia decide to interact sexually with this other person of their own free will?' The question: 'To what extent is there abuse of power, or just abuse?' must be asked in such situations. Having developed a close, caring relationship with a person with dementia will help you to sense when your client is being abused. Carers have very important roles as 'signallers' of possible abuse. Concerns should be directed to one's supervisors, and related to the client's family doctor.

Sexual disinhibition

Spouses of persons with dementia sometimes tell carers about the complaints they have about their spouse's sexual behaviour. For example, a spouse might relate that their partner is making 'sexually laden comments in public to perfect strangers'. Or, a spouse might complain that their partner 'is suddenly becoming so sexually demanding that they cannot, or do not wish to satisfy such demands'. The spouse may continue to explain that, for understandable reasons, no logical discussion about this situation is possible with the person with dementia. In some circumstances, dementia can lead to sexually disinhibited sexual behaviour. Sexual impulses are given free rein and can no longer be controlled or managed or 'braked'. The person with dementia is no longer able to react adequately to the dismissive reactions of their partner. In such situations, expert help should be sought. When such behaviour occurs because of brain or other damage, it is sometimes possible to dampen such sexual impulses with medication. Sometimes medication is a 'blessing', not only for the spouse, but also for the person with dementia. It can suppress sexual behaviour and protect the person with dementia. This is not to say that every sexual expression or advance (for example, in a nursing home) should be frustrated or interrupted with medication.

Finally

The spouse of a person with dementia exists in an incredibly difficult situation. For outsiders it is often very endearing to see that the partner is 'always there', ready to offer any practical help needed, even though it isn't an easy situation. The emotional problems that really exist are more difficult for outsiders (sometimes even closer friends and relatives) to see. The process of gradually becoming 'widowed', though the spouse still lives, is not evident to all. Generally speaking, the healthy partner loses not only their 'mate', but also their 'friend' and 'sexual partner' gradually. Out of such emotional and physical need, it is understandable that spouses of persons with dementia sometimes project their feelings onto carers. This can be expressed not only by seeking intimacy and trust in the carer, but sometimes, also by making sexual advances towards them. This can happen without the spouse being conscious of what they are doing. In this sad situation, it sometimes happens that the spouse is intensely moved and touched by the presence of an energetic, refreshing, or young carer. If this leads to undesired intimacy, it is important for the carer to immediately call a halt to such behaviour. Just as with the person with dementia, carers can do this with nuance through gestures, tone of voice and posture, so that the spouse 'gets the message' without being compromised or ashamed by it.

15 Aggression

Case history example

> When he rolled his sleeves up to help with the washing up I saw marks, but I had no idea his wife had given them to him. One morning he came in with a black eye. I asked if he had fallen and he suddenly started crying. I didn't know how to react.

Since the first day that Eva started working at the Randal's home, Mr Randal's devotion had touched Eva greatly. His wife had been a dementia sufferer for years already. Now, she forgot everything, could barely make herself understood, wandered around the house at night like a lost soul, and, if given the chance, on the street too. The police had already found and returned her a few times. Mr Randal never so much as made a comment or complaint, until Eva had asked about his black eye.

> Thinking back on it, I could kick myself that I didn't notice things sooner. He told me what had been happening in bits and pieces. His wife didn't recognise him any more at times. This was especially true in the morning. When he wanted to help her to get washed and dressed, she sometimes suddenly hit, pinched and swore at him. What bothered him most was that she also sometimes scratched. He had always loved her and tried to do his best to care for her. He had wanted to talk about it earlier with me but hadn't dared because it made him feel as though he was betraying her.

Although Eva believed him, she had trouble with his disclosures. Eva had never seen Mrs Randal be aggressive. Eva couldn't imagine that Mrs Randal could actually hurt her husband who treated her with such kindness.

Eva couldn't really believe Mr Randal until she was confronted with the same behaviour. Mr Randal had to go to the doctor and had asked Eva to help Mrs Randal out of bed and to get dressed. He'd be back at ten o'clock.

> After his story, you can imagine that I was a bit nervous. To start with, it seemed as though nothing could go amiss. She was lying in bed, awake and looked at me with large, friendly eyes. She let me help her wash her, standing at the wash basin. I couldn't understand what she was saying exactly, but I noticed that she wanted to go back to bed. When she was sitting on the edge of the bed, trying to get her dress on, I could tell she was getting annoyed. Since everything else had gone well up until then, I had let down my guard somewhat. When I was squatting down in front of her, trying to help get her panties on, she suddenly kicked me hard in the chest. I got a terrific shock and it was very sore. I remember thinking, as my first thought, 'What did I do wrong?' Then, I became very angry and started shouting at her.

When Mr Randal returned from the doctor, Eva acted as though nothing had happened. When he asked if everything had gone well, she had assured him it had. Eva had been feeling terribly guilty about yelling at his wife in the meanwhile.

At Eva's home, after dinner that evening, when she and her husband were sitting in front of the television, Eva finally found enough courage to tell her husband about what had happened at work that day. Her husband reacted by saying, 'What on earth does that woman think she's doing?' and 'Look for another job!' Eva didn't tell her husband any more. The next morning Eva went to her supervisor for a talk. 'I'd like to speak to you, as long as our discussion doesn't have any consequences for Mrs Randal. I don't want her to be admitted somewhere because of me.'

Layout of the chapter

In this chapter we shall begin by examining the causes of aggressive behaviour in persons with dementia. There are a range of causes: someone can be aggressive by nature; they may be reacting to fear or frustration; or the aggressive behaviour may be a direct consequence of particular kinds of brain damage. In the next section, we shall discuss the reactions of the carers to such aggression. It will depend in part, on whether they know the cause of the behaviour and can recognise it. If the carer sees it as 'a game', or, if this aggression activates 'old pain' in the carer, it will be more difficult to deal with. Finally, we shall look at possible ways of dealing with aggression. Try to look for the cause, but also look at your own reactions to what is happening.

Introduction

Persons with dementia can display aggressive behaviour. Whether the carer is able to deal with it depends in part upon whether they have a sense of attachment to the person. Is the person often whimsical or impatient? Has the relationship always been awkward and 'stiff'? Is the carer able to detect small moments of tenderness and humour? If aggressive behaviour occurs with a sense of 'deliberate intent', or happens totally unprovoked, it is very difficult to deal with. It is important to note that many feelings can be evoked by an aggressive encounter. While one carer may be angry, another might feel frightened or powerless.

Do you first have to experience aggression before believing that it is occurring? Even after Mr Randal's unexpected and emotional confession, Eva wasn't completely convinced. It didn't even occur to her that Mrs Randal might have been reacting to unpleasant behaviour on the part of Mr Randal. Eva thinks of him as a 'sweetie', 'kindness itself'. When she encountered aggression herself, she was very taken aback, but she didn't exclude the possibility that she might have done something wrong. That is not very surprising, because even in other situations in daily life we often don't know how to deal with aggression.

Carers working with people with dementia at home or in care facilities have often had, and continue to have, great difficulty with aggressive behaviour. 'It's something that you never get used to.' Carers do not readily or easily speak about it, but when they finally do, it appears that almost everyone has encountered it. What is understood by aggressive behaviour varies widely; from someone pushing you away from them, to being sworn at or hit. The feelings that such behaviour evokes in a carer are very diverse and sometimes very complex. While one carer may feel compromised or humiliated, another feels angry; others feel frightened, sympathetic, powerless and anxious. Sometimes the intensity of a carer's reaction to aggressive behaviour (and the difficulty they have in speaking about it), is influenced by their own personal experiences with aggression outside the work place.

The important point is that aggressive behaviour causes carers to keep a safe distance from persons with dementia. They may think literally: 'In a minute I'll get another swipe!' and figuratively: 'Suit yourself!' This conflicts with the perception that carers have that the person with dementia needs their presence. Because the client is so dependent on others, it is difficult to 'leave them to it'. To build up contact with the person again, it is necessary to get physically close to him/her again.

Aggressive behaviour

According to the dictionary aggressive behaviour means 'prone to attack, conflict seeking, injurious'. Usually, it is behaviour that damages another physically and/or mentally. Such behaviour can occur in a variety of forms: verbal (swearing and shouting); gestural (threatening, raising one's fist, tapping one's forehead with a finger); or physical (hitting, spitting, pinching, thumping, scratching or kicking). There are differences in seriousness and degree.

Causes of aggression

There are a number of causes that explain the origins of aggression: it can be part of someone's general makeup; a reaction to frustration; a reaction to being frightened; a reaction to another person's aggression; or a direct result of brain damage. We shall examine each cause briefly in turn.

Aggressive by nature

Each person is born with a certain amount of aggression that is innate. In our upbringing, we are taught that it is not socially acceptable to express aggressive behaviour. Sometimes, the aggression that is 'bottled up' inside us spills over. A socially acceptable way of expressing our naturally aggressive behaviour is by watching violent films, or watching or taking part in competitive sports. When aggressive feelings are released in unacceptable ways, for example, if they are not checked in social interactions with others, it indicates a degree of disorder or disturbance in psychological functioning.

Having an aggressive nature is also influenced by a person's early social environment. Aggression can develop through the behaviours that children observe or experience within family life, for example, an older brother who always behaves aggressively when he doesn't get his own way. Sometimes children grow up in a neighbourhood where aggressive behaviour is frequent and acceptable.

Persons with dementia can be aggressive because such behaviour has always been a part of their lives. They have always been aggressive. The life history of a person provides the carer with the key to his/her behaviour. If this were the explanation, Eva would not be able to do anything about Mrs Randal's behaviour. The social rule 'that aggressive behaviour is unacceptable' has become vague, or has been forgotten by Mrs Randal. She has little or no control any more over the aggressive tendencies that she has always had and the aggression will be expressed freely. Eva can do little to change this.

However, if Eva knows that Mrs Randal has behaved like this since she was a child, and that it is a part of her normal 'coping' repertoire, then Eva doesn't have to 'take it personally'. It will help Eva in that she does not have to take the blame for having provoked this behaviour needlessly.

Aggression as a reaction to frustration

Another cause of aggressive behaviour is frustration. Frustration is the feeling that occurs when you have not achieved what you wanted to, when you have had a setback, or when something is blocking you. One person may react (on the inside) by developing physical symptoms, stress or apathy. Another may react (on the outside) by taking it out on others. This is the type of aggression usually seen in persons with dementia, especially early in the course of the dementia process. They are limited in what they can do, or need to do, but at this stage, they are still aware of this. Here, aggressive behaviour results from a sense of loss, because of this awareness of mistakes and limitations, and because of the realisation that they are losing their grip on reality.

If this is the cause of Mrs Randal's behaviour, Eva might be able to do something about it. Where possible, she can try to look for the cause of Mrs Randal's frustration, and help to remove it. Sometimes this can be done by offering help, for example, when someone cannot find the right word they are looking for. It might be helpful to ask a question that requires the person to simply nod or shake their head in order to respond. By not asking too much or too little (which is usually intended as a means of protecting the person with dementia), carers can minimise his/her frustration. The biggest problem in the early stage of dementia is that the person denies, or will not admit to having difficulties, or will not say what is causing the frustration.

Aggression as a reaction to fear

Aggressive behaviour can also arise when persons feel frightened (unsafe), and deceived or cheated. In Chapter 9, we discussed at length that persons with dementia can feel unsafe because they are aware, and remained involved with everything that is happening to them. Their cognitive (mental) deterioration gradually brings them into a different perceptual world. This can bring them to the point where, sometimes intermittently, sometimes continually, they feel utterly alone, displaced and abandoned by all. It is well known that persons can behave aggressively when they feel frightened. Such aggression can be compared to the 'anger stage' of the grieving process following a deep personal loss. The aggression of the person with dementia is a reaction to the feeling of loss, not the awareness of the loss.

Finally, in thinking about this third explanation for aggression, Eva could try to think of ways to make Mrs Randal feel less frightened. She might do this by giving Mrs Randal more of her 'closeness', by staying near her, where Mrs Randal can sense (see, hear, feel) her presence. There are many times when Eva cannot sit with Mrs Randal for any length of time because of her work duties. This emphasises how important it is to be consistent by making one carer available to the person as much as possible. Eva can also try to ensure that Mrs Randal does not react aggressively as a result of something she does. For example, aggressive behaviour is often expressed when persons are being washed and showered in the morning. This behaviour might be triggered by the sudden and abrupt change from being in a warm bed, to standing (unsafely) in a cold bathroom, with all of the accompanying movements involved in getting there.

Things can be even more complicated by 'new losses activating old losses', 'personality' and 'life history'. Examples might be, if someone has had more disappointments or frustrations in life than they could process; or if a person with dementia very often felt insecure or frightened in the past. Such experiences can strengthen the feeling of aggression, which itself results from having dementia and feeling displaced. If this were the reason for Mrs Randal's aggression, it would be a way of saying that she is projecting and carrying her past unresolved feelings over to her present situation. Something similar is happening in the following example.

Mrs Gerrard was in the habit of 'snarling' and 'falling out' with Miriam, who didn't understand any of this behaviour. Miriam had already told her supervisor and colleagues that this sometimes made her sad. She was starting to feel guilty that she was doing something wrong. Why otherwise would Mrs Gerrard behave like this? One day, Stella came to take over from Miriam. As it happened, Stella had been talking to Mrs Gerrard's neighbour, who mentioned in passing that Mrs Gerrard had a daughter who was tall and blond, just like Miriam. This daughter had fought with her mother for years before leaving home and didn't visit her any more. Stella started to realise what the difficulty might be. Because Miriam resembled this daughter, Mrs Gerrard was projecting her negative feelings about her daughter onto Miriam. When this was discussed, it was agreed that Miriam should move to work in another family.

Aggression as a reaction to aggression

Aggressive behaviour can also occur as a reaction to the behaviour of others. If you are feeling attacked or threatened, or have the feeling that you are being betrayed or deceived, or are being roughly dealt with, then you may 'hit back in defence'. Sometimes, the carer's behaviour can be the cause of the aggression of the person with dementia. The reasons are numerous: because you are in too much of a rush and keep telling the person with dementia to 'hurry up'; or you grab someone's arm to help them get their cardigan on (but the person doesn't know that you are trying to put his/her arm in the sleeve); or because you are using a tone of voice that the person interprets as 'insulting', even though you meant well.

If this explanation of aggression is true for Mrs Randal, Eva will need to think very carefully about 'how' her behaviour is 'coming over'. It is very helpful to watch when such aggression occurs. In this instance, it was when Eva was putting Mrs Randal's panties on. Is the posture (squatting in front of her) the problem? Is it the personal nature of the help Eva is giving? Is the rapid succession of getting out of bed, washing, dressing (involving changing posture from sitting to standing, etc.), too much for Mrs Randal? Eva might observe how Mrs Randals reacts if she is washed 'below' in bed and her panties are put on while she is still lying down. Perhaps she could then be left to potter around in her bedroom for a while in her housecoat before she is helped with the rest of her toilet.

Aggression as a direct result of brain damage

Some aggressive behaviour is the result of specific damage to the brain. The aggression occurs unintentionally. It can happen for no reason, without provocation. It would be more correct to use the term 'aggressive disinhibition' to describe such occurrences of aggressive behaviour, in the same way as the term 'sexual disinhibition' was used in the previous chapter.

Aggressive behaviour in some persons with dementia can sometimes be traced to specific types of brain damage. It is usually not immediately evident that this might be the cause of aggression. Sometimes, this conclusion is only reached when all the other explanations (and possible solutions) have been examined/attempted and failed.

Assuming that this fifth reason is the explanation for Mrs Randal's aggressive behaviour towards Eva, then there is no way of changing or influencing it. Perhaps medication might help. However regretful it is, sometimes there is no other way of protecting yourself than by temporarily avoiding or excluding yourself from the person's company. What inevitably arises in such situations is where the person can best be cared for. At home and in residential settings such behaviour can be unmanageable. The problems may be easier to control in a nursing home or a psychiatric unit, but can the latter settings care for persons with dementia without giving them the feeling that they have been 'left out in the cold?'

Reactions of carers

Carers are better able to deal with aggressive behaviour when they can identify the cause. How carers then react depends on their own feelings and experiences.

Different feelings

Carers react differently to aggression. Some feel sad, others feel aggressive and yet others feel powerless. One carer becomes angry and hits back at any type of aggressive behaviour whereas another reacts by being 'panic stricken' and frightened. Some carers react somewhat laconically, and aren't particularly bothered – at most, it makes them feel a little impatient.

It is not unreasonable that feelings such as fear, panic and anger are related to an individual's life history. Some carers will have seen or experienced violence, even if it did not in their home life. The next example illustrates what is meant by this.

> One day, a carer no longer dared to go to Mr Silver's room alone because she said that he had made her feel very uncomfortable. After enquiring what had happened, the carer said that he had a 'wild look' in his eyes and that had tried to hit her. Her father, who was often moody and angry, also had had this look when he was upset with her. A severe beating usually followed. In terms of counter-transference: the carer found herself in a situation that caused her to project unresolved feelings towards her father onto Mr Silver. This caused her to react in an overly fearful way to the aggressive behaviour of Mr Silver.

Mixed feelings

There can be large differences between carers in terms of the feelings they experience as a result of the aggressive behaviour of persons with dementia. It can also happen that a carer feels several, even opposing, emotions when confronted with the aggressive behaviour of a client. A carer might feel both frightened and vulnerable, but at the same time feel understanding and compassion for the client.

When carers can't say exactly what they feel when a person with dementia is behaving aggressively towards them, this can be a sign that they have mixed feelings. This sometimes points to the difficulty some carers have in admitting that they are experiencing strong feelings, and that these feelings have a special personal meaning for them.

For example, a carer may not readily admit to feeling angry or panic-stricken because, as she admits, she has difficulty in keeping these feelings under control. Perhaps some feelings bring back too much pain and it feels safer not to talk about them and therefore not to let them 'hurt' again. This is one of the reasons why certain carers may tend to hush up all the conflicts they experience at work. If they don't, sometimes so much aggression surfaces that they are overwhelmed by it. You only have to have experienced aggression once, for it to have such negative consequences in your life. You'll do anything to avoid being confronted by it again.

Extra difficult: unresolved old pain

When a carer tries to avoid the aggressive behaviour of persons with dementia, for example, by refusing to work with a client any longer, it can be a sign that he/she is trying to protect him/herself from strong negative feelings. If aggressive behaviour makes a carer feel very powerless, it may result in thoughts like: 'I can never do anything right', or, 'She doesn't like me.' It often happens that such a carer feels rejected by other people as well, and keeps looking for the blame inside him/herself. The inevitable consequence is that this carer will continue to have difficulties with aggressive behaviour. Any number of things can lead to a reactivation of unresolved old pain, and then to 'counter-transference'.

Extra difficult: devoid of emotional credit

For a carer, it is even more difficult to deal with aggressive behaviour if they have never been able to build up a good relationship with the person with dementia. We see this in instances where, every time the carer tries to make contact or help the client, he/she responds aggressively. 'You have to help them, but there's no joy or satisfaction in it.' This can lead to the situation where the person with dementia, at an emotional level, has no 'credit' left with the carer. That makes it difficult to find any solution. It can make the carer feel disheartened, uninterested and also indifferent. Note the indifference in the following comment: 'I was hardly shocked, actually I had to laugh inside to see him making such a fuss.' Sayings such as: 'Of course it was very annoying when it happened, but I won't let that influence my feelings', indicate that the client's aggressive behaviour is being tolerated because they don't have any 'emotional credit' left with the carer. To receive a sudden snarl or swipe from a person with dementia whom you like, is usually easier to deal with than receiving the same from someone whom you dislike.

Extra difficult: unexpected and apparently deliberate

When the aggressive behaviour of a person with dementia comes 'out of the blue', it is often very difficult for the carer to deal with. This is also the case when such behaviour is (justly or unjustly) seen to be 'a game', or deliberate.

Unexpected

Someone suddenly starts shouting at you. Then they kick you. You turn around and get a slap in the face. If a carer has developed a certain trust with a client and a certain physical intimacy, the carer 'dares' to be close to the person and feels safe and comfortable in helping. This 'safe' feeling, and its resultant 'spontaneity', suddenly vanishes when aggression has been shown. The carer thereafter remains 'at a safe distance' and is cautious. He/she must always be 'on their guard'. The carer wants to be close, but out of self-concern, must remain at a distance. This feels unnatural, at least for a time, because the trust has been broken. It takes time to re-establish trust.

Apparently on purpose

The person with dementia starts to yell at you, to scratch you or bites your arm. This can feel as though the client is terminating the existing emotional bond between you. You were counting on their trust and there was already a certain amount of intimacy. Although you wanted to be close, you must now remain 'at a distance', although there has been no apparent reason for this change. This is what appears to be happening at the end of Chapter 12, where Mrs Turner appears to be 'cutting Ann off'. Recall that, on closer examination, the opposite is true.

Dilemma

Aggressive behaviour is difficult for carers to deal with because it presents them with a dilemma. It brings them into a 'conflict of loyal-ties'. In the previous chapter we saw that persons with dementia exhibit 'proximity/closeness-seeking behaviour'. As a rule, this even-tually leads to an emotional bond, even sometimes to a sort of adoption process and a trusted relationship within which a certain type of physical intimacy occurs. Aggressive behaviour forces carers to remain at a distance and become defensive, not only for self-defence, but also so as not to become overwhelmed by fear, panic, humiliation or anger. The aggressive behaviour of a person with dementia can cause a conflict between 'drawing closer' and 'pulling away'. Although increasing closeness is needed, sometimes a safe distance must be maintained. This can lead to considerable damage to an existing emotional bond, or, at the least, to cause it to stagnate. What remains especially difficult for a carer, is knowing that the client is actually being deprived of what they need.

It is rare for carers to have little or no difficulty with the aggressive behaviour of persons with dementia. Aggression almost always causes the 'receiver' to (temporarily) distance themselves. Shock, fear and astonishment often cause the same reactions. It leads to the carer asking the question: 'How secure is my attachment to this person?' The problem in brief is: aggressive behaviour forces carers to distance themselves, even though they don't want to. This creates negative feelings, but also discredits the previously existing positive ones. The latter observation is even harder to deal with than the first shock, or feelings of fear or astonishment.

How to deal with aggression

Know your own reaction patterns

Speaking to colleagues and supervisors is necessary, not only to identify and work through one's first emotional reactions, but also to help to sort out your conflicting emotions. This means that the persons you speak to need to be motivated and have time to listen to you seriously. To be helpful, they need to have time to listen to you (without coming to simplistic conclusions like, 'Get another job', as Eva's husband did). It usually isn't enough for colleagues and supervisors to act as 'sounding boards' though. Meaningful questions need to be asked which take you further than 'just letting off steam'.

Questions need to help you to identify and formulate the problem as specifically as possible. Questions that might have helped Eva are: 'What was worse, the pain or the shock'? and 'Which word would best describe your first feeling: bewilderment, humiliation, fear or anger?'

Eva has already said that she was first shocked, and then, that she asked herself whether she had done anything wrong, and then, that she got angry. Actually, that order of things is quite remarkable. Shock and anger are pure emotions. Asking yourself whether you did anything wrong is a 'thinking activity'. Or was it? Perhaps it was, but we don't know because no proper evaluation of the incident took place. That is why Eva wrestled with the situation for so long. Perhaps if there had been, Eva would have discovered that 'asking yourself if' is not a true account of a feeling. Perhaps the shock immediately activated a feeling of guilt. If that were the case, she could have taken either a 'therapeutic' or a 'pragmatic' approach to the situation. She could have looked at the mechanism and history of this 'shock–guilt' relationship. She could have come to accept that, given her previous life experience, shock leads directly to feelings of guilt. Even being aware that such a relationship between feelings exists is often enough to 'disconnect' them.

In team settings, the pragmatic approach is usually the most suitable. The team does NOT continue to ask questions like: 'Why do you think that happened?' or 'What feeling from your past do you associate with this situation? Instead, the team should ask questions like: 'Do you think that you would be just as shocked if this happened again?' 'Would you feel just as guilty?' This example needs some clarification to show how 'talking to colleagues' is only constructive if they can listen constructively. (Those of you who are afraid that your team does not yet have enough ability or experience to 'listen' well, could begin by starting with yourselves. Try to listen carefully and identify what is happening when, for example, one of your colleagues, is referring to a problem. Team members often learn more from experiencing one real example than from looking it up in a book.)

Taking time for a collegial exchange of ideas to look for the possible cause of aggression in a client should not be 'a great luxury'. To come to an exact diagnosis of, and to be able to identify exactly what the cause of aggression is, is rarely possible with regards to a person with dementia. Too many factors cloud the issue. Colleagues will identify and interpret the aggressive behaviour from many different viewpoints. One will look for explanations in life history, another will ask about physical problems such as urinary tract infections, constipation, etc. Another might look at the noise levels in the environment and the possibility of sensory overload.

All those different ideas make it impossible for the carer voicing the problem to have a clear oversight and look for a solution. Problems are usually complex. However, in practice, it does appear that meetings (whether 'team', 'client' or 'care planning'), do have a positive effect on how carers try to deal with the aggression of clients in the future. Such meetings help because you can learn that others are wrestling with similar problems, and that your problem is being taken seriously and not 'dismissed out of hand'. This increases your self-confidence.

The starting assumption, however, is that collegial discussion takes place in a constructive atmosphere. It isn't about who has access to 'the truth'. Rather, discussions are about 'asking' and 'listening', to be able to consider possible solutions for helping a care-giving relationship that has 'gone sour'.

Trying to find out why

Understanding and identifying possible causes, gives carers the chance to step into the shoes of the perceptual world of the person with dementia. The process of trying to understand 'why', often provides carers with possible handles to prevent aggression. In this way, the person with dementia will not be 'written off' as an 'unappreciative stranger'. Also, the carer is less likely to blame themselves for the aggressive behaviour of the person with dementia. Feelings of uncertainty and guilt will be reduced ('It must be my fault!'). Hopefully this will allow a carer to continue to think of the person as being likeable, kind, or sympathetic.

That is not to say that no measures should be taken by carers to protect themselves from aggressive situations. Understanding the possible causes of aggressive behaviour helps carers to be better prepared when it is encountered and to continue to accept the client as a person when it occurs. This can help prevent damaging the emotional bond between carer and the person with dementia. The unarticulated and rude shouting of a client can be better accepted when the carer realises that the person is no longer able to say what he/she wants and feels powerless. In the same way, it can help to realise that unresolved feelings from the past can resurface and make someone angry again. For example, seeing an oriental carer might evoke associations for a person with dementia of being in a Japanese prisoner-of-war camp.

Carers, overall, do accept aggression in persons with dementia very well. The proof of this is that in day-to-day life outside work, they generally do not accept the same type of behaviour from persons who do not have dementia.

Reducing external stimulation (triggers)

In almost all of the causes of aggressive behaviour, external triggers play an additional role. (Triggers usually 'give rise to' aggressive expression, rather than being the 'cause of' the aggression.)

Although you are not doing anything wrong, the very thing that you are doing, or your very presence can create an overload that takes the person with dementia beyond the 'breaking point'. In general, carers are unaware of how much energy they emit to their environment. When they are talking, they very often continue doing things that have nothing to do with the topic of the conversation. For example, a carer might be removing the flowers and crumbs from the table ready for setting the table and at the same time is asking her client whether they need to go to the toilet. Or, while putting one person's shoes on, a carer might be calling over her shoulder to someone else. Often, carers' movements are fast. Their voice is some-times loud. Both in your actions and conversations, you might use many gestures. In general, carers would do well to reduce their speed and energy levels somewhat, when in the presence of clients. When someone is threatening to become, or is already, aggressive, a 'calm, quiet presence' is the best way of reducing or preventing aggression.

Hallmarks of calm, quiet behaviour

A few hallmarks of quiet, calm behaviour are the as follows: smooth, slow, graceful movements; a calm voice, a little lower than normal tone of voice. Use this tone of voice consistently. Use short, clear sentences/phrases/interrogatives such as, 'It's not that easy is it?' 'Don't rush.' 'Life's strange isn't it?' These aren't exhortations, but a sort of calming 'background music'.

You can also try to reduce every action to small, manageable pieces. For example, in helping someone to get out of a chair, first make eye contact, explain what you are going to do, give them the time to look around, offer your hand or arm, wait to see if the person accepts it and then invite them to stand up (more with your own posture and gesture than through words or commands). Try to remain calm when the person becomes upset (by shouting, being obstinate or making insinuations), with a hint of agreement if appro-priate, certainly without disagreement. The agreement is meant to acknowledge the feelings of frustration and upset, not the content of the insinuation. If agreement is inappropriate, remain silent. Do not ask for explanations of aggressive behaviour (avoid asking why), or demean, or punish the person.

It isn't easy. What makes it even more difficult is that you should not give the person with dementia the impression that you are ridi-culing them. If you are getting the feeling that you are 'playing a little game' and not taking the person with dementia seriously, it is better to go away for a few minutes. Persons with dementia can sense 'off-handedness'. It is also important that others do not interfere with the situation, thereby bringing extra 'stimulation' and 'busy-ness' with them. It is better for them to retreat from the visual field of the person for a while until things have settled down again.

Finally, sometimes carers are confronted, directly or indirectly, with the aggressive behaviour of a spouse or a child towards the person with dementia. Sometimes, vice versa, where you witness your client reacting aggressively to another. For the 'receiver' it can be an incomprehensible and sad confrontation. For example, a mother, whom the children had always regarded as a 'peacemaker' and the person who resolved conflict, is unrecognisable to them at times now because she swears so forcibly. 'She was never like this', the children say, ashamed.

This latter situation (the client behaving aggressively towards their family) is generally easier to deal with than the opposite. The carer is not the victim and can 'pick up' and console the family member/s. Thereafter, try with the help of a third party, to work out what led up to the aggressive behaviour. This can bring about a better understanding, and possibly even the insight into how to avoid the behaviour being repeated.

The first situation (the family being aggressive towards your client) is usually more difficult to deal with. Carers, as a rule, side with the 'weakest' party, the victim. Even though carers may understand the behaviour (for example, a partner yelling out about feelings of powerlessness, or hitting out because of feelings of disappointment that the plans for retirement have been thwarted), they cannot accept it. Quite simply, the person with dementia has no way of defending him/herself. It is an unequal fight. It is not easy to discuss such matters with a family. You will have to wait for the right moment, comment and 'atmosphere'. It is often better to wait until your own emotions are under control before reacting to such a situation. Whether you deal with this situation by yourself, or after consulting with colleagues, or involve colleagues, will depend upon the gravity of the situation. Is the person with dementia being shouted at 'only incidentally', or is he/she being more seriously victimised?

16 A basis for tomorrow

Eileen has been working with families of persons with dementia for years.

> Through trial and error, I have learned what I can and cannot say to family members. In the beginning, for example, I didn't realise that I could sometimes get the sufferer to do things that the family members almost couldn't. I just did my work. I never really stopped to think how the family members felt about it. It was only later, after thinking about it more deeply, that I started to realise what my 'success' must feel like for the spouse or child.

Eileen admits that, however welcome her help is from a practical point of view, she is sometimes viewed with a degree of scepticism by family members. As a carer, you can suddenly find yourself within the intimacy of a family. Not only that, but whether you want to or not, you become a spectator of a long-existing relationship, complete with all its patterns and idiosyncrasies. Whatever else happens, the family watches while a perfect stranger becomes 'attached' to their loved one. Eileen says:

> The spouse or child, naturally, has asked for help, but they aren't exactly bargaining for having to deal with a new person in the house. Usually such jealousy goes away after a while. But in the beginning, I sometimes had the feeling that I could never do things right, as far as the family were concerned. They could react to every single thing I did. If you were bathing someone, they kept on hovering around – giving one instruction here, another there, getting an extra towel for you and so forth – all the things that you can do, or find out, for yourself. I understood that it was difficult for them, having a stranger around who 'takes over', but on the other hand, I kept thinking: 'Man, just go and do something with the time you have now. Do something you can't do when I'm gone.' They all complain about that you know – that

they don't get a moment's rest, no chance to do anything 'for themselves'. I'd go crazy, too, if my husband kept roaming around me and getting underfoot all day long.

At the moment, Eileen visits a couple every other day of the week. The husband is the person with dementia. Mrs Storey, a somewhat fragile woman, wants to keep her husband at home as long as possible, whatever the cost. She says that her husband is sick and needs help, but his dementia isn't really that bad. The couple have two sons. One lives in Canada and the other in New Zealand. They hardly have any contact with neighbours. When Eileen is working, she has to constantly be on her guard to avoid having arguments with Mrs Storey, who finds it very difficult to hand over the care of her husband to another. She would rather have done everything herself, but because she can no longer lift her husband, she had to ask for help. Even so, at every chance she says, 'I haven't got a life any more with this man in this condition.' To speak to her in order to convince her to let others help more, or to enrol her husband for day care is impossible. She sees it as her duty, she says, to care for him herself, to the end.

Eileen says:

> On the one hand, I can understand her feelings. Deep in my heart, I have a great respect for her. But on the other hand, she sometimes irritates me no end. It's all so complicated: she says that the dementia isn't really that bad, but at the same time she complains that she has to do so much for him. She moans about her life, but refuses all help. She complains about how tired she is of the situation, but won't take on board any information whatsoever. It seems that Mrs Storey will first have to become really ill before she gives in and accepts more help for her husband.

Layout of the chapter

First, the relationship between carer, family and the person with dementia will be discussed. The family suffers a personal loss because of the changes that are happening to their partner, father or mother. Caring for the person with dementia usually means some sort of additional burden, on top of all of the other/normal problems and duties that they have. When part of the care is handed over to a professional carer, a whole new situation comes into being. Everyone has to find their own way of dealing with this, not only in practical terms, but also emotionally. Thereafter, the first phase of this 'new situation' will be discussed. Carers begin by getting an impression of the persons in the household, their needs and expectations. How can carers, within their own abilities make sure that they are 'doing their best'? The request for care, initial discussions and arrangements are usually made without the carer being present. Of course the carer will try to get as much information as possible beforehand, but the mutual process of getting accustomed to one another only begins when the carer enters the home. How do carers present themselves?

This chapter (and hence, the book) ends by taking a look at the future. In the relationships between family, person with dementia and carer, each day will bring its own specific cares and worries. The way in which these are dealt with depends upon a person's past, but also their future perspective. The future holds one thing for certain. There will come a time when this present period of caring is finished. You never know when or how. What happens each and every day will later affect how carers look back at the person with dementia and the family.

More than loss

In the previous chapter, we looked closely at the emotions generated in families when one of them is affected by dementia. We discussed the grieving that occurred over the loss of the person that they knew, who had a very special meaning for them, and who is disappearing into an unreachable world. What makes it even more difficult is that the person with dementia continues to live with them. They cannot 'say their good-byes' in the same way as at the graveside. This process of loss is rather similar to that of a 'missing person', where hope, against all better judgement, gets in the way of grieving.

We also discussed the different kinds of coping mechanisms, which, especially in the uncertain, creeping progression of the first stage, lead to tension. The strange behaviour of father may be denied and/or minimised (for the sake of the children). The children may later blame the mother for withholding the truth, which will only add to her grief. Or, instead, a mother may confide in her children about the problems she is having with father; but the children think she is exaggerating. Whenever they visit, father is always pleasant. Sure, he sometimes 'gets the wrong end of the stick', but who doesn't. So then, mother remains isolated with all her problems. She also wonders why her husband is able to be so 'normal' when the children are around, but cannot 'hold himself together' when they are alone. The 'confusion', of which she is so frightened, but cannot see clearly with her own eyes, can lead to confrontational 'memory tests'. 'Do you know who I am?' 'What is the name of the monarch?' 'What did we have for lunch today?' Perhaps, she reproaches him when he makes a mess, or makes inappropriate comments, obstructs her as he walks in front of her, distorts the television image or sound, and sits in the armchair, doing nothing but drumming his fingers on the arm rest. When family members can no longer deny the reality, regrets often arise. The only person who can forgive you, is yourself. When you are able to do this, you have already come a long way.

We also looked at the changing future perspective. For the partner, a dream of living peacefully together into old age, perhaps, even 'a second youth', is shattered. The possibility of becoming ill yourself, which most older persons have thought about, becomes unthinkable. Almost every partner caring for a spouse at home, or visiting them in a care home says: 'I cannot allow myself to become ill.'

Care never comes alone

A widow first helped her mother-in-law to care for her sick husband. Shortly after his death, the mother-in-law began to suffer from dementia. As they had experienced so much loss together, the widow took her mother-in-law into her home, against the protests of her only daughter who, with her son, had come home to live with her mother after her divorce. There were many conflicts: about the boxes of incontinence material that took up space everywhere, and about who should stay at home during the holidays. The widow could not care for her grandson as well as her mother-in-law, although the daughter wanted a free hand to do what she wanted to. This is one story. There are thousands like it.

For children who are carers, often the caring is an additional task on top of many others: housekeeping, maintaining relationships and working. Sometimes a family shares the work evenly because everyone has an equal understanding and motivation to share the load. That isn't always the case though.

A young partner of an older person with dementia sometimes still has children at home who also need a lot of attention and time. It is a bitter defeat when the children go elsewhere and no longer bring their friends home. One's sexual life, normal bickering sessions and even the deep discussions cease. In a short period of time, the partner, who has no desire to relinquish normal life, is 'forced to follow the rhythm' of the person with dementia. This often feels not only like a 'loss', but also a great 'injustice'.

When one member of a couple gets dementia, the whole of life seems to revolve around caring and grieving for that person. Just at this difficult time, other 'life issues' can surface. Take Mrs Storey, for example. She has certainly always been sad that, first one son, and then the other emigrated. Possibly she and her husband found comfort in the fact that their sons had good jobs. Perhaps, the increasing unemployment in Europe gave them some solace: 'It was wise of the boys to go where the work was, it was for the best.' But such musings are intellectual arguments to suppress unpleasant feelings. Now that her husband is emigrating to a world that is incomprehensible and unreachable, probably all of the old painful questions are surfacing again.

> Why am I alone in caring? Wasn't I a good mother? I know I have a surly character, but I couldn't do anything about that could I? I've never had my grandchildren on my lap. The one and only time I saw them, all one could talk about was pop stars and the other about baseball. Henry was good at talking about that, but I wasn't. I think I would have turned out quite differently if the grandchildren had been born here and I had had the chance to visit them regularly. I wish I could talk to Henry about it, but I can't. We're not 'together' anymore.

A snooper

Receiving help in doing housework or caring for a person with dementia, is usually a welcome relief for family. It helps solve a number of practical problems. This is especially so when family members live elsewhere. They see the care as a 'lightening' of their daily or weekly programme of activities. It is important that family members agree with one another that the help is needed, and what kind of help is needed. It is not uncommon for 'other' family members to have a different opinion from the person running the home and doing all the daily caring. For the primary carer, receiving help can mean more than an outsider could imagine at first glance.

> Mrs Worth is the primary carer for her mother, who lives about a 15-minute journey away. When they were all living at home, her two brothers, her sister and herself, she always felt that she was 'the least successful'. Even later, when everyone had left home, and only saw each other for special events or celebrations, she couldn't compete with the 'success stories' they told about their children and careers. When mother turned eighty, everyone turned up to visit. Mother didn't seem to notice much of what was going on and spent most of the time dozing in a chair. Everyone was very nice and caring. They paid more attention than usual to Mrs Worth. Perhaps, because she wanted to have something interesting to talk about, she elaborated about how 'heavy' the care for mother was becoming, and how she was almost breaking down under the strain of it all. The result of this was that the family called an emergency meeting and decided there and then that mother had to go into a nursing

home. In anticipation of a place, a carer had been found. No matter how much Mrs Worth protested and then tried to minimise the comments she had made during mother's eightieth birthday party, fourteen days later, a carer arrived on the doorstep.

Mrs Worth viewed the carer with mixed feelings. In fact, she had not exaggerated about mother at the birthday party, and the care really was becoming too much for her. On the other hand, since the onset of the dementia and all of the caring, a much more intimate bond between herself and her mother had come to exist than that between mother and the other children. Her feelings of responsibility gave her a certain feeling of importance. The arrival of the new carer gave new life to her feelings of 'insignificance'.

Also an extra burden

For children and spouses, regardless of how much the carer's help is needed, an extra feeling of 'burden' also accompanies the help. They have to get used to a different daily routine and another way of working.

Mrs Storey, for example, will probably get up earlier than she used to. She wants to be washed and dressed before Eileen arrives. It isn't just for reasons of pride that she doesn't want to open the door in her night-gown, there is also a very practical reason. When Eileen goes to help her husband, the bedroom and the bathroom are in use. She might have to wait half an hour in her night-gown before she can use them again. By that time she'd like to make a cup of tea for everyone. The fact that she used to 'have to' get up early still influences her mood in the morning. She needs a lot of time to 'get into the swing of things' and she is easily distracted. That makes her 'edgy', and that prevents her bowels from opening, and then she has a sore tummy for the rest of the day. There are also 'deeper-seated' feelings of discomfort at having a carer take over the care of her husband. Perhaps she feels that he is the only one who still needs her. He doesn't react much, but when he smiles, that's all the reward she needs. Recently though, it seems that he smiles more at Eileen than he does at her. That makes her feel jealous. Sometimes she'd like to have a long, good cry; but she doesn't know how to any more. It was never her 'strong point'.

With Mrs Worth and Mrs Storey, the carers feel negative emotions directed towards them. These feelings can be better accepted when carers know that they are not directed against them personally, and when they can understand the reasons. It doesn't make for a pleasant working environment, though. Above all, this isn't a very beneficial environment for the person with dementia to live in, because the tensions do not go unnoticed, and can 'unnerve' (distress) them further.

Help where it's needed

When a partner or child of a person with dementia has to 'share' or 'hand over' the caring, there are usually some difficulties. Most families wait until they are desperate before asking for help. They have already used up all of their emotional and physical energy reserves. In such situations, a sort of 'numbness' can be present. This makes it difficult for family members to adjust to the new situation, even though it brings some relief. Most of them are past being able to be 'defensive' and hence, are especially vulnerable. It is also common for help only to be arranged when the family has reached their limit, and is in crisis. This point is not easy to determine. Take the Storey family, for example. When is help needed there? What type of help is needed? Often, the care that is really needed can only be determined once a carer is in place. To do this, it is best at first to wait and see where the problems lie. Only then can the type of help that is most needed be determined. Is it taking on the care of the person with dementia or supporting the family? Such things cannot be determined by merely objectively looking at the 'care load'. For example, how much extra work does the increasing dependence of the person with dementia really make for the primary carer (partner or child)? The 'ability to carry the burden' also plays a role: for example, does the primary carer have physical or psychological problems?

More than an 'addition' problem

In the beginning, Eileen used to plan her work like the adding up of a sum:

> If I reduce Mrs Storey's workload, and burden, then she is free to do the things that she otherwise could not do. This will allow her to cope better with the rest of the care she has to provide during the remainder of the day. Perhaps she could have a nap in the afternoon so that she can make up for some of the sleep she loses at night because of her husband. She could use the time to go and see a friend, or she could go to the shops.

But it wasn't that easy. Mrs Storey continued to walk around the house beside Eileen, 'on her last legs', even with her help.

A mistake that is often unconsciously made, is that the family carer is seen as a sort of 'unpaid worker'. This is expressed in very small things. For example, on the very first day, the carer might say to the spouse, 'If you just show me where everything is, and which clothes your husband is wearing today, I can manage just fine.' The carer is treating the spouse like a colleague, from whom she is 'taking over'. It is as if the morning ritual has no meaning for the spouse. Perhaps, it is only during these moments of close physical contact, that the spouse has found a means of expressing her close attachment to her husband.

There are other ways in which family carers are sometimes placed in the role of 'unpaid helpers'. On entering the home a carer might ask: 'Was your wife a bit more settled last night?' The carer knows that the wife is often very restless during the night. The husband has already told the carer several times that this is what is 'doing him in'. The question appears to be sympathetically intended, but in fact, it is only an invitation for the husband to talk about the unrest of his wife. If the carer, instead, had asked: 'Were you able to sleep a bit last night?', then the husband could have received some direct attention and may have started to talk about himself. Perhaps he would have said, 'I couldn't get to sleep. I was actually happy that my wife got up to go to the toilet. That, at least was a bit of a distraction.' Perhaps he would then feel the carer's interest, and say a little more – that he had been anxious and fretful all night. Perhaps he would continue to tell you even more. But it might be that he only returns to talk more about himself much later. The important thing is that the question asked should be about him, and not only about the observations he made as a 'helper'.

Extending a hand

When a family has cared for a person with dementia for a long period of time, the carer can never really 'take over' the care. The carer can try to divert the problems and/or share the care. This is usually a slow process that can be 'steered' only one step at a time. The carer can only extend a hand here and there in order to take the next step together.

The first day, Eileen could only ask Mrs Storey if she would show her a few times how she did things to help her husband. That, at least helped Eileen to know how Mrs Storey wanted things done. After all, Mrs Storey knows best how her husband likes things done. Naturally Eileen wouldn't say this within earshot of Mr Storey, because he might have a different view of things than his wife. Perhaps he is no longer able to express this in an 'effective' way. Furthermore, the relationship between the Storey couple is none of Eileen's business. What is important is that Mrs Storey probably thinks that she knows what is best for her husband, and that this is acknowledged. When Mrs Storey is hesitant about things, this is the best time for her to gradually start to talk/share her thoughts with Eileen.

If, after a few days, Mrs Storey entrusts Eileen completely with the morning care of Mr Storey, it would not be very clever of Eileen to say triumphantly afterwards, that it was 'a piece of cake'. Mrs Storey would be much better served by hearing: 'I don't know how you have managed to keep doing all this for so long.' This is an invitation for her to talk about her feelings. Perhaps Mrs Storey was pacing through the house for a whole hour, frustrated beyond belief while Eileen was with her husband. The previous days were already 'different', but now, the old familiar pattern has definitely come to an end.

With the question: 'Do you have to get up earlier, just for me?' Eileen is suggesting that Mrs Storey is doing something for her. Perhaps Mrs Storey would answer by saying that she has always been an 'early riser'. 'Whether I get a little or a lot of sleep, I always wake at six and then get up immediately. That's still in me from the days when my sons were little and my husband had to get off to work early.' Perhaps, unintentionally, Mrs Storey will be a little proud of herself, think about the past and remember some of the things that gave her a sense of satisfaction.

It could also be that Mrs Storey explains that her 'early rising', isn't at all easy. 'When my husband has been restless during the night, I'm dead tired of a morning.' Eileen could then pick up with, 'Then actually, my coming here on those mornings isn't much of a help to you.' Mrs Storey might reply, 'Yes, but even before you came I had to get up early to help my husband, so it doesn't make any difference.' Regardless of how Eileen responds to this, she will likely not get much further in the conversation at this very moment. It doesn't matter. Eileen has given Mrs Storey a signal that she can talk about her fatigue, and the feeling that 'nothing makes much of a difference' anymore. Merely talking about such things isn't enough. But at this moment, it is still too early to look for a solution together. Mrs Storey has been 'ploughing along' for so long that the 'ploughing' is part of her.

In the beginning, 'when the territory has to be explored from both sides', it is important for the carer to refer back to the comments that family carers have made about themselves. 'You were saying yesterday that your old friend was planning on coming over for a visit. Has she been?' 'You were expecting a phone call from Canada on Sunday. Was your son able to phone?' 'Did you get a chance to make the steak and kidney pie that you were hoping to have this past weekend?' Such small comments show that the carer is listening to the person and is taking them seriously. It is also a very sensible way of finding out whether there are small problems that the carer and family could possibly solve together. For example, 'I know that your dentures are bothering you. You said they weren't fitting properly any more. Do you want to go to see the dentist?' Then, the carer might discuss which time is best, so that she can look after things at home while the spouse goes to keep her appointment. Mrs Storey said a while back, that she wanted to buy her husband a pair of warm trousers for the winter, but she hasn't done anything about it yet. Eileen has found out in the meanwhile which store Mrs Storey likes to go to, and so she says: 'The sales are on this week. I'm here on Monday anyway, so if you want to go then, at least you'll be one of the first ones through the door.' This is how Eileen tries to gain the favour of Mrs Storey. It is these small successes that are so important for family members. It helps them to break through the feeling of 'numbness', of 'being on a treadmill'.

Becoming a partner

If family members have been caring for someone for a long time, their 'care' doesn't evaporate when a carer steps through the door, or when the person with dementia is admitted to a care facility. Up until that moment, the practical caring gestures were a sort of 'vehicle' for their care. Caring helped them to express their concern for the person and to keep a line of communication open. Now, there is only emptiness.

Different reaction patterns

People react differently to the arrival of a carer. One will withdraw and lick his/her wounds in secret. Such persons will probably initially appear to be reserved towards a carer. The chances are, that when such a person goes to visit their spouse or parent in a residential or nursing home, they will barely greet the staff or ask how they are doing. A carer who already has a certain relationship with the new resident is easily tempted to make small demonstrations of their successes. 'We had such a good lunch, didn't we Mrs Baker?' It is intended to be information to allay the concerns of Mr Baker. He is then almost obliged to say, 'So, you had a good lunch then!' His body language is saying 'You can go now nurse!' Mr Randal, whom we discussed in Chapter 15, was also reserved and business-like with Eva at first. He made a sort of a 'work agreement' with Eva and for the rest, kept quiet about the real difficulties. Later, Eva regretted her 'unsuspecting' demeanour. It is probable that she wasn't entirely 'blinkered' to what was going on, but likely unconsciously was respecting the boundaries that Mr Randal had put in place.

Not everyone works through their feelings of loss in silence. Carers can receive waves of 'mistrust' and 'complaints'. 'Did you clean my wife's glasses?' 'Will you make sure that my husband drinks enough?' 'Why is father wearing his Sunday trousers in the middle of the week?' 'Mother's cardigan is full of stains. Why don't you put a napkin on her?' Even though you understand that this is one way in which families 'let off the steam' because of their frustration, it remains difficult to deal with such behaviour. The first step, is naturally to take the remark seriously. 'You're right to be making sure the glasses are clean. It's so important, and it's these small things that others might not notice.' Don't say: 'That was the only pair of clean trousers that were hanging in the closet.' That might be picked up as a criticism of the person's wardrobe. Saying, 'I'm sorry about the trousers', without any other defensive comments, leaves more scope for conversation. Perhaps the family won't take this opportunity to speak further. But it is human nature to express regret. The other person is apologising for circumstances. 'Perhaps I should buy some more trousers.' This offers the carer a beautiful handle for further conversation. 'Do you think that is necessary? Maybe we could look through the closet together for a minute to see what's there.' Together, you can have a look, and a discussion. Afterwards, if the family have gone shopping, they will likely tell the carer about the outcome. Sometimes it is such very small things that unlock a person's heart.

Small presents

A carer is also a person. It is easier to work when people think you are pleasant and like you. Family members also need to be liked. Some families are immediately jovial and generous. They make jokes, offer biscuits and show an interest in all manner of personal information about the carer. That isn't always easy to deal with. Sometimes, if the carer tries to be a little bit withholding, the family re-doubles its efforts. If the carer still does not respond, the family sometimes suddenly labels them as an 'old misery'. If the carer plays along with the game of: 'Isn't it lovely that we all get along so well', a number of serious misunderstandings can arise. There appears to be an 'intimate' relationship although the contrary is true. It is the person with dementia who stands the chance of being left on the sidelines in such situations.

In a care home, where colleagues work beside each other and relieve each other at shift changes, unintentional 'popularity' contests can arise. This does nothing to help 'team spirit', and this also can be to the detriment of the care of the person with dementia. Once a pattern has come into existence, it is difficult to break it. Prevention is better, even though it is easier said than done.

It is usually better for the carer to be a bit reserved in the beginning, even with families who are inclined to be 'a bit over the top' in their friendliness. It could be that the 'bottled friendship' that we just referred to, will disappear and make room for a more realistic interaction. When this doesn't happen naturally, it might help if the carer says: 'I'm amazed by the way you keep up your spirits.' That may have the consequence that the family member starts to give you any number of examples of their 'high spirits'. That doesn't matter. What is important is that the person is now, not being jolly, but trying to give you an image of themselves: 'Never one to feel defeated.' 'Ever robust, even though it's not always easy.' Sometimes, unintentionally, such families will change their mood into one more suitable in which to care for the person with dementia. They were able to talk about themselves. Perhaps that gave them some peace. Perhaps it also helped to bring some peace to the relationship that the carer had with that family.

In conclusion

In Chapter 11, we said that carers can come to feel like a family member. In this chapter, we have looked at the situation from the perspective of the family. They carry a portion of the care, and therefore, because of all of the past losses they have endured, there is a new emptiness. The carer tries to offer them a hand in such a way as to bridge an 'emotional chasm' between them. That can only happen when both parties have patience and respect for one another's difficulties and boundaries. This is also a kind of an adoption process. There will inevitably be an end to the relationship between carer and family. Perhaps, after the death of the person, there will be a time when both parties need to see each other. As a carer, you need to be aware that at some time the family will want to 'have the feeling that this period of their life has been closed'. This will include ending the relationship with the carer. This is why carers are well advised to continually maintain 'their place', even when a bond of trust has been established.

Carers will have to 'create a bit of distance' from time to time, so that at the end of the journey they are not 'burnt out'. This distance is necessary to keep an oversight of the situation, but also, to be able to continually find the right way to deal with the changing course of things. Carers cannot 'take over' responsibilities that belong to the family. They can help to 'carry' the responsibility and to give it shape. In such circumstances, both family and carer will be able to say goodbye to the person with dementia, despite all of the sorrow. Usually both carers and family have increasingly taken the person with dementia into their hearts 'as the person they now are, in all their fragility'. It becomes increasingly quiet around the person. Perhaps it is in this quiet, that the real encounter with the person with dementia takes place.

Related reading

Jones, G. M. M. and Miesen, B. M. L. (1992) 'The need for an interdisciplinary core curriculum for professionals working with dementia', in G. M. M. Jones and B. M. L. Miesen (eds) *Care-giving in Dementia*, London: Routledge/Tavistock, pp. 437–53.

—— (1992) (eds) *Care-giving in Dementia. Research and Applications*, London: Routledge/Tavistock, 481 pp.

Miesen, B. M. L. (1992) 'Attachment theory and dementia', in G. M. M. Jones and B. M. L. Miesen (eds) *Care-giving in Dementia*, London: Routledge/Tavistock, pp. 38–56.

—— (1992) 'Care-giving in dementia: review and perspectives', in G. M. M. Jones and B. M. L. Miesen (eds) *Care-giving in Dementia*, London: Routledge/Tavistock, pp. 454–69.

—— (1993) 'Alzheimer's disease, the phenomenon of parent-fixation and Bowlby's attachment theory', *International Journal of Geriatric Psychiatry* 8 (2): 147–53.

—— (1996) *'So blöd bin ich noch lange nicht'*, Stuttgart: George Thieme, 144 pp.

—— (1997) 'Awareness in dementia patients and family grieving. A practical perspective', in B. M. L. Miesen and G. M. M. Jones (1997) (eds) *Care-giving in Dementia Volume II. Research and Applications*, London: Routledge/Tavistock, pp. 67–79.

—— (1997) 'Care-giving in dementia: the challenge of attachment', in B. M. L. Miesen and G. M. M. Jones (eds) *Care-giving in Dementia Volume II. Research and Applications*, London: Routledge/Tavistock, pp. 337–52.

—— (1998) *Leben mit verwirrten alteren Menschen*, Stuttgart: George Thieme Verlag, 190 pp.

Miesen, B. M. L. and Jones, G. M. M. (1997) *Care-giving in Dementia Volume II. Research and Applications*, London: Routledge/Tavistock, 388 pp.

—— (1998) 'Attachment behaviour in dementia: Parent orientation and parent fixation (POPFiD) theory', in G. H. Pollock and S. I. Greenspan (eds) *The Course of Life*, vol. VII, Madison: International University Press Inc., pp. 197–229.

—— 'Psychic pain resurfacing in dementia: from old to new trauma', in L. Hunt, M. Marshall and C. Rowlings (eds) *Past Trauma in Late Life. European Perspectives in Therapeutic Work with Older People*, London: Jessica Langley Publishers, pp. 142–54.

Munnichs, J. M. A. and Miesen, B. M. L. (1986) (eds) *John Bowlby, Attachment, Life-span and Old Age*, Deventer: Van Loghum Slaterus, p. 39.

Index